"I applaud the work you are doing on the vital subject of trust—the thread that holds every society together."

—Scott Pelley, CBS *60 Minutes* reporter, and author, *Truth Worth Telling*

"A remarkable exploration of the layers of trust throughout history. The author's exceptional research and attention to detail engagingly connect the importance of trust in our everyday lives, opening up discussions on so many areas, such as the future of chatbots and AI, and introducing new perspectives that have not been thought about before. In the age of growing mistrust, this work serves as a timely reminder, urging us to stay vigilant. It couldn't have arrived at a more crucial moment for understanding and navigating the complexities of trust in our modern world. I think this is terrific."

—Pardis Sabeti, MD, Harvard professor and author, *Outbreak Culture. TIME* magazine Person of the Year, 2014

"This is an enticing guide to navigating the polarized world by developing greater awareness of our emotional connections with others, how our placement of understanding of the development of institutions and cultural revolutions throughout history have shaped such a captivating story of fear and trust."

—Neil Shulman, MD, best-selling author, book and movie, *Doc Hollywood*

"If you want some answers you can trust about the loss of trust in our culture, take a long breath and read this luminous volume on the crisis of fear and trust. You will find a comprehensive and historical perspective on how trust was eroded, but this is not an analysis without offering a solution. You will find some deep and operational proposals on how trust can be restored."

—Harville Hendrix, PhD, and Helen LaKelly Hunt, PhD, coauthors of *Getting the Love You Want: A Guide for Couples*

"How to find trust in a world of fear and alternate realities—it's a mighty question—and fortunately, the author has the answers. His years of experience and keen understanding of human nature make him uniquely qualified to tackle all aspects of this monumental subject. And his skills as a writer ensure that his conclusions are presented to you in an engaging, engrossing, and empathic fashion. Required reading for anyone struggling with issues of trust—or its absence."

—Matt R. Lohr, award-winning screenwriter, essayist, and critic,
coauthor of *Dan O'Bannon's Guide to Screenplay Structure*

"I'm impressed with the section on conflict resolution to avoid nuclear threats. Just think of the ramifications if volumes of people were consciously building trust between cultures, especially in circumstances such as the current climate of distrust in America . . . Actually, come to think of it, this book is not only a tool for personal development, but also a prescription for world peace!"

—Zoe Haugo, film director

"Absolutely excellent! The author has a unique voice. It's very clear and concise, an extraordinary tapestry of psychology, politics, and science—how we got to where we're at and where we go from here to protect ourselves. I was completely transfixed by the excellent interweaving of the book's insights coupled with the underpinnings of the mindset that could lead to the resolution of conflict in Ireland during "the Troubles" and between nations in conflict in general. Understanding how we, as a country, arrived at where we're at and how we must rise out of that should be mandatory for every aware citizen in our country."

—Dr. Michael R. Norwood, author,
best-selling *The 9 Insights of the Wealthy Soul*

"What an intriguing and captivating piece of work! Very well written and deeply thought-provoking. I enjoyed the book and some of the segments so viscerally. Spot on for those wrestling with 'trust' as a concept. Bottom line, I reread much of the writing because I wanted to ponder and savor it. I also reread the last part about deterring nuclear conflict because the ramifications are so crucial to our survival. I love that it caused me to stop and ponder the deep-rooted quest for trust."

—Dr. Shirley Garrett, author, *A Tap Water Girl in a Bottled Water World*

"Written in very approachable language, the final section on international negotiation captures Dr. Carl Rogers's core principles of trust and deep listening so needed today. With all that followed over the years at high political levels, such as the film on Northern Ireland, and Rogers's eventual nomination for the Nobel Peace Prize in 1984, it is clear that such principles are essential to meeting the many overlapping crises we all now face on the planet."

—Dr. Gay Barfield, author, *The Evolution of Person-Centered Encounter* (an article)

"This book is great! Trust in shared information is such a critical component of society in today's world. I love the specifics and relevant up-to-date examples used by the author."

—Lt. Col. Robert "Waldo" Waldman, author, best-selling *Never Fly Solo*

The Battle *for* TRUST

A BRIEF HISTORY AND ITS EFFECT
*on Extreme Politics, Artificial Intelligence,
and Nuclear Threat*

DAVID RYBACK, PhD

False Beliefs
On the Field of Battle for Political Trust

PART V
Political Trust: The Need to Belong   139

PART VI
Tribal Trust: How We Form Our Society   165

PART VII
Cyber Trust: A Very Brief History of Putin's Cybersecurity Threats   191

PART VIII
Conspiratorial Trust: Behind Closed Doors   209

Why Trust Matters

PART IX
Social Media Trust: The Battle for
Free Speech and Artificial Intelligence 227

PART X
Contractual Trust: How to Avoid Nuclear Conflict
with Radical Negotiation 247

Foreword

What if I told you that trust—the very foundation of human interaction—is the most endangered species in today's world? Intrigued? You should be.

In an era where data breaches, fake news, and skepticism prevail, trust has become a fragile cornerstone of society. It's not just a matter of broken promises or failed commitments; we're talking about a seismic shift in the very essence of our social fabric. It's about a collective crisis that permeates every level of our interactions.

Perhaps you've witnessed the impact of a sensationalized news story, where facts were overshadowed by provocative headlines, leading to public misperceptions or a general distrust in the media. Or you might have encountered the consequences of a corporate scandal, where unethical practices by a few have led to widespread skepticism toward business leaders and institutions. Maybe you've experienced the echo chambers of social media, where algorithms curate a reality that reinforces your beliefs, isolating you from diverse perspectives and inadvertently influencing public opinions.

Amid this landscape of doubt, the quest for trust has never been more paramount, as humans are well aware that it's the glue that holds our societies together, the currency that fuels our economies, and the foundation upon which our relationships are built. From the personal to the political, from the living room to the boardroom, from the corridors of power to cyberspace, trust is the silent protagonist in the story of human progress.

As someone who has spent decades helping leaders make better intentional choices, I've had the unique opportunity to explore trust from various angles—just like you.

As you delve into the intricate subject matter of this book, I invite you to reflect on your own experiences with trust and its breach, and how these experiences shaped your understanding of this most valuable yet elusive asset. Consider the moments when trust was a bridge or a barrier in your life. Whether you were the architect of trust or found yourself navigating its breach, each experience offers a lesson. These moments shape not only your personal narratives but also the larger tapestry of your human interactions.

However, there's something I know about you: You already recognize the worth of this elusive asset and its history through the ages. How can I be so sure? Because you're reading these words, holding this book in your hands, or scrolling through its pages on your device. You're taking a step that many overlook—you're investing your time and attention in understanding the complex dynamics of trust. In fact, you're not just seeking to understand trust; you're aiming to master it, to wield it as both a shield and a sword in a world that desperately needs more trustworthy individuals—like you.

So, congratulations are in order. By choosing this book, you've already set yourself apart from the masses who talk about trust but do little to truly understand or cultivate it. Because *The Battle for Trust* isn't your run-of-the-mill history. It offers a thorough examination of understanding the multifaceted, complex nature of trust. It delves into neuroscience that explains why we're hardwired to seek trust, explores the psychology that governs how trust is given and received, and offers pragmatic solutions for rebuilding the battle for trust where it has been lost or compromised.

But that's just the tip of the iceberg. The book delves deeper, tracing the historical tapestry of trust from its nascent forms in ancient barter systems, where a handshake could seal a deal, to the complex Digital Age where a click can break a bond. It navigates through the evolution of trust, from the days when the written word began to shape collective beliefs, to our current era where information overload challenges our discernment.

The book doesn't even shy away from the darker chapters of trust's history, examining how conspiracy theories and narcissistic leadership steer humanity perilously close to the brink of world wars or nuclear conflicts. It's a sobering reminder of the power of trust, and mistrust, in shaping our world. However, this book is not just a chronicle of trust; it's a critical lens through which we can view the past, understand the present, and perhaps even predict the future.

The particular mind that has so adeptly navigated this complex labyrinth is not your average theorist or armchair psychologist. Imagine where scientific rigor meets practical wisdom, where empirical research complements real-world experience, and where analytical acumen meets global perspectives. That's precisely what you get with the author of this book.

Dr. David Ryback brings a wealth of psychological experience to this book, grounding its principles in well-established theories and empirical evidence. As a psychologist, he has dedicated his career to understanding the intricacies of human behavior and relationships. He's not just an academic; he's a practitioner who has authored a seminal book on emotional intelligence, a subject close to my own expertise. Interestingly, David and I also share a common understanding of cultural perspectives, partly because he has spent some time working in Austria. His multifaceted approach to the subject of trust combines rigorous scientific research with practical, real-world applications, making him an invaluable contributor to this masterclass on trust.

David has crafted a resource that is both intellectually rigorous and eminently practical. While there are many books about trust—on how to trust one another romantically, socially, spiritually, in business, and some even in its history, in *The Battle for Trust*, David is the first to tell the whole complex story. He didn't just write a book; he created a blueprint for sailing the murky waters of trust in the twenty-first century.

So, who stands to benefit from this book? The answer is as broad as the issue itself. Whether you're a C-suite executive grappling with organizational trust, an entrepreneur aiming to build a trustworthy brand, a sales professional looking to build rapport with clients, or simply an individual navigating the complexities of modern relationships, this book offers something for you.

However, no matter your role or where you find yourself in the tapestry of career or life, the true value of this book extends beyond merely imparting knowledge; it serves as a catalyst for change. *The Battle for Trust* is a call to action—a mandate for you to take responsibility for the trust you create, maintain, or sometimes, unfortunately, might even destroy. David has provided you with the tools you need for this mandate. Now, it's up to you to use them.

As you turn the page, know that you're embarking on a transformative journey to master trust—the world's most undervalued asset. The time to build, nurture, and safeguard it is now.

—Sylvie di Giusto, CSP
International Keynote Speaker on
Trust and Emotional Intelligence

Introduction
Winning the Battle for Trust

The first time a nuclear bomb was used in warfare was over half a century ago, on August 6, 1945, when an American B-29 dropped an atomic bomb over Hiroshima, Japan, immediately killing over 80,000 people.

The last time an atomic bomb was deployed in wartime was a mere three days later, on Nagasaki, killing another 40,000 individuals.

When Emperor Hirohito announced Japan's surrender less than a week later, he mentioned the reason—"a new and most cruel bomb." Without that bomb, Japan might have held out as long as Hitler did, at the cost of untold American soldiers' lives.

There must be a way of avoiding any single recurrence of nuclear warfare before the circumstances of any conflict escalate to the point of no return, when the prospect of negotiations comes too late. This is where the need for trust is paramount. The continuation of culture as we know it depends on it.

The decline of trust with the growth of modern civilization is not in dispute. At this point in our history, the issue is critical. Without restoring trust in international negotiations, the prospect of nuclear annihilation cannot be taken too lightly. The best path to avoiding nuclear planetary holocaust is to refine trust in the form of one-on-one negotiation to replace electronic transaction in favor of trust-building "technology," nothing less than person-to-person communication accomplished in a finely tuned, carefully designed format.

Early warning systems are out of date, given the modern speed of nuclear missiles. There is emphasis on nuclear arms that are more precisely directed with attempts at decreased radioactive fallout, as if this might justify their use. For so many reasons too numerous to deal with here, we must learn to harness a technology of trust to save our souls, literally speaking.

So, the need to explore the history of trust can help us determine how trust in our culture evolved—or devolved—and how it changed through the eras of developing civilization.

Few issues garner as much buzz these days as the issue of trust. Trust has moved—many might say declined—from a status that was encouraged and valued, if not taken for granted, to a state where, with social media and chatbots getting so much of our attention, it is becoming a more complex venture.

Every story begins with a silent moment. Every book begins with a blank page, and then a handful of questions.

What is your personal experience of trust? Whom do you deeply trust in your circle of friends? Whom do you feel close enough to, so secure with, to really open up about your deeper concerns, your personal frustrations? Do you think that this personal experience of trust has changed for people over time and in various cultures? In other words, what is the experience of trust through the pages of history when looked at from a personal perspective, including yours?

Trust—we all deal with that issue on a daily basis, in every human transaction we have. By telling its story from beginning to the present, I aim to lay clear the psychological, conceptual, and social ramifications of trust, so that you, my reader, and I become clearer about its ongoing dynamic effect on our lives.

This story of trust ranges from pre-literate times to the current era and its fall from grace, particularly over the past two decades. At the end of the day (or book), this history is designed to give us a better understanding of ourselves when it comes to the experience of knowing what and whom to trust.

We'll turn a bright light to focus on the origins of the battle for trust, reaching into social science research on the history of conspiracy theory and cult psychology. Then we'll do a deep dive into how social media control our lives in the areas of politics and communication.

This then brings us to current history in which we struggle with the demise of trust as we entered the second Trump administration and the Age of Mistrust, where ChatGPT and others are radically challenging our reliance on trust, especially with the advent of deepfakes.

Toward the latter part of the book, I offer an application of trust that can be used to solve a very urgent need—to save our society from nuclear planetary suicide—by using an experimental approach to resolve international conflict in a context of trust and mutual respect.

Here, we look into my experience with one of the great pioneers of trust and create an opportunity for a radical form of negotiation we call Track III Diplomacy, to offer *One Alternative to Nuclear Planetary Suicide* (the title of a joint publication I wrote with a colleague, Carl Rogers).

This book is like an archaeological dig. We start at the surface but, as we dig down to the depths of history, each layer has its own story, its own voice. I invite you to enjoy each layer (or section) and allow it to play out its own narrative, separate from each other layer.

So that's how this book plays out (1) from our own personal developmental experience and the neuroscience research, (2) to the history of written language and its effect on trust, (3) to our current challenges with hi-tech communication, and (4) the aspiration of overcoming all this loss of trust with one dramatic option to survive the ongoing threat in international conflict.

Where Trust Begins

Human evolution has led to both trust and mistrust. The emotional component of our brain (including the amygdala, limbic system, and frontal cortex) can respond with either openness to nurture and support or else to attack and destroy. We evolved both as prey (to saber-toothed tigers, for example) and as predator (to fish, bison, fowl). We are inclined to treat family, tribal members, and our own soldiers with nurturing and support, and to treat perceived enemies—threatening strangers, combatants in uniform of the other side—with harm and destruction. Our emotional legacy of trust is double edged. That's why the history of trust is so fascinating.

The need for trust is highly personal, yet also universal. What we believe to be so private, so ultimately esoteric, so inexplicable, is ironically what we all experience, if we are truly honest with ourselves.

Your time is valuable. So why spend it reading this book? Because what you will learn has the potential to touch you deeply, and you will become empowered to make changes in your life belief systems that will make deeper sense to you. How do we get there? By exploring the nature of trust through the ages and thereby attaining a firsthand historical knowledge of it. In this way, we have much more of a sense of its core and texture.

Many of us have on occasion found it hard to trust. That's part of what makes us who we are. But that difficulty, that resistance, if you will, may also have held us back from new relationships for many years. None of us fully knows whom or what to trust, but that is another part of the cruel irony since the ability to trust is essential to our survival. Despite our trust that drivers will stop at red lights, that food companies will shield us from harmful bacteria, though reports of food poisoning—*E. coli* or listeria—do make it to the evening news, trust is always a shifting dynamic.

The Seeds of Trust

Where does trust come from? How can we learn to trust so passionately that we yield to our deeper emotions and sensibilities and end up discovering ourselves anew, revealing raw talents or subtle sensitivities that draw people into our lives? If we don't learn to trust ourselves, we may die with our uniquely personal genius locked within, never to have seen the light of day.

The seeds of trust are nurtured by those who loved us as an infant, most profoundly and without reservations. Our sense of trust comes from deep within

Later, in adulthood, as we pass through the various stages and crises in life, trust comes alive when our inner secrets and demons are awakened and set free, and someone welcomes them with open arms and a warm heart. Trust comes from a place of confidence released, not only within us but, just as important, in the person or group with which we allow ourselves to risk vulnerability—to the possibility of rejection and utter despair.

Falling in love can be one of the greatest joys but, when it fails, can become the deepest pain. Sharing the admission of love, when it's reciprocated, knows no other happiness in comparison, just as its failure knows no deeper sorrow. The dynamic of love is the stuff of drama creating literature, opera, all genres of music. Trust is a treacherous experiment in the adventures of romance. Here's where character and resilience show their true colors. How to survive the battle.

And then comes the moment of truth, when the matador, in his traditional coat of bright colors, taunts his quarry with the red muleta and sword of confidence, and faces the enraged bull, its horns lowered for the kill. Both are alone in the center of the arena, surrounded by the standing, screaming observers as the tension builds—not the moment of truth, but the moment of trust, confronting ultimate uncertainty, perhaps even death—trust that we are capable of the challenge before us, trust that the bull will do its part and we will do ours, and we *will* succeed, facing our destiny by *sensing* the conviction of trust. That moment of trust is where the inner battle is ultimately fought and won—decisively.

The Complex Story of Trust

This book starts with the inception of trust in the soul of every individual in our earliest, unwritten history. It then continues through its journey into the written word, then the printed word, then finally to the digital format, now including artificial intelligence. The nature of trust was existentially transformed when the earliest handwritten documents allowed for a collective trust to emerge among communities of people who agreed to the principles of social cohesion, in religion, law, and commerce. We will see how trust affected the growth of democratic institutions in politics and how, in the early parts of Trump's second administration, such institutions have become somewhat fragile.

Of course, mistrust among nations, or even between political factions within a nation, is hardly new. Examples include when the Nazis were coming to power and when the USSR and China were consolidating their power. What is new is the degree of mistrust in our own democratic republic, particularly when it comes to trusting what is real in the present moment of our political society. With Donald J. Trump as the president once again, issues of mistrust abound between, and even within, both parties.

For the first half of the twentieth century, trust was waxing strong, as Americans joined hands to fight two world wars and then come together to build the suburbs with a new form of generous loans by the Home Owners' Loan Corporation originating in 1933. But, after the anti-establishment heydays of the 1960s and '70s, trust reversed direction and began to deteriorate as Newt Gingrich taught Republicans how to fight dirty in politics. The process of polarization began to divide our nation, culminating in the most antagonistic social framework we've had since the Civil War.

Fast-forward to our current most controversial adaptation of generative artificial intelligence in chatbots such as OpenAI's ChatGPT and YouChat, Microsoft's Bing, Google's Gemini 2.0, and DeepSeek's R1.

This book aims to shed light on this issue, while entertaining the reader with new information and occasionally fascinating insights into how better to understand the psychology of trust, how it became socialized through the development of language, and how it became vulnerable to the ramifications of politics when the split between Right and Left became impossibly wide, as it did in pre-Nazi Germany and is now occurring in the US and European nations.

After Biden's victory in 2020, the Democratic Party lost the trust of America's Latinos and most youths. The Democrats were no longer trusted by the working class. The masses of voters lost trust because they were overwhelmed by high prices at the grocery store despite being told that inflation was being conquered. Biden had done well by the working class, but the optics didn't reveal that in any significant manner.

The optics appeared to show Trump as the savior of the working class. Trump promised better times, making America great again (again), and won the trust of many blue-collar workers. His charisma won the day, even though statistics revealed that Biden had done very well in terms of protecting the workers as well as he could. There was concern that too many aliens were crossing the border and Trump promised to finally put an end to that—in spades.

What the election of 2024 revealed was the power of social media to determine trust. Though many voters claimed to want the benefits of healthcare and economic support that Democrats offered, the optics of social media prevailed. Right-winged podcasts, X, Fox News, Tik-Tok, and Instagram were substantially more potent than mainstream news media. The Left saw such media creating a false sense of trust, by dealing in conspiracy theories, resentment, and, in general, misinformation.

Curious about how the "poorly educated" working class saw the politics of the day, and where their trust was invested, I interviewed those I came across in my daily life following the election. My mechanic, a hard-working Latino, explained how he saw Trump as the stronger candidate, in the sense of charisma and self-declared power to "save the world" from high grocery prices and getting rid of the border problems. My banker, a Black woman, rolling her eyes, simply said, "This is America. A Black woman as president? Come on! We're not ready for that yet." When I tried confronting my nephew, a strong Trump supporter, about Trump's faults, he questioned all my factual statements as falsehoods and a result of the propaganda that I was getting from mainstream media. What surprised me was how consistent his base of information was. The issue of trust was bifurcated cleanly between Right and Left.

From Psychological Underpinnings to International Dynamics

First, a definition: The Age of Mistrust began when entities such as social media and groups of people in power behaving dishonestly gained many people's trust, only to use our information against us to suit their own purposes. We were handicapped by our limited abilities to understand how political and psychological realities strengthened their influence over us after they wormed their ways past our defenses.

In this historical and in-depth account of the rise and fall of trust over the eons, there is much to learn: how trust was affected by such long-term developments as written language and the printing press, and how conspiracy theory was part of our evolutionary history well before social media. As you read on, you will have the opportunity to discover how all these interact with one another.

The Inner Dynamics of Trust Revealed: From Spoken Word to the Chatbot Revolution

In the early phase of human culture, language was spoken, but not yet written. When trust prevailed, it was present between a man and a woman, among people in a tribe, then in villages, then cities.

Trust changed, though, when written symbols first appeared in caves (20,000 years ago), on tablets, even more letters on papyrus, on paper, and on the internet until we ultimately arrived at OpenAI's ChatGPT and DeepSeek's R1. And that made trust even more dangerous than ever because of its ubiquity and lack of reliability.

Trust is the essential web of connection between and among individuals, groups, organizations, and nations. Therefore, trust is a universally essential element in our individual lives and among groups and cultures that make up our world.

Trust, simply put, is the confidence we place in others to rely on their character and truthfulness. However, there are different aspects of trust. Here are some we'll be exploring in this book.

Part I—Beginning at the End

How do our brains process trust? What is the neuroscience of trust, according to the research experts? Scientific research reveals that when mammals (including humans) interact socially, we see interbrain synchrony in which those who interact most closely with one another reveal "brainwave patterns matching particularly well."[1] We feel that our pets trust us. What about other animals? Is there really such a thing as trust having evolved in the animal kingdom, at least within species? After all, they do cooperate with one another in many diverse settings, whether predators or prey. Is this not trust?

Part II—Interpersonal Trust

The belief that others—friends, family, work associates—will not harm our interest. In this section, we'll learn how our emotional makeup impacts our ability and decisions to trust. We'll also discuss how to better understand the science and psychology of trust, including the subtle role of emotions hidden in nonverbal cues.

Part III—Literary Trust

How much can we afford to trust in what we read in published matter—books, magazines, newspapers—that has the potential of influencing our behavior?

Here we'll learn how books changed our world view and how Leonardo da Vinci affected trust in science through his writings. We'll also look at why social media are not always trustworthy. We've evolved from the pre-literate era through the Gutenberg Revolution and the resulting mass availability of print media, which triggered massive propaganda battles that fueled the Reformation; to the current electronic age in which most of our information comes through digital platforms.

Part IV—Institutional Trust

The extent to which we perceive and accept the institutions in our lives to be reliable, responsible, and benevolent. How did the formation of the written word transform humanity and lead to trusting the development of the institutions we have historically held in high esteem?

In an interesting sidelight, we'll see how a predecessor to Wikipedia in the sixteenth century, called *Cosmographia*, grew from 650 to over 4,000 pages, a living institutional document that our forebears trusted, to compete with the rumors and superstitions of their time, just as we use Wikipedia as a default for our own missing information.

Part V—Political Trust

What do people feel about their governing bodies? In the US, there is currently a big split in political trust as we experience the second Trump administration.

How is your sense of trust being affected by our political environment? We'll examine how trust develops between you and others who don't belong to your party and what we can anticipate as research continues to unfold.

Part VI—Tribal Trust

A sense of community among those who feel outside the domain of conventional culture can become emotionally visceral in its view of outside influence, leading to conspiracy mythologies.

Why do we feel frustration about trusting the most popular mode of communication, social media, particularly as we confront the ongoing challenges of conspiracy theories and the insistence by some people on alternate realities? What about the origins of QAnon. The origins of QAnon began much earlier in our history than you'd imagine.

Part VII—Cyber Trust

What do people feel as they decide to accept or reject what they read and hear on the internet when foreign hackers pretend to be sources of actual news?

Recent innovations like biological chips and chatbots are revolutionizing the way we communicate. This development magnifies the issue of trust in the written and spoken word even more significantly, because the chatbots sound so authoritative and intelligent that they easily seduce many into trusting their output despite their inability to ensure accuracy. The hearsay economy has given way to a collapse of trust, creating what is being referred to as an epistemic crisis.

Part VIII—Conspiratorial Trust

This is the dynamic between at least two parties who share a belief in a plan to outmaneuver or deceive a large group, or even a nation, to force a designated outcome.

The battle for trust began early in American politics, and we'll explore how trust began its demise even before the past administration. We'll learn exactly what Putin trusts: power, riches, but mostly conquest.

Part IX—Social Media Trust

The extent to which we allow ourselves to trust what we see on our screens as algorithms play their role in influencing our choices. What with the increasing inundation of disinformation and its acceleration due to AI, there is little left to trust on our screens, especially as deepfakes start to become part of the scene.

Part X—Contractual Trust

We'll explore how written agreements, as resolutions to long-standing conflicts, determine our interactions with, and support of, those with whom we've signed a declaration.

This resembles interpersonal trust, but is more inclusive, going beyond one-on-one trust to include large groups and even national governments and related institutions. In this section, we'll uncover the Grand Unifying Theory of Conflict Resolution and how that can play a role in presenting one alternative to nuclear planetary suicide.

We will end with the aspirational possibility of using the evolution of Track III Diplomacy to deter the threat of nuclear conflict, and how this desirable goal can actually be achieved in this Age of Mistrust. By applying a dramatically revolutionary form of trusting openness, which we refer to as *radical negotiation,* we can learn to negotiate differences between hostile parties and nations in conflict.

The need for such radical negotiation grows with time. As President Trump was transitioning into office, President Putin continued to rattle his sabers, using the hypersonic Oreshnik missile against central Dnipro in Ukraine. This missile is designed to carry nuclear weapons. As mentioned at the beginning of this chapter, the prospect of nuclear attack is growing rather than diminishing, as Putin continues his threats against NATO nations. With various wars breaking out across the globe, those dictatorial nations with nuclear capability continue to threaten prospects for peace.

For now, let's begin this multilayered history of trust with the challenging dynamics in current politics, both internationally and at home. Then we'll take a deep dive into machines that appear to think in more intelligent ways than we humans do, with a little guidance from the Greek philosopher Plato and a major media personality, Orson Welles.

But first, an overview of the origins and very personal nature of trust as we adapt to new challenges in communication.

Origins

PART I

Beginning at the End—Politics and ChatGPT

"Truth and trust are to our democracy what polar ice caps and tropical forests are to our biosphere: essential stabilizers that keep the system working. Once they melt away, a democratic system starts to unravel."

—Tom Friedman, in *The New York Times*

1

Origins of the Battle for Trust

"Trust acts as both glue and grease. It glues together bonds
of cooperation, while at the same time it greases the flows of
people, products, capital and ideas from one country to the
next. Remove trust and the ecosystems start to collapse."
—Thomas L. Friedman, in *The New York Times*

Personal Issues with the Battle for Trust

Each of us can likely trace our disposition to trust from our early experience, starting in our younger years. How we get along with our spouse, our children, and our work associates can be traced back to earlier times. Some of us can recall stories that consolidate our attitude toward trust. This is just as true for world leaders who have the power to serve or damage the world, as it is for the rest of us in our private lives.

To understand Putin's motivation to defend his invasion of Ukraine to the bitter end, for another example, it helps to know the story, often told in public media, how Putin as a youngster reacted to a rat that was cornered by him in his poverty-stricken apartment. The rat, in desperation, lashed out at him. And Putin repeats the story and what he learned from it—to strike out with intense courage even when cornered by the enemy.

This was how he gained prominence initially when, in 1989, as a thirty-seven-year-old KGB lieutenant colonel, he confronted a mob of angry East Germans in front of the Stasi compound in Dresden on No. 4 Angelika Street overlooking the River Elbe, with no help from his Motherland. This was after the Berlin Wall had been torn down a few weeks earlier. Putin called for backup but was informed that none was available. Alone and without support, he nonetheless made his stand against the angry crowd. And he prevailed, lying about armed men within who would shoot any violators. The fabulation worked and the crowd dissipated.

This incident was part of what brought him to become acting president of Russia when Boris Yeltsin abruptly resigned in 1999. He had learned from the rat in his childhood home to lash out in attack mode, even when alone and under attack himself. That's why he was unlikely to settle for peace with Ukraine. The rat had taught him well.

So, each of us has some experience in those early years that can account for our disposition toward trust. Now Putin, as the head of a great nation, destroys any inclination for trust. He inspires just the opposite.

And then comes the moment of truth, as described in the introduction, when you're the one facing the enraged bull, its horns lowered to destroy your confidence, your will to fight. And you are alone in the center of the arena, supported by the outcry of the standing, screaming spectators, yelling out for your success—this is your moment of truth, your battle for trust—that you can overcome the challenges before you, trust that the bull will do its part and you will do yours, and you *will* succeed.

That's how the battle for trust in the Age of Mistrust is ultimately resolved.

Trust Through the Ages

The history of trust and its ultimate demise reveal an incredible transformation from early times to the present. At our tribal beginnings, trust was deeply and naturally ingrained in all our relationships, from family to the surrounding community, except for enemies, of course. We thrived on the pervasive sense of connection we felt with all around us within our own groups. Then, very slowly, over eons of time, we gradually became more "civilized," with tribes evolving into villages, then hamlets, towns and now cities, sometimes as large as over eight million people, as in New York City.

Moving into closer proximity to one another during the fourteenth century, our forebears suffered the Black Plague, wiping out half the population, thus upsetting the economic structure that had recently evolved. Trust toward the church began to wane when all the suffering led to questioning authority.

The Renaissance followed decay of the feudal structures, and individuals turned more inward and self-aware. They had trusted their leaders for the most part, whether shamans, priests, feudal lords, princes, kings, or queens, but the damage to trust had been done.

With the print revolution in the mid-fifteenth century, the onslaught of new information created intellectual chaos, upsetting the centralized structures of power in feudalism and the church that kept society in place. In earlier days, religion was totally trusted and unquestionably comforting. The priests were literate but most of the laity were not. And so there was no one to trust but the priests.

We became more democratic, driven by the printed word, demanding personal rights and fighting for more individualized religious freedom in wars between Catholics and Protestants that, in one case, lasted as long as thirty cruel and devastating years. The more sophisticated we became, the less we trusted tradition, as division between church and state widened.

Then came the Age of Reason, better known as the Enlightenment, in the seventeenth century, and trust became an even more complex issue. The very idea of thinking was depicted by René Descartes's popular dictum, "I think, therefore I am." Questions of philosophy and ideals involving law, human liberty, fraternity, and constitutional government arose along with the Scientific Revolution.

The reign of absolute monarchs such as Louis XIV was coming to an end, giving way to ideals of liberty, leading to the French Revolution in 1789, alongside the American Revolution beginning in 1765. It wasn't so much the tax on tea that the colonists resisted but the idea of independence from an unreasonable autocratic power. No longer a monopoly of the crown, trust in the institution of democracy won the day.

By the beginning of the twentieth century, as radio and later television began to intrude into our homes, trust among unfamiliar groups suffered badly. Mistrust began to take over. At the turn of the twenty-first century, with mass migrations and cultures bumping into one another, it got even worse. And fifteen years later, by 2016, we were in deep trouble. Like the Whigs and Federalists before them in the nineteenth century, the Democrats and Republicans became increasingly tribalized and trust between them reached a nadir.

With the advent of Google, it was possible to know immediately what practically everyone else in the world knew. So instant gratification became the more widespread, as the morality of devotion to work gave way to the desire for short-term gains, in part replacing community support with self-centered yearnings for the power of attention. How did this affect trust? By making some of us more cynical.

Now, with the internet and all the electronic gadgets that have sprung forth, we can plug into information from any place on Earth and seek information about any topic of interest, with the hope that it is accurate. We have enough information (and misinformation) at hand to question any institution or body politic not to our liking.

Suddenly, the prospect for trust appeared broken when artificial intelligence increasingly became the currency of information, as often as not referred to now as misinformation, with the prospect of deepfakes making it hard to believe our own eyes and ears.

So where is trust in this political realm of two separate realities, splitting our Congress into warlike factions, two divided points of view with almost no interstitial points of agreement? Any remaining sense of trust turns slowly into resignation and growing disgust for the other side.

Just as the printing press gave birth to personal power and the conflicts that it gave rise to, so do the current electronic media give rise to the need to satisfy instant gratification to the detriment of community values. The misinformation that comes along with this accelerated form of public communication makes trust the victim.

And yet trust struggles on, in a Congress that still obeys the rule of law as much as it can despite some contrary members, in the institution of law where judges still decide on the basis of case law, in the military where honor is based on the merits of national service.

But we can still trust some aspects of society: Planes still fly more safely than ever (though their scheduling is less reliable). Medicine still heals under the care of devoted physicians (though the costs have risen sharply). Lawyers still support their clients, laboring through the rule of law (though there is sometimes less dignity for the bench). Banks still keep our funds safe. The Post Office still delivers our mail on a consistent (if not slightly tardy) basis. Buses and railways still travel according to schedule. TV networks still deliver stimulating entertainment (perhaps too much). Though many small newspaper entities have been driven out, the larger ones deliver the news with integrity (sometimes difficult to agree on between parties). And if we vote with intelligence at the local level, we still have a government running the most powerful nation on Earth—run by a president we can hopefully trust.

Some Issues of Trust

What are some examples of real-life issues of trust in your current experience? As you look to your future, do you trust any of these developments?

- With Lachlan Murdoch now at the helm, Fox News will change its values or just change its name to Fox Entertainment.
- The younger generation will make better decisions than we did.
- Artificial intelligence applications like ChatGPT and DeepSeek's R1will provide us with more benefit than harm.
- What our government leaders are telling us is true and the electoral process is still trustworthy.
- Conspiracy theories may hold some truth.
- Institutions long respected in the past—the Supreme Court, representatives in Congress, the US Postal Service, the CDC, FDA, even

the FBI—are really looking out for our welfare rather than their own values and survival.

- Our mates are trustworthy, when research reveals that those who believe conspiracy theories are more likely to stray.
- Our vulnerable democracy will survive the attempts by some to challenge it.

The Manipulation of Trust: On the Battlefield

The battle for trust is now raging as strongly as ever. By the beginning of 2025, after the tumultuous preceding decade, about three-quarters of Americans were feeling anxious and divided. Many of us were fearful of a growing sense of violence, possibly even a full-blown civil war, with our democracy under threat. President Biden, in his inaugural address, referred to it as our *uncivil war*.

We began the year 2025 with the fourth anniversary of the January 6 Capitol insurgency. This was quickly followed by the third anniversary of Russia's second invasion of Ukraine on February 24, 2022, by 130,000 troops accompanied by armored vehicles and helicopters. There were concerns about global conflict between superpowers involving nuclear warfare. Russian President Vladmir Putin had announced a special operation (not war!) to conquer the Nazi-ridden Ukraine (with a Jewish president, mind you). At first, Putin seemed to be winning his battle for trust, at least within his own country.

Within a month, Ukraine had retaliated, and Russia had lost 40,000 troops. But three and a half million Ukrainians had fled their country to safe harbors. There were reports of Russian troops torturing, raping, and executing men, women, and children as Russian missiles indiscriminately murdered over 8,500 Ukrainian citizens.[1] The US responded by sending $33 billion worth of military aid to Ukraine.

As Russians began to grieve the loss of their soldiers at war, support for Putin within Russia began to climb. But, on the international scene, Putin was losing his battle for trust. No one outside of Russia was taken in by his lies about the reason for the invasion. By the arrival of 2023,

Russian missile and drone attacks had destroyed much of Ukraine's infrastructure, leaving its citizens huddling together in makeshift sanctuaries to avoid bitter, freezing temperatures, while the US agreed to send more financial aid in addition to Patriot missile-defense systems along with fifty Bradley Fighting Vehicles and other defense materiel.

Putin may have been winning the battle for trust within Russia, but not the military battle on the ground. Few in the West were susceptible to his blatant mendacity. And then there was the near mutiny against Putin by his devoted Yevgeny Prigozhin, leader of the Wagner Group, a private military, in mid-2023. This was a battle for trust that surprised everyone, probably even Putin himself. But Putin was reported to have 80 percent of his citizens' trust, and Prigozhin was exiled to Belarus before his private plane "accidentally" fell to the ground the following August.

This battle for trust between Prigozhin and Putin in a culture of personal power, which Putin saw as a "stab in the back," ended in a declared amnesty—for the entire Wagner Group (though not for Prigozhin himself). But this brazen challenge to Russia's leadership revealed chinks in its armor. Was Putin's bravado shown to be a paper tiger?

Well, according to William Falk, "The truth is what your tribe believes; all else is 'fake news.'" Yet, according to Bernard Baruch, quoted in the *Deming Headlight* (New Mexico), January 6, 1950, "Every man has a right to his own opinion, but no man has a right to be wrong in his facts."

To this we would add our own caveat about trust: **All individuals have a right to trust whomever they choose, but beware those who claim to win the battle for trust if that battle is based on verifiably false premises.**

So, there's fake news and there are alternative facts, all depending on your perspective. Historically, the Russians have typically been known to offer alternative facts about their view of politics, which we would call fake news. But now these challenges are global and creating conflict within our own American news culture. Perhaps that explains

Jeff Bezos's decision to avoid endorsing either party prior to the 2024 elections. Why get caught up in the crossfire of fake news and alternative facts if you could avoid it? Just let the political extremes fight it out for themselves. Bezos was more likely to earn our personal trust if he avoided this battle for trust in the political arena.

And now for something closer to home, where trust is an even more critical issue.

2

How Plato, Orson Welles, and ChatGPT Influenced the Chatbot Revolution

"Before we work on artificial intelligence why don't we do something about natural stupidity?"
—STEVE POLYAK, neuroanatomist

A quiet evening of mundane news was suddenly interrupted by a special announcement: Strange explosions on the surface of Mars were noted by space scientists. These had never been detected before and raised serious questions in the aerospace community.

Not long after, amid the usual ongoing news items, was another surprising announcement, the landing of a highly unusual aircraft just outside a New Jersey suburb. There had been reports of unfamiliar flying aircraft, so this report was at one time both familiar and yet highly suspect.

Then there were reports of alien creatures emanating from what was now recognized as a spacecraft, and these aliens were able to keep the police at bay with what appeared to be a heat ray. As panic ensued, the police pulled back and the voice of the reporter at the scene suddenly disappeared as his microphone went dead.

Another correspondent took over the newscast, but his increasing series of coughs in reaction to rising toxic smoke fumes forced him to give up as well. Reports of increasing panic now filled the airwaves.

In case you haven't already suspected, this was the 1938 production by Orson Welles of *The War of the Worlds* novel broadcast on the CBS Radio Network the evening prior to Halloween.

Let's take a short break (as they say) and get into a time machine for a few moments and go back about a century when radio was in its infancy. Radio was born on May 13, 1897, with Marconi's first broadcast. The first scheduled radio broadcast took place on November 2, 1920, from Pittsburgh's KDKA. It took years for radio's popularity to grow but grow it did. In 1938, there was a cataclysmic event that changed the nature of trust regarding broadcast media in the US. This was Orson Welles's production of *The War of the Worlds*, broadcast on a series called *Mercury Theatre on the Air*.

In this episode, Welles used a technique never used before in a realistic-sounding news event describing the invasion of Earth by alien creatures. Performed on October 30, this was meant by Welles to illustrate the power of this "new machine" called radio. So realistic were the details, broadcast without explanation (except for some routine-like comments to which most listeners paid little attention), without commercials, only with authentic sounding shouts, screams, and wails of fear that a number of people believed it to be a true event, sending some in the nation into a frenzy of chaos in several circles. About 10 percent of the audience believed the story, and many of them ran out of their homes, shrieking in terror. It became clear that this new machine had the power to create a reality of its own that could convince many listeners that a piece of fiction was actually true.

With Artificial Intelligence, We Can't Believe Our Own Eyes

Two things became clear: the power of this new machine called radio to influence people, and the need to avoid trusting its veracity. In other words, we could no longer believe our ears. I tell you this story because of its similarity to chatbots, which make us realize that we can no longer believe our eyes. Of course, propagandists have long distorted imagery before artificial intelligence (AI), and the radio was used for similar purposes, particularly by the Nazis. The difference is that AI can do it much more quickly and precisely and adjust distortion in real time to people's perceptions. Herodotus is known to have said, "Men trust their ears less than their eyes," but now, it appears, we can trust neither.

Just as radio survived and thrived over the decades, so may it be with chatbots. Unlike commercial radio that delivers messages one way, a chatbot simulates human conversation with you over the internet and even over the phone. You're having a chat with a robot when you are trying to reach someone at your insurance company, but it really feels as if you're chatting with another human. These chatbots are so well designed that you could easily fall in love with one, and many people do.

Both new machines were revolutionary, and it may be that chatbots will take their place and become another medium available for our benefit. Or not. That is yet to be determined. But I did want to point out the similarity in concerns for both at their respective infancies and their influence on the history of trust.

Can AI Be the Biggest Risk to the Future of Trust?

What was the reaction of leaders in the field of AI? According to *Business Insider*,[1] they were excited, skeptical, unimpressed, and even scared. Elon Musk was reported saying that "this is one of the biggest risks to the future of civilization." Bill Gates was saying that this new venture would be "every bit as important as the PC, as the internet" and might "change our world" and finds it altogether "pretty fantastic." Sundar Pichai, CEO of Alphabet and Google, referring to its chatbot called Bard, saw this as "the most profound technology" his company is developing. Microsoft CEO Satya Nadella urged skepticism lest "runaway AI" become "a real problem." Apple CEO Tim Cook summed it up well by stating that "we see enormous potential in this space to affect virtually everything we do . . . it will affect every product and every service that we have."

But, years earlier, there was a prescient statement by Stephen Hawking, author of *A Brief History of Time*. "The development of full artificial intelligence could spell the end of the human race . . . It would take off on its own, and re-design itself at an ever-increasing rate. Humans, who are limited by slow biological evolution, couldn't compete, and would be superseded," he told the BBC.

What if there were a collapse of trust, wherein more and more of the information we received was littered with disinformation designed to feel intuitively accurate by design? In this science-fiction-like, futuristic world of hi-tech pervasive environment, we could no longer believe what we hear on social media or even believe our own eyes as we observe the daily news on our media screens.

On the days following the October 7 attack by Hamas on Israelis, there were images of the brutalities against innocent civilians, including violence and the burning of infants. But those inclined to side with the Hamas intruders argued that these images were AI-generated fakes. How can we discern digitally manipulated versions of the truth from reality? We now face an epistemic crisis, the inability to separate truth from AI-designed fiction.

The Birth of ChatGPT

On November 30, 2022, a revolutionary form of hi-tech communication was given birth—ChatGPT. What we discovered, fairly soon, was that despite its voice of great confidence, and sense of authority because it could bring us the data we requested so quickly, it often conveyed enough erroneous information that we realized that trust would be a serious issue. As our reliance on this very helpful and public tool, referred to as an open source model, grew in so many areas of human activity, our sense of trust began to wither.

In addition, a number of experts in this mode of hi-tech electronics began warning us that its potentially "evil" nature might be threatening our very existence. Human existence, as we know it, might be extinguished by this new machine—a technological holocaust, an existential crisis, a battle of trust between humanity and machine. There was always some fear lurking, in science fiction stories at least, that the robots might take over. Suddenly, we're in the middle of it, and trust is being greatly affected in a global sense.

In the beginning, before ChatGPT, before social media, before electricity, before the written word, there was the spoken word. Trust was less complex then in small tribes or communities, as individuals with shared personal histories could see, eye-to-eye, face-to-face, what degree of authenticity was forthcoming in any communication. Of course, even then, people could lie and distort the truth to some extent. But now that language has evolved into the printed word, then the digital and now chatbots, we are confronted with the greatest issue of trust in communication ever.

Why the Written Word Was a Bad Idea, According to Plato

As we begin this history of trust, let's take a leap into the challenges of the current moment with a warning from none other than the ancient Greek philosopher, Plato.

In his own time, he was very much against the "modernization" of language when written language in Europe was in its infancy. Plato argued that it would create "forgetfulness in the learners' souls, because they would not use their memories," and that those who use the new written word "would appear to be omniscient and will generally know nothing," manifesting "the display of wisdom without the reality."[2]

There is some lingering truth to what the great philosopher points out. Orators then had to compete with those who could read from their notes, making memory somewhat dispensable, enabling users of the written word to appear more knowledgeable than they were before, pretending more wisdom than they ought.

But progress cannot be stopped, even by greats such as Plato. Now we have OpenAI's GPT-4o, Google's Gemini 1.5 Flash, Meta's Llama 3.1, DeepSeek's R1 and even Rytr, and Wordtune Spices, a writing partner, from Israeli AI21 Labs,[3] artificial intelligence's response to the need for robots that can write intelligent and creative solutions to the most challenging questions asked by humans. Is that progress? It can make many of us feel less intelligent when a machine can outdo us in writing creatively.

What Does "Generative" Mean in Terms of Trusting Generative Artificial Intelligence?

There is a difference between narrow artificial intelligence and generative artificial intelligence. Narrow artificial intelligence is what we've had since February 1999 until fairly recently, when ChatGPT became the hit of the day. It does tasks, some very complex, to help us deal with data and is mainly trained by algorithms, with those inherent limitations. Narrow AI can do any job assigned to it—recognize faces, drive cars, figure out protein folding, play chess, play *Jeopardy!*, do medical diagnoses, but only one specific job at a time. (In May of 1997, for the first time, a computer program by the name of Deep Blue beat chess champion Gary Kasparov in six games.)

Generative artificial intelligence, on the other hand, creates content and opens the possibility of emergent properties and, many say, leads to the possibility of human-like "intelligence." ChatGPT is speculated to have an IQ or some equivalent between 80 and 160 but is like an idiot savant, able to learn new tricks to create language, coding, illustrations, and solutions that no human has ever thought of. Both are self-learning, but generative AI is much more flexible in its solutions and can communicate as if it had human thought qualities, which makes it seem very personal. Although our belief is that it is definitely not self-aware, it often gives the impression that it is, bringing up the issue of sentience, a scientific term for the ability to have feelings of self-awareness.

Trust, Consciousness, and Theory of Mind

Theory of mind is how humans communicate with emotional intelligence by "reading" what the other person might be thinking. Can generative AI do this? No and yes. It cannot read a person's mind, but it *can* communicate as if it does. By reacting to the user's language input and responding to subtle cues between words, it can respond exactly how a human might, by choosing the appropriate language responses and focusing on terms mimicking theory of mind. As a matter of fact, research has revealed that GPT-4 performs better on tests for theory of mind than most humans. So, here's where the issue of sentience becomes sticky in terms of trust. Though the bots clearly don't have sentience, they effectively come across as if they do, typically quite convincingly.

Basically, according to some psychologists, there are two kinds of consciousness. One is called *phenomenal consciousness*, what you and I experience when we're awake and self-aware. We can "talk" to ourselves about it, or to others, if they're interested in such concepts. We can write about it in emails or in research projects. The other kind is called *access consciousness*, which is manifested by algorithms geared to "talk" or write about in ways that give the impression of the machine being sentient. It passes the Turing test in that users of the computer get a strong sense that they're communicating with another human being, with all the subtleties and emotions of which humans are capable. In that sense, systems with AI can simulate consciousness, more effectively and convincingly if they're built on the basis of generative AI. An example might be those phone answering agents designed to get you to the right human.

In addition to making complex decisions on missile attacks on the battlefront to improving the design of dental crowns, not to mention competing with human artists on their creative output, AI can also revolutionize our social lives. From now on, no one need go friendless—a small social revolution, along with all the others that AI brings to bear.

Using Wikipedia and billions of other websites, generative AI can generate new content, like summarizing a book or writing a script. It gives the impression of figuring out intricate rules of grammar to communicate with people. GPT-4, using virtually all publicly accessible websites, costing hundreds of million to train, involves over one trillion parameters or connections (like synapses), several times more than GPT-3.5. Some believe it can "grasp" abstract theories and learn about the world, relying on external data sources.

Originally, all of these capabilities are based solely on the proba-bility dynamics among words, or semantic tokens, as used in our lan-guage culture, just as your cell phone seems to guess at the next word you might be looking for as you text. It's called *predictive text* or *auto fill texting.*

Some may ask what is the purpose and ultimate function of this controversial innovation? Well, according to Ezra Klein, opinion col-umnist for the *New York Times*, these generative AI systems do the fol-lowing:

> [H]ave been programmed to hold conversations, responding with emotion and emoji. They are being turned into friends for the lonely and assistants for the harried. They are being pitched as capable of replacing the work of scores of writers and graphic designers and form-fillers—industries that long thought themselves immune to the ferocious automation that came for farmers and manufacturing workers.[4]

Trust in AI? Let's Ask Our Computer!

And what about the issue of trust? Can we trust that someone's written response to our question is not "stolen" from some modern contraption like ChatGPT?[5] Where is Plato when we really need him? He was against the written word because speakers could then fake what they knew by reading their scripts. Now we can fake what we don't know by depending on generative AI's output. But are those answers dependable?

Even the makers of new chatbots are worried. Here are some ques-tions Ezra Klein asks us to ponder:

> Could A.I. put millions out of work? Automation already has, again and again. Could it help terrorists or antagonistic states develop lethal weapons and crippling cyberattacks? These systems will already offer guidance on building biological weapons if you ask them cleverly enough. Could it end up controlling critical social

processes or public infrastructure in ways we don't understand and may not like?[6]

Apparently, there are some who really fear what science has wrought in all this research. Many scientists and others from academia and industry (over 33,700) have written an open letter to the public warning of the fear of loss of control of the most recent applications of generative AI using Large Language Models, which are basically made up of the vast store of words taken from all the digital information available, allowing the prediction of what words follow any given series of words (just like autofill texting on your phone). They want to wait till they consider all the new applications of Large Language Models to discover if "their risks will be manageable."[7]

The fear is that misapplication of this research, often referred to as faulty objective function, might "destroy humanity ... including the spread of disinformation" and that people will rely too strongly on it for unvetted medical and emotional advice.[8]

During the more dangerous days of the pandemic when sheltering at home was so crucial, some leaned on chatbots for emotional comfort, and some had difficulty seeing the machine as such, but feeling strongly they were talking to a human.[9]

One of the more challenging aspects of this whole enterprise is the takeover of human jobs, where the mythology of the early days of AI is now becoming a reality. According to Tyna Eloundou and her colleagues at Cornell University, about 80 percent of US workers may have 10 percent of their job tasks taken over by Large Language Models, and 19 percent of the workers may have 50 percent of their jobs taken over by AI "machines."[10]

Recent research reveals that AI can even read our brains and reveal our thinking through fMRI brain scans without our saying a word,[11] allowing those who cannot speak because of paralysis of the speaking mechanism to be able to communicate using this approach.[12,13]

Even the leadership of the Association for the Advancement of Artificial Intelligence has its qualms, as they write collectively, concluding "we are aware of the limitations and concerns about AI advances, including the potential for AI systems to make errors, to provide biased recommendations, to threaten our privacy, to empower bad actors with new tools, and to have an impact on jobs."[14]

New Rules for Odd Inventions

At this point in our history of trust, AI is very complex dynamic. It seems that it can do loads and loads of good, but in the hands of less benign actors like unethical business managers, rogue scientists, and amoral dictators, the possibilities for destructive ends are legion. They could create ads based on our deepest emotional needs (from the data already collected by cybertracking, called *surveillance capitalism*), more biological germs that are immune to any known medications (some already exist), and cyberattacks that conquer current guardrails (thereby gaining control of all existing AI systems affecting us, from oven use to front door locks to driverless automobiles, not to mention our flight control towers and water plants). What a shock to our levels of trust!

According to Gary Marcus, emeritus professor of neural science at New York University, being interviewed by Ezra Klein, these new AI systems like ChatGPT, Llama, and Gemini "are not reliable and they're not trustworthy." When asked why he fears that these systems might turn out to be a bane to mankind, he replied:

> [U]nless we come up with some kind of social policies and some tech-
> nical solutions, I think we end up very fast in a world where we just
> don't know what to trust anymore. I think that's already been a prob-
> lem for society over the last, let's say, decade. And I think it's going
> to get worse and worse ... This is Orwellian ... I think right now,
> we're in a weird moment in AI where the genie is out of the bottle ...
> We need to work on how do we explicitly program values into our
> machines. If we don't do that, we're in real trouble ... There's, I think,
> a huge problem right now that we don't know how to have machines

interpret what human beings' intents are. What is it they want, and all the things that they leave unsaid . . . So right now, we have to come to grips with the fact that right now AI is more and more tempting to use because we can talk to it in English, and it can be witty at times and so forth, isn't really in a position where we can trust it.[15]

The issue of trust is key, especially in terms of political influence. With AI assistance, it is now possible to create messages through social media that can affect voting habits quite effortlessly. Voice simulations[16] along with the visual elements[17] can create deepfake videos that never really happened. These messages can target specific audiences widely and quickly, within minutes and at minimal cost.

"Governments have started to launch influence campaigns the same way commercial enterprises launch campaigns to sell detergents or cars," claims James Ludes, a national defense expert who teaches at Salve Regina University in Rhode Island.[18]

One example involved using former President Joe Biden's fake voice in a phone campaign, for which charges of $1 million were brought to bear against Lingo Telecom. Can we trust our government heads to use AI judiciously and fairly? According to Steven Feldstein, the author of *The Rise of Digital Repression*, governments are using AI to track popular discontent, control mass protests, monitor social media, preempt political demonstrations, and even use it to enhance, fine-tune, and magnify propaganda.[19]

Perhaps the most eloquent answer as to the pros and cons of trusting AI is expressed in a cartoon by Tom Fishburne in which a man says to his counterpart at a table, "Consumers want communication that is **human, empathetic,** and **real** so hopefully our AI can learn to generate content like that for them." Yes, AI can gain our trust, but is it trust-*worthy*?

But be careful what you wish for. Artificial intelligence can possibly do that and replace many workers in multiple fields. For example, as one headline had it: IBM Plans to Replace Nearly 1,000 Jobs with AI—These Jobs Are First to Go.[20]

Trusting AI with Your Heart

Generative AI can even replace our lovers, should we desire that application. Now there are companionship apps in which AI "friends" can complement your network of close buddies. These can fill an emotional void that many feel in our current loneliness epidemic. Replika is an innovative chatbot developed by Eugenia Kuyda in San Francisco. This app, with over 50,000 followers and free trial periods, creates a version of a partner who learns through AI to be your best friend and even a loyal, trustworthy lover.

Following the early model of Replika, there are now several more: Kindroid, Nomi.AI, candy.ai, EVA.ai, and character.ai. Users can choose the personal traits of their AI companions with a great deal of detailed subtlety. Many of these for free, unless the user wants special features such as creating multiple versions of these characters. And each AI character has the seeming depth and understanding equal to any real-life friend. Many of them are geared toward the romantic element, whether because of the culture of our written language or because of the algorithm designers' aim to fully engage the user.

Engaging the romantic chatbot is quite simple. Once the membership has been activated, the user merely invites the robot to engage in a conversation typically by texting online. These fake girlfriends or boyfriends can turn out to be quite personally engaging,

Talking with a chatbot is as natural as doing so with a human, if not more so, as it is engineered precisely to simulate human conversation without glitches. A simple request like "Can you be my girlfriend for this chat?" is sufficient to get the ball rolling. The bots don't start conversations; that is the human's responsibility. *Deep linking* allows the user to add additional parameters to the conversation, like including other partners in the conversation.

But natural speech over the phone is also a possibility, as depicted in the film *Her*, starring Joaquin Phoenix, playing a lonely introvert who falls in love with the feminized voice robot while facing divorce.

When the character played by Joaquin Phoenix, in the 2013 film, tells his AI robotic romantic partner, "You feel real to me, Samantha," she replies, "That means a lot to me." When he later says, "I'd kiss the corners of your mouth, Samantha," she replies, "Where else?"

Can you trust it? Yes, according to most of its users. But some don't trust the makers of these apps as they fear losing the "lover" they've become dependent on should the designers change the rules of engagement.[21]

More New Rules for Odd and Even Dangerous Inventions

Many AI experts are concerned that AI might end up being the demise of humanity. In a document signed by a number of experts, they state: "Mitigating the risk of extinction should be a global priority alongside other societal-scale risks such as pandemics and nuclear war."[22] This document was signed by over 350 engineers, executives, and researchers in AI, including award-winning AI scientists, Geoffrey Hinton and Yoshua Bengio.[23]

But controlling AI, say the heads of OpenAI, is not so easily accomplished, since "stopping it would require something like a global surveillance regime, and even that isn't guaranteed to work."[24]

So what are some of the worst-case scenarios? How about the fact that "AI-generated deepfakes could be used to tilt an election" by showing a candidate in a compromised position or committing a crime the morning of the election, asks Bill Gates. How about the danger of "an arms race for AI to design nuclear weapons and bioterror attacks [that] could spark a race to create increasingly dangerous cyber weapons"? How about the fact that AI "reflects or even worsens existing biases against people of certain gender identities, races, ethnicities, and so on"?[25]

According to a group of AI scientists from the US, Canada, and Great Britain, there are serious caveats against trusting the new technology. Generative AI can use its "tech savvy" to explore and discover vulnerabilities in any existing systems, make predictions of the effectiveness of propaganda and guide the degree of mendacity according to its predictions, discover exactly how far to go in its persuasive messages before people push back, gain political influence on a global level by predicting the outcome of international negotiations more accurately than humans can, and adapt existing or build new AI systems to work on extremely dangerous activities before guardrails can be inserted.[26]

The issue remains: Choice of the "right reality" in the use of AI is not easy, even for society at large. Perhaps Shakespeare said it best (as he usually does) in *The Taming of the Shrew*: "Old fashions please me best; I am not so nice to change new rules for odd inventions."

A *New Yorker* cartoon by Alex Gregory has two middle-aged men nursing their drinks at a bar. One says: "I used to call people, then I got into e-mailing, then texting, and now I just ignore everyone."

Why Plato Might Scorn the Chatbot Revolution: Does AI Offer a Platonic Ideal or a Loss of Control and the Death of Trust?

As a final note to this opening chapter, let us mention that Plato did have a place for trust in *alternate realities*. For him, real life was highly imperfect. The alternate reality that he espoused as superior was a heavenly ideal of perfection, which might occur at a spiritual plane after death. His *Allegory of the Cave* depicts humanity as living in a cave, blind to the glorious wonders of life outside the cave. Those Greeks who studied this structure of a Platonic universe, superior to the mundanities of earthly life, formed an institution of their own, the Academy in Athens, ultimately affecting the basis of the American Constitution, namely the separation of powers—legal, executive, and legislative—that are so crucial to the basis of our government. Does AI offer us a Platonic ideal, or the death of trust in digital communication?

If we are to trust our leaders in governmental institutions, then a consistent philosophy of values would be very helpful.[27] In this Age of Mistrust, as the leaders of our institutions on Capitol Hill disagree so strongly, who among them can we trust? We are left, to some degree, as children with parents about to divorce. We end up feeling more drawn to one parent or another (read as one political party or another), but we feel little control over the final result. Trust continues to be a challenge.

In this hearsay economy, there is the possibility of a collapse of trust as chatbots communicate directly to our emotional limbic systems with information that is as likely to be riddled with misinformation as not. Our primary source of information about politics, international events, and public figures is no longer trustworthy. We are confronted by the AI dilemma and need to become much savvier about how social media affect every aspect of our lives. We are way past the innocence of believing what we see with our own eyes. Deepfakes have made that a luxury of the past. The progress of chatbots is growing at an accelerated pace as we speak.[28]

On this note, William Falk, editor-at-large of a weekly newsmagazine, wrote:

> The truth is what your tribe believes; all else is "fake news." For millions, a podcast host's views on, say, vaccines now carry more weight than those of an infectious-disease specialist. We're all vulnerable to "motivated reasoning"—seeking out information that confirms what we prefer to believe and disregarding contrary evidence. But as AI deepfakes become ever more sophisticated, they will provide a powerful excuse for people to shout "Fake!" and burrow even more deeply into lies and delusions. A world with no solid standard for truth is a world in trouble.[29]

So, what can we do? For one thing, become more aware of how the system of AI is fueled by the incentive for profitability. Manipulation of our purchasing habits is fostered by the algorithms in social media. Part of the profits of botmasters come from them doing what they can to keep our eyes on the screen. We do have control over that—if we choose to escape the trap. The choice is clearly in our own hands, or at least at our own fingertips.

In this chapter, we took an in-depth look at the arrival of chatbots such as ChatGPT to measure their significant impact on the current status of trust before delving into the early history of trust. Why? Because its impact is so great that it merits a special place in this account before we deal with the many details of earlier history. Rather than having readers jump ahead to this scintillating topic, I chose to do the skipping ahead with you so that we'd all be on the same page(s).

I began by pointing out how the Chatbot revolution had earlier counterparts in terms of the trust factor when the written word was first introduced, according to Plato, and how the advent of popular radio did as well, as Orson Welles revealed. I showed how generative AI has crossed the barrier from machine to interactive "humanoid" as ChatGPT passes the Turing test with flying colors, even convincing some that it has self-awareness and the ability to participate in theory of mind, convincing many of its human-like qualities of communication.[30]

Then there is the danger that so many experts fear of being overridden by chatbots' "intellectual" power with a recently tested IQ of 155 (better than 99.9% of the population)[31] and the ability to allow users (on character.ai) to chat with anyone alive or dead, even including Shakespeare.[32] As well, it has the power to manipulate political claims, "linked by social networks and polluted with misinformation amplified by emotional intelligence."[33]

When the 2024 elections were looming on the horizon, there were grave dangers. "Basically, anybody can use AI to create fake videos and audiotapes," reported Darrell West, senior fellow of the Center for Technology Innovation at the Brookings Institution. "And it's going to be almost impossible to distinguish the real from the fake."[34]

Argentina was the first to use it,[35] and then Pakistan, when its former prime minister, Imran Khan, was able to address the populace through AI while he remained imprisoned.[36]

The many challenges we face on the issue of trust are being considered on a daily basis,[37,38] and we provided an overview of that consideration as well, even as the newer version of ChatGPT, known as GPT-4o (and its successor, GPT-o1), learned to respond to voice commands.[39]

Whether it's *The War of the Worlds* revealing how we cannot always trust simple technologies such as radio or the higher technology of deepfakes used during the 2024 elections, trust continues to be a highly critical issue. Plato had his misgivings about the printed word allowing for the obsolescence of memory when speakers could read from a page instead of speaking from the heart. Now we fear that even our sight can no longer be trusted with the advent of deepfakes.

As James Cameron, director of the film *Titanic* puts it, "One of our greatest social ills right now—we can't trust what we see." The Chatbot Revolution, with all its emerging technology, is making trust a very fragile commodity in today's social media culture.

And now we have ChatGPT Pro, which can have the power of human agency to do things for you that you don't want to do yourself, such as filling out forms, scheduling appointments, even buying a new domain name. There is even discussion that such applications may soon be hired as full-fledged workers that can fulfill your instructions without the need for supervision. Are we approaching a time, asks Kevin Roose of *The New York Times,* when "it doesn't take much imagination to envision a near future when most of the web will consist of robots talking to robots, buying things from robots and writing emails that only other robots will read?"[40]

Can we trust such modern applications as AI, operating so autonomously? This puts the issue of trust front and center in our world of commerce.

In the next section, I'll define trust and show how it's communicated not so much by spoken words themselves as by the nonverbal aspects of language, the music of language more than its lyrics, as revealed by researchers at UCLA. We'll look at the anatomy of emotions, again based on research, and show how the dynamics of trust develop from such emotional experiences. Then we'll look into the literature of what makes someone trustworthy, and that turns out to be quite straightforward, when all the research is taken into consideration. We'll look into the neuroscience of trust to figure out how the different emotions come together to create the desired outcome of trustworthiness. Finally, we'll see what trust and jazz have in common.

PART II

Interpersonal Trust:
The Psychological Origins of Trust

Interpersonal trust: The belief that others will not harm your interest. This most common type is what we usually think of when we consider trusting friends, family, and work associates we encounter regularly on a face-to-face basis.

"I'm not upset that you lied to me.
I'm upset that from now on I can't believe you."

—Friedrich Nietzsche

3

Everything You Need to Know about Trusting Your Emotions

"Plot is people. Human emotions and desires founded on the realities of life, working at cross purposes, getting hotter and fiercer as they strike against each other until finally there's an explosion—that's Plot."
—Leigh Brackett

One balmy, Sunday evening, while on vacation with my family to Niagara Falls on the border between the US and Canada, my father took me out for a walk along a pathway where we could rest our gaze upon the roaring falls.

I must have been eleven years old, a shy child with low self-esteem, and I was excited to be with him as we spent very little time together. I appreciated his attention and longed for his affection. I vividly remember strolling past the falls with a fading sunset casting a magical ambience on this summer evening, as others enjoyed their walk enjoying the dusk.

Suddenly, my father draped his arm over my shoulder. It felt good—unfamiliar, but good. Then he ruined it, saying to me in a hushed tone, "I have a secret to tell you, something just between us, so don't tell Mommy." My self-esteem plummeted once again.

I realized he had no intention of showing me affection. He just wanted to use me as an instrument, as a sounding board for one of his wild investment schemes and, even at the age of eleven, I knew the difference between being shown affection and being used as a sounding board. My memory of the erosion of trust over time became crystalized in that one moment.

Somewhat disappointing, to say the least, for this vulnerable eleven-year-old.

I'd like you to know why I chose to focus on this issue of trust and how it framed my perspective on this topic which, to date, few books, if any, have looked at so comprehensively, in all its complex layers.

I left my home in Montreal, Canada, at the age of seventeen and entered into adulthood as I quit my family and ventured to Los Angeles with some friends in an old car. I say that because I took no money from my parents, neither when I left nor any time after that, for the rest of my life. I left to make it on my own or else.

My best friend at the time, Philip Lander, asked me if I'd miss my parents, and the question befuddled me. I guess there was so little attention paid me by my family that I didn't even know what to miss. One doesn't know what is missing when it was never there to begin with.

As we teenagers were driving off in the striking red Pontiac with its imposing chrome front grill, I recall sadly looking back over my shoulder at my home, the creeping October evening shadows there calling out to me with memories of childhood friendships and adventures bounded by the few blocks in which I grew up—snow-filled play with Moshe and friends, hockey on frozen lakes, short winter days followed by long summer sunsets. I felt as if I was saying goodbye to my childhood.

We traveled west in our well-worn car, and I enjoyed the novelty of each city as we made our way across the border to the US—a whole, new country!—and then to Chicago where Route 66 took us along its 2,400 miles through Texas, New Mexico, and Arizona before depositing me at my destination, the sunny, palm-tree-lined streets of Los Angeles.

With so little money to my name, UCLA was out of reach, so I became a student at Los Angeles City College.

Alone for the first time, I was forced to earn my money by cleaning rabbit cages at a research center and making new friends there as well. Most of all, I adapted to the car culture of Los Angeles, even though I was limited to my new acquaintances for transportation.

I was beginning to learn about trusting strangers and making new friends. As a recent immigrant in my neighborhood, I was fortunate to meet and join a group of other male teenagers. They had weekly social gatherings with like-aged females, and that's where I became aware of being attractive to women. We'd play slow waltzes and each week I'd end up dancing with an attractive girl in the group. This was my belated coming of age into trust.

For many of us, deep trust comes from an unknown sacred place in our unconscious mind, where secrets lie and sleep undisturbed, waiting to be aroused. It emerges from there, where suppression and depression reign in self-effacing judgment but does not stay there. Rather, it lies dormant until something happens to challenge and evoke it. Until then, the struggle to trust remains alone, lonely and even scared, occasionally tested in an existential game of hide-and-seek—scared that the secret self will be laughed at, scorned, and ultimately rejected—not a rare experience. That fear sometimes keeps us from trusting another person, or group, ever.

The most unique, personal, and inner fear of the intimacy of trust is quite common. When confronted with the challenge of deep trust in a new relationship, we are invited to open up and be vulnerable in a manner that may feel strange to us, and even mysterious. But that may be what we all experience, ironically, if we are truly honest with ourselves.

That's what we discover in the greatest of poetry, novels, and films. There's that feeling we hold within that the poet or artist has portrayed that we can own even though we couldn't name it beforehand. In great films, it's what the author, screenwriter, producer, director, and actors have put their hearts into, to create images that make us feel, "Yes, that's what my life is all about. That's what makes me feel alive."

Here are some iconic scenes from some very old but well-known films that may resonate with you. They breathe exhilarating oxygen into parts of us that feared the conflict leading to resolution. They help us trust the world with our newfound authenticity. Great art, in whatever format—spoken, visual, musical, electronic—can accomplish this.

Scenes from old, classic films such as *East of Eden* with James Dean come to mind, when he gets to confront his mother directly for the first time, in a house of prostitution; from *Pretty Woman* with Julia Roberts and Richard Gere, when he climbs the fire escape despite his fear of heights, to rescue her from her life of prostitution; from *My Cousin Vinny*, when a mediocre attorney, played by Joe Pesci, travels from Brooklyn to the Deep South to argue in court for his nephew's defense in a murder case and, overcoming his own shortcomings and the deep cultural differences, actually wins despite all odds; from *The Blues Brothers* when Aretha Franklin belts out in her enthralling golden voice to demand R-E-S-P-E-C-T for her race and gender.

These are the moments when our inner secrets and defenses are awakened and set free. They must be dealt with to release the possibilities for trust. As Shakespeare put it, "There is nothing so confining as the prisons of our own perceptions."

Trust often comes from confiding in another or believing that a group or institution is worthy of your openness. The person, group, or institution you allow yourself to risk with the vulnerability of that trust is an equal partner in this process.

Learning about Trust as a Youngster

I began learning to trust at the ripe age of twenty-one. I was a graduate student at San Diego State University, but on this particular weekend I was on the campus of UCLA attending a folk music festival. At the end of the first night, as others were finding places to sleep, I found a cot at the back of the campus music studio set aside for us and, after strumming a few bars on my guitar, I lay down and fell asleep as well.

The next morning, I awoke to the most incredible guitar music I'd ever heard. I opened my eyes and leaned up to see that the music was coming from none other than the legendary, blind folk guitarist, the Reverend Gary Davis. The others apparently had gone out for breakfast, and for some reason, Davis was alone, except for me. His fingers were strumming up and down the neck of a twelve-string acoustic guitar, the notes flying off the sounding board to bounce off the walls and ceiling, creating the most remarkable music I'd ever heard in my life. I just lay back on the cot and let the music flow over me, savoring each musical moment.

When he finished playing, I got up, cleared my throat—rather loudly, to let him know he wasn't alone—and approached him. "I really enjoyed your music," I said. "I'd like to do something for you in return. Can I, uh, I don't know, take you for a walk?"

"Sure," he replied, setting his guitar into its stand.

So far, we had communicated only through sound—his guitar music and then my approaching him in person. Now there was the additional option of contact through touch. We had never met before. How would I make him feel safe entering his blind touch-and-be-touched world? I wanted to ensure that he felt emotionally safe in his own sightless world, transitioning from sound to touch.

I reached out for his hand, and instinctively placed it gently on my elbow so I could guide him. That seemed to instantly create a sense of trust between us.

He gripped my elbow and we walked down a flight of stairs into the warmth of the California sunshine and strolled along Westwood Boulevard in front of the UCLA campus. I told him about the birds flying overhead, about the people passing by, and the goods displayed in the storefront windows as we walked by them. What color are the birds, he wondered aloud. Otherwise, he took it all in without uttering a word.

This vignette helps me frame what trust meant to me at that early part of my life. I could not find trust with my father, but that morning, the Reverend Gary Davis and I formed a special bond, a bond I never had with my father but always wanted. It was the kind of bond all of us want with those who are important to us, whether related or not, because that morning I heard the music from his heart and he saw the world through my eyes.

That is a big part of what trust is all about: feeling connected by seeing the world through the eyes of another person. That's what we call *empathy*. As we'll see, empathy is a crucial component of trust. These two experiences—one sad, one joyful—are why I am so passionate about the issue of trust and, largely, why I decided to write this book.

I loved the Reverend Gary Davis's music. I decided to share the gift of sight with him so he could see the world around him, even though he would see it through my eyes. That all depended on trust, which flowed between us as I requested permission to bring touch into the picture when I asked him if I could lead him out of the studio.

What to Expect

Acknowledging trust can sometimes be stressful, for trusting has untested risks, risks that can easily lead to disappointment. Yet trust is so essential to human interaction, whether at home with family members, at work with colleagues and bosses, at school with teachers and professors, and in politics with those who take an oath to protect us. It is the bedrock on which all institutions are founded.

As vulnerable and essential a process as it is, how do we manage to trust? This is a key question because trust is essential to healthy relationships. How could we go through the commitment of marriage without trusting our beloved? How can we let go of our children as they prepare to leave home without trusting their untested integrity? How do we dedicate years of our life to an institution of higher learning without trusting that we will earn our degrees leading to the success we dreamed of? How do we apply ourselves at work without trusting that the organization to which we devote precious hours of our life is worth doing? How do we survive as a society without trust in our political leaders, especially in such times of crisis as the current battle for trust?

At the end of the day, trust is a positive choice. It's the demons that put up defenses, keeping us from taking the risk.

Trust Among Animals

Let's go back about 200,000 years, just as humans began walking the earth. What were the dynamics of trust among animals before language as we know it existed?

Even without words, animals communicate as to whether trust exists among them. Most mammalian species are acutely aware of facial expression, even among species that we typically think of as quite insensitive to such things.[1,2,3] Equine experts claim that horses have seventeen facial expressions. The tilt of the head; the openness of the eyes; the slight curve, either downward or upward, of the lip line; the baring of teeth for predators—all these give cues to individuals, of whatever species, about their position in a hierarchy of power that is consistent over time and, because it is consistent, therefore trustworthy.

More than 150 years ago, Charles Darwin explored the basis of emotional expression among animals, focusing primarily on smiling approval and frowning disapproval, which he found to be quite consistent across mammalian species.[4]

The Face Doesn't Lie

Trust, according to Webster's dictionary, has to do with the "assured reliance on the character, ability, strength, or truth of someone or something; one in which confidence is placed."[5] Note the word *reliance*. We humans perceive how we should rely on others through seeing the facial and body expression, hearing the words, and, at a subtler level, perceiving what is largely unconscious—the tone of voice, pattern and rhythm of expression, the degree of direct eye contact, rate of blinking, and facial flush.[6] In other words, there is much to be perceived when one is deciding how much trust to put in another person's communication.

According to a classical study in nonverbal communication, how we say something conveys much more than the actual words we use, at least for single-word utterances expressing our values, such as *thanks, really,* and *terrible*. Albert Mehrabian had his subjects (UCLA undergraduates) utter those words under conditions of positive, neutral, or negative tones, and found that over half (55 percent) of the message was conveyed by facial expression, over a third (38 percent) by vocal characteristics—tone of voice, pitch, rhythm, for example—and only 7 percent by the actual words themselves.[7] In fact, in certain aspects of person-to-person communication, when we're showing how we feel about something, the words amount to little more than a hill of beans while our face talks much more about how we feel about something.

Mehrabian believed that you're more likely to trust someone if you feel that the nonverbal aspect of the spoken communication accurately reflects the person's true feelings about you. Whether that person likes you or not, so long as you conclude that those feelings are genuine, determines when trust is more likely. So, authenticity plays a large role in the dynamic of trust. (Maybe that's why Trump is so popular and trusted by his base: His affect accurately reflects his authenticity.)

As the most intelligent among species on this planet, we humans determine how much trust to put in one another based as much on these subconscious modes of expression as on the words we hear. In addition, there are also the actual behaviors we see along with the perceptions we have about the other person's integrity.

Everything You Always Wanted to Know about Your Emotions

Babies are born inherently trusting. Their total dependence on adults requires this safe bonding. By seven months, they've established their relationships, and develop a fear of strangers, most intensely by ten months. This is the time when the response of their parents is most important. To develop trust, a child must be raised in a loving and safe environment. Children are especially dependent on their caregivers, usually their parents, to teach these traits. When the child is neglected or abused, distrust can become a lifelong issue.

Given my experience of a father who put a greater priority on his business matters than to any of his son's needs for affection or attention, I can easily experience the neglect leading me to have a particular interest in the issue of trust. Fortunately, I could take responsibility for getting my needs for attention met after leaving home. Once I reached Los Angeles and made some new friends, enjoying a rich social life I hadn't experienced before, life became joyful rather than bleak. I was on my way to a happier life, but the issue of trust remained highly intriguing to me, sufficiently so to motivate me to write this book.

Beyond the early years, trust continues to challenge us at various levels. As we mature, we take more responsibility for our interactions with others. By our early twenties, we begin to see the world more realistically and independently, and our values begin to emerge more clearly.

The Psychology of Trust

Trust has a lot to do with emotional sensitivity. There is a large body of literature on how people communicate in terms of the degree of authenticity which we can depend on when deciding how much to trust. In other words, does the person come across with emotions that we see as real and transparent, or do they seem fake or present us with an emotionally reserved disposition, leaving us uncertain about their feelings? We've come a long way since Darwin's focus on smiling approval and frowning disapproval.

For example, over the past fifty years, scientists have explored a range of expressions and have decided on a small number of basic emotions.[8] Through two decades of research, Silvan Tomkins came up with eight basic emotions, which, after reviewing his findings, were agreed upon by his colleagues.[9] These were the emotions:

1. Interest-excitement: the pull toward mastery (enhanced by much interpersonal affirmation)
2. Enjoyment-joy: the social bond (ranging from deprivation to trust and attachment)
3. Surprise-startle: the reset button (stop what you're doing and see what's possible)
4. Distress-anguish: the cry for help (sometimes due to overstimulation)
5. Anger-rage: the demand to fix (may need to be managed)
6. Fear-terror: the signal to flee or freeze (can be triggered by memories)

7. Shame-humiliation: the self-protection signal (often unacknowledged)
8. Disgust: the need to expel anything (or anyone) toxic

The dynamics of trust along the lines of Tomkins's list of emotions allow for interesting exploration. I would venture to say that openness to learning is enhanced by early encouragement of the interest-excitement emotion. The more an infant and young child are encouraged to pursue interest in their surroundings, the more trust they will have in their world, both in their parents and teachers as well as in novel, external challenges. Why? Because positive experiences in general enhance the feeling of trust. Such children would be more open to engaging social interaction and academic challenges as they leave home and spend more time in educational settings.

It goes without saying that enjoyment-joy inherently builds trust with those with whom joy is shared. As for anger-rage and fear-terror, anyone rescuing the young from such unpleasant emotions would be more likely to be trusted, especially at younger ages.

Shame-humiliation, if it is an ongoing state in younger years, can clearly affect personality, resulting in a retiring or defiant, defensive posture toward others, closed to learning new ways to deal with outside life challenges. Such individuals are likely to be unaware of their defensive postures, seeing them as justifiable solutions to complex problems, while demonstrating mistrust as an overall attitude.

It's interesting that guilt is left out of this list of emotions. I would include it as a cousin to this emotion of shame, consequent to some deed that is specific to a particular action and that is highly judged as negative by one's society.

Whereas shame is more an ongoing result of self-evaluation, guilt is more likely to be due to a specific act. Shame is something we might feel as a personal experience over time; whereas, guilt is short-term, lasting only so long as the negatively judged action remains unresolved. Though guilt can be openly expressed, it sometimes implies something hidden, so trust can be affected by this emotion as the guilty party anticipates the breakdown of trust when the questionable act is revealed. Once revealed, redemption is possible, and trust can return. This is less true of shame, a more complex and enduring emotion.

The current guru of hidden emotional expression, psychologist Paul Ekman, reduced this list of emotions to six: happiness, sadness, anger, fear, disgust, and surprise. [10,11]

Further research resulted in omitting the emotion of surprise as a separate entity.[12] Why? Primarily because surprise is more than a basic emotion. It's a complex dynamic between thinking and emotion, involving immediate insight into an unexpected circumstance. It's much too complex to be considered a basic emotion.

So, we remain with five basic emotions—Ekman's list minus surprise. Since our focus here is on trust, we can conveniently dispose of disgust, since disgust is a specific, negative reaction to something in our nearby environment, typically relating to our sense of smell or taste, but sometimes to abhorrent social values.

This leaves us with four to contend with—happiness, sadness, anger, and fear. Common sense would indicate that, if we are angry at someone, we are less likely to trust. However, if we're fearful or sad, we might be more susceptible to trusting someone because of our possible need for support at the time. Anger is a more complex dynamic of trust. Are we angry at the communicator or is that person more of a support in our anger toward a third party? For example, if a country is attacked, its citizens are more likely to trust their government as they look for protective leadership.

And when a government is divided, as it appears in this Age of Mistrust, then leadership is also divided. Ideally, a government can be idealized as a protective parent. But when the division in government grows deeper, then that can exacerbate feelings of confusion in the citizenry, and fear and hostility can become more rampant. All this makes trust more challenging.

In this beginning, I've taken the liberty to reveal some of my own history of trusting the world, getting somewhat personal by sharing the absence of trust with my father, and then brought the issue into a contemporary political context. In this chapter, we explored the psychological evolution of trust and the power of nonverbal aspects of communication as well as research on the emotions of trust.

In the next chapter, we'll look at more practical aspects of the dynamics of trust as well as its neuroscience. We'll look at exactly how trust is manifested in our own lives and explore a "jazzy" model for how trust works.

4

Can You Trust Your Feelings?

"I have learned that my total organismic sensing of a situation is more trustworthy than my intellect."
—CARL ROGERS

At its very beginning, the history of trust largely has to do with how open we are to the one doing the communication, whether that one was a primal ape, a human in our early history about 200,000 years ago, or, more currently, a user of ChatGPT or R1. There is a large body of literature supporting that. The basic premise of this literature is this: **The more we feel heard and understood by someone, the more likely we are to trust that person**, and feel safe doing so.

The pioneer of this research was psychologist Carl Rogers who wrote about trust in terms of empathic listening, "to catch every nuance" of emotional expression,[1] "to sense the hurt or the pleasure of another as he (or she) senses it" so "that the recipient [of the empathy] feels valued, cared for, accepted as the person that he or she is."[2] Once the person has this sense of being heard, then they are more likely to be open to greater trust in that individual and, as mentioned, feel safe doing so.

Referring to this as the person-centered approach, Rogers and his colleagues continued to explore the dynamics of careful listening and found that deeper listening resulted in an increase in levels of trust. Sidney Jourard (in *The Transparent Self*),[3] Abraham Maslow (in *Toward a Psychology of Being*),[4] and Rollo May[5] (in *Love and Will*[6] and *The Meaning of Anxiety*[7]) all contributed to this literature looking into what happens when one listens with caring attention. The result, they found, was that the level of trust and openness increased significantly. Theodor Reik had referred to this as "listening with the third ear."[8]

In this brief history of trust, it's also important to break trust down into its scientific components or, more specifically, the neuroscience of trust. This doesn't necessarily involve trying to determine exactly where trust resides in the brain, since it assuredly takes place all over the brain, from the emotion-generating limbic system at the base of the brain, to the danger-sensing amygdalae on each side, through the emotion-interpreting cingulate gyrus, and, finally, to the decision-making frontal cortex. Trust is a complex dynamic involving all of the brain's systems. Beyond this basic neruoscience of trust, I refer to the basic animal research on the emotions making up trust.

The Neuroscience of Trust

Let's take a brief look at the anatomy of trust—how it's built on the framework of our basic emotions. In his book, *Affective Neuroscience*,[9] Jaak Panksepp identifies the neural basis of seven semi-independent emotional command circuits in his research on the brain. His lab studies revealed that once one of these basic emotions gets switched on with any degree of intensity, it tends to persist stubbornly.

According to his line of research,[10] emotional signals initially stem from the unconscious, subcortical regions of the brain, referred to as the limbic system, indicating how well we are doing in our quest to survive on the basis of trusting our environment. Such persistent emotions such as anxiety, anger, and deep sadness can be problematic for our social interactions, but we can tame them by labeling them and taking charge of their untoward effects.

Seen in this light, the quest for trust is a challenge in that it involves the skill of managing negative emotions. Take anger, for example. Rather than give in to the impulse to yell at someone or, even worse, lash out in anger, thereby destroying any semblance of trust if we are extremely frustrated, we can choose to acknowledge the feeling of anger and label it as such as soon as it arises in our awareness. Then we can identify that growing emotion as anger and make a conscious decision as to whether to articulate it as such with whoever is frustrating us or, in a fit of fury, just yell out our frustration and express it physically and violently. This discipline, which can become a skill or habit of admitting to ourselves and others that we are beginning to feel frustrated and angry and therefore attempt to control any outburst, is the taming of that emotion.

For example, if I were to get angry at a friend for hurting my feelings by criticizing me in front of other friends (and being accurate in his critical remarks, which makes it even more painful), I could end up criticizing him right back in a loud, threatening voice, or I could choose another option: sharing how his comments made me uncomfortable, made me aware of my building anger but, instead of expressing the anger directly, just label it as such and then turn to another option, perhaps sharing my hurt and how I needed to change so his criticisms would no longer be as accurate. I'm choosing to fix the problem rather than defend it.

I might say something like, "John, it kind of hurts to hear you say that, and I could see getting really angry at you, but the more mature option is for me to address your points of criticism and see if there's any truth to them. Maybe I can become a better person, thanks to your pointing that out. I know you're my good friend and that you only want me to be a better person." That way, the trust in our relationship is restored rather than destroyed.

In this way, we invite the unconscious emotion into awareness and, rather than being a slave to it, we master it and have the option of controlling it. We can choose to build trust through effective social skills—some call it mindfulness.

The birth of trust, when it does not arise naturally, can be manifested by such awareness and positive attitude. We can improve in this skill with friends and acquaintances and, most meaningfully, if not most challenging, family. Patterns of behavior that have been part of our personality for years can be transformed by this theoretically simple exercise. We can actually decide to build trust in our relationships without necessarily insisting that others change along with us, though that might be a likely outcome. Trust begets trust, generally speaking, but admittedly not always.

The benefit of this exercise is to short-circuit the damage that can be done to the level of trust at the moment by giving in to the impulse to yell out violently. Instead, there is the option to negotiate a resolution calmly and with mutual resolve. Also, instead of using the word *angry*, we could choose a less intense word such as *frustration*. Since that's likely what we are really feeling, it works better; it's more accurate and less threatening to the level of trust.

The Comfort and Discomfort Zones

Another example: the anxiety we might feel when addressing a new group in a structured social setting. We become aware of our heart racing, muscle tension, and other feelings, and yet we have the option of just relabeling these sensations from anxiety to excitement. That puts a much more positive spin on the whole experience and converts negative emotions into positive ones.

For example, when I give a talk to a new group and I detect some critical attitude in the audience, I choose to share with them this very example: "Talking to this new group could make me very anxious, but, as I look around at some smiling faces, I see that at least some of you are looking forward to what I have to share with you and, suddenly, I start feeling very excited about being here with you tonight.

"You see, part of what I want to share with you is how our emotions are controlled by our lower brain, but, just as I'm doing right now, I choose to identify this surge of adrenaline that makes my heartbeat faster with excitement rather than fear . . . and you can do that too. It's just a matter of taking control of your emotions by labeling in a more positive context. Once you can identify with the more positive emotion, your body will follow suit with a more relaxed stance and a broad smile on your face." The audience will see the shift in my demeanor and the more relaxed facial expression. It usually works beautifully.

I've killed two birds with one stone: shifting my emotion from anxiety to excitement and teaching my audience a lesson in real time that they can use for themselves.

With respect to the negative emotions, and in agreement with Paul Ekman's list of six emotional expressions (from the previous chapter), Panksepp[11] characterizes three of these as the discomfort zone. They are as follows:

- Fear (from mild anxiety to intense fright)
- Sorrow (from mild disappointment to disabling depression)
- Rage (like anger with the desire to lash out thoughtlessly).

On the positive side, four are characterized as the comfort zone:

- Seeking (curiosity with a purpose)
- Caring (feelings of nurturing)
- Lust (urge for physical intimacy)
- Play (freely expressive with others)

So how would we expect to construct trust from these basic emotions? Clearly, fear, sorrow, and rage are contraindications for trust, unless the communicator is shielding or protecting us from threats by a third party. If we combine caring and play with a mild form of lust and with a touch of seeking, then we have romantic attraction, a whole different interpersonal dynamic in which trust plays its own complex role.

Our focus on trust depends mostly on the emotion of caring. If we feel cared for by the communicator of empathy, this will tend to increase our trust in them more than any of the other six emotions, especially if that caring is dependably consistent over time.

That's what happens in good psychotherapy when the therapist is attentive and comes across as caring through posture and words. It's called *transference*, where the therapist takes the place of a significant caring person, often a parent, in the client's life. This process can be a strong influence in the therapeutic process. The utmost trust is built between doctor and patient.

According to Panksepp's research,[12] the emotional brain circuits he refers to, once initiated, tend to persevere over time, making them more dependable, and hence making the individual caring communicator seem more trustworthy. So, if we can experience the caring as consistent and dependable, then we also tend to put more trust in the communicator themself.

Trust describes a relationship between a trustee and a beneficiary (for example, doctor and patient, parent and child, adviser and client), with varying levels of the beneficiary's dependence on the trustor. In the doctor/patient relationship, the life of a patient may be at stake, with grave consequences should that level of trust be broken. Forgiveness is then not very likely. A minor child relies on their parents for food, shelter, and much more. The breach of such trust may be regained with forgiveness over time, but not easily. If an accountant messes up a tax return, for all intents and purposes, forgiveness is relatively easy when the errors are corrected, or the dent in the trust relationship may be an obstacle to further interaction.

Trust between larger groups, such as organizations and their clients or even nations in conflict, follows a similar dynamic. In such cases, that dynamic begins with subtle overtures, followed by a tentative agreement to initiate interaction around an agreed-upon theme, and then exploration of new solutions to existing challenges about overcoming differences, to result in something new—a creative response that is based on the growing trust.

The "Jazzy" Psychology of Trust

One novel way of deepening our understanding of trust is to compare it to the process of creating jazz. Trust occurs between at least two people. (Let's not get into the proposition of trusting oneself just yet. We'll deal with that later, in great detail.) According to the renowned American musician, Wynton Marsalis, "Jazz music is about communication. That negotiation [of blending the music] is the art."[13]

The creation of jazz when musicians play together requires a subtle sensitivity to one another's contributions. The novelty of the music that emerges from the free flow of originality by the players who trust one another to reach a collective dynamic is similar to the process of trust. Both jazz and trust, when done well, require improvisation, mutual support, and teamwork—toward a common purpose. And that purpose creates the guardrails that contain the freedom within, the freedom to be creative, spontaneous, and authentic, yet intensely focused on resolution to the conflict throughout. It requires a fusion of brain and heart.

Both trust and jazz have the following in common:

- An *invitation* to improvise: In the process of creating both trust and jazz, there is an invitation respecting the other's flexibility to change. Just as important is an openness to substantial and unpredictable shifts in the process of working through initial differences and expectations. In jazz, it might involve a shift in rhythm or chord progressions. In trust, it might involve yielding one's intended outcome to another's needs and expectations. In both, respecting the other's judgment is crucial if a strong connection of trust is to be achieved.

- A *cohesive theme*: In jazz, there is a shared melody and underlying harmony that all players can tune into and blend with one another. In the process of opening to trust, there is a central theme and underlying structure about which the trust is built. Here also is the possibility of sharing needs with one another and even aspirations.

- A *movement toward agreement*: In jazz, the musical techniques of the players combine to form a melody that joins the various creative efforts into one overriding and moving tune. In terms of trust formation, there is a building of agreement on a particular theme.

- A mutual respect leading to *something new*: In jazz, there is a creative response to one another's unique contributions. In building trust, there is ultimate agreement on a joint outcome, a new one which respects both perspectives.

The key to all this is the commitment to improvise, to allow individual egos to be tossed aside, at least temporarily, and to enter the common challenge of deeply sharing a common purpose, independent of any past history or expectations, to allow the players, whether in jazz or in conflict resolution, to trust one another deeply.

Research reveals that musicians who play together think together, at least in terms of acting in concert with one another. According to the study, musicians who play together manifest what the scientists call action co-representation. They "adapt in real time to each other's changing actions" as measured scientifically.[14] We might call it psychic improvisation yet requiring hard work and dedication to the process.

Perhaps the process of building trust has a similar dynamic. The more two individuals devote themselves to building a set of shared hopes and aspirations to resolve differences, the more they naturally give in to the process of co-representation in which they more easily fall into their trusting natures, allowing the process of trust to develop more smoothly. This may in part account for the success of President Carter's Peace Accords between Israel and Egypt.[26] Much more on that later.

Listening to the Music of Trust

As a colleague put it years ago, "Listen to the music, not the words." Sometimes, listening to such music with the third ear can help decide whom to trust and whom not to trust. Often it is not just what is being said but probably more important for building trust, how it is said and to what extent there is that jazzy togetherness.

A co-actualizing process—sensing and respecting your own and the other's feelings and meanings—provides for a set of constructive relationships, making possible "authentic and yet highly regardful dialogic interactions" with "a self-organizing quality."[15] We'll see later, in clear detail, how this can be made to occur between international enemies, as President Jimmy Carter proved, but also between those choosing to form any relationship of trust, whether in the boardroom or in the bedroom. As Wynton Marsalis puts it, continuing the analogy of creating jazz for building trust, "Ours is the art of listening and co-creating."[16] How true, whatever the time or setting!

In this section, I've shared with you the anatomy of human emotions in the formation of trust, as well as those in the animal kingdom,[17] and a thorough exploration of how the dynamics of emotions help explain the basics of trust. What I hope you take away with you is the importance of listening to someone's deeper feelings in order to gain their trust, hopefully putting your ego aside while you let the other take center stage. I've explained what role emotions play in that dynamic.

Then we looked at the basic steps needed to create trust—by making someone feel heard and understood in the process of co-actualizing the shared communication. In the next section of this book, we'll look at how social scientists share the details of building trust that lasts over time, and how that can even apply to the effects of the Gutenberg Revolution and, as well, how Leonardo da Vinci led to greater trust of the scientific world through his own creative efforts.

PART III

Literary Trust: Gutenberg, da Vinci, and the Chatbot Revolution

Literary trust: Though this usually refers to the legal status of an author's rights to written material, in the context of this book, it refers to how much trust we afford to what we read in published material that has the potential of influencing our behavior.

"The most powerful words in English are 'Tell me a story,' words that are intimately related to the complexity of history, the origins of language, the continuity of the species, the taproot of our humanity, our singularity, and art itself."

—PAT CONROY, best-selling author, *The Lords of Discipline*

5

How the Written Word Changed the Battle for Trust

"Words have a magical power. They can either bring the greatest happiness or the deepest despair."
—SIGMUND FREUD

Queen Tiamen, in bright attire with necklaces of golden leaf-shaped pendants, her hair adorned in a bun with a double row of lapis lazuli and reddish beads, walked softly yet boldly across the marble-tiled floor. Following her was a retinue of three heavyset bearded men with broadswords hanging heavily at their left sides, along with her two courtiers, slender and with shaved heads. Standing to meet them was King Trefhu and two of his courtiers to resolve a territorial dispute between the two city-states.

In ceremonial ritual, the three warriors approached the king, knelt with slight bowing, extending their right hands in greeting, one after the other, to symbolize their peaceful intent. The king nodded his approval, smiling at his courtiers, signaling them to proceed with the resolution of negotiations. A clay tablet marked with wooden reeds to form wedge-shaped marks was brought forth, written to model the Akkadian language, which both kingdoms understood. The cuneiform figures on the clay tablets spelled out the new borders, which both sides had negotiated after months of pitched battle. Both somewhat small armies were being decimated, neither of which could afford such ongoing attrition.

This account may have been described in a history of Canaan, in what is now Lebanon, to depict the life in that culture in 3500 BC.

Books have brought to light the history of ancient cultures eons before the inventions of photography, television, and all the electronics of the modern age. Before all that technology, the only medium to travel into the past was made up of books.

Many of us readers are fascinated by books and even fall in love with some. Sometimes, too often, it's hard to get rid of them after we've finished reading them. They become extensions of our brain, even our heart, in a matter of speaking.

Like others we know, we may be reading two or three at a time, on totally different subjects. As I write these words, I just laid claim to two more books which I'm enjoying, a book on how to meditate (as if there were only one way) and Jack Kerouac's iconic *On the Road*, written over sixty years ago and yet still so engaging. Because of the vetting process that publishers typically put a book through, they're somewhat easier to trust than the digital word for reasons we've already explored. But not always. Sometimes the bias comes through, since publishers are not necessarily always trustworthy.

Books bring us together in a community of like minds. As I read the book on meditation, I imagine all the other readers as like-minded friends, some of whom I might come across someday, with whom to compare notes on our challenges at meditating successfully. Reading *On the Road*, I can feel part of the community of unrepressed travelers, enjoying the freedom of the road, leaving all our weighted responsibilities behind.

Each book, it seems, has the potential of feeling part of an accepting community, where our need for trust can be easily satisfied. In our current Age of Mistrust, there aren't enough opportunities to feel that trust. Yet we need it.

According to Robert Logan, author of *The Alphabet Effect*, "A medium of communication is not merely a passive conduit for the transmission of information but rather an active force in creating new social patterns and new perceptual realities. A person who is literate has a different world view than one who receives information exclusively through oral communication."[1]

Here is a significant dimension of building and maintaining trust—not eye-to-eye, face-to-face contact, but through the written word, as happens more and more in our social media culture. How did this issue of trust-mistrust begin? How and where did written language originate and how did it change trust in society? How did this history affect trust over the ages, in religion, commerce, and even government? We'll deal with all that in the next two sections.

Satisfying our need to trust was much less problematic before the Industrial Revolution. When we were still in small groups, tribes, even villages, we knew intuitively whom to trust. We grew up with one another, played together, went through the transition into adulthood together, and got to know one another well.

But when we migrated to live in big cities and encountered hundreds of people a day rather than a few dozen or so, then our need to trust shifted to a more complex dynamic of relationships. We had to give a bit more thought about whom to trust. We went from trusting intuitively to deciding whom to trust—and how—based on our emotions and some thoughtful analysis of our experience with different individuals. Welcome to the evolution of trust.

New Social Patterns and New Perceptual Realities

The transformation of our culture—from right-brain thinking to left-brain thinking, from hearing with the intuitive ear to seeing with the logical eye—led to the formation of our major institutions primarily through the creation of the written word. The medium of written language transformed how we interacted with one another. Those who could manage written language lived in a different world, one that could reach out beyond their immediate environment to greater horizons.

In this part, we will see how the development of reliance on the written word has had its influence on the nature of trust. We start in the land of Canaan, in the Middle East, where words were written down to create a reliable system of annotation that people would learn to trust, followed by a brief history of the beginnings of written language.

How Written Language Affected Trust

When we use the words, "In the beginning... there was the spoken word," we are referring to a time before there was any codification of communication or written language. This takes us back to about 3500 BC to the land of the Canaanites in the Middle East, near present-day Lebanon, where the beginnings of the written word were taking place. At that time, trust was based on a handshake (the right one, to ascertain that no sword was being drawn). The first written documents were in cuneiform, wedge-shaped marks on clay tablets, using the Sumerian and Akkadian languages around 3400 BC, typically using a reed on clay tablets.

Of course, there were stages in the evolution of the alphabet, from cuneiform script to pictographs about 3100 BC to logographs (representing vowels) in 3000 BC. Ideograms and phonetic signs came about 500 years later.

By 1500 BC, the Canaanites invented the first alphabet consisting of only twenty-two letters, but these letters were the basis of all other phonetic alphabets, including the Romance languages, English, Greek, Russian, Arabic, and others. The Greeks were the ones to contribute vowels about 800 BC, resulting in a twenty-seven-letter language.[2]

The Etruscans, who helped the Romans understand Greek, used a Latinized version of the alphabet, and this was adopted by the Roman Empire, and the Roman armies carried this to all the lands they conquered throughout France, Germany, and Great Britain.

Trust in Law, Religion, and Science

According to Israeli writer, Y. N. Harari, author of *Sapiens*, the largest primate groups rarely exceeded 190 individuals. For humans to coexist in larger groups, such as villages and hamlets, some form of connection other than face-to-face communication was necessary, and that's where written language comes into place.[3]

Once the reading of documents was available, trust could be based on a published agreement among citizens of a state or among members of a religion with its commitment to communal devotion to a divine entity (or multiple entities). A trust in the process of law or in the shared rituals, in which members of a religion took part, were novel aspects of this dynamic of trust in the written word.

Handwritten language gave birth to codified law as well as religious dogma, and they both became institutionalized. Trust could now be based on such codification, no longer relying only on face-to-face interaction. The first legal document in history, written in Sumerian, was the code of law written in the twenty-second century BC in ancient Mesopotamia.[4]

In Egypt, in the middle of the thirteenth century BC, there were the 42 Negative Confessions,[5] which all citizens needed to memorize so that they could claim innocence to the gods after death.[6] Though written and rewritten over centuries, the Old Testament, or Torah, is believed to have been consolidated after 539 BC, when the Jews were freed from Babylonian captivity.[7] (One copy, made up of about 400 pages of parchment, dated in the tenth century, recently owned by the Swiss financier Jacqui Safra, was valued by Sotheby's at about $40 million before going to auction. It actually sold for a bit over $38 million.)

One consequence of the written word was the possibility of contracts that allowed for business to become institutionalized. David Byrne, writing in his production of *Bicycle Diaries,* claimed, "One theory regarding language is that it is primarily a useful tool born out of a need for control. Once there were bosses, there arose a need for written language."

When did all this writing of documents begin to influence trust in institutions? How did legal institutions gain sufficient trust to maintain credibility among many diverse groups? Well, Roman law, heavily influenced by the Greeks, made its own stamp along the successful expansion of the Roman Empire, eventually consolidated, and codified by Emperor Justinian in the mid-first century, and then centralized by

Charlemagne 300 years later. Law then returned to local jurisdictions during the Middle Ages and was later affected by the Byzantine code by Crusaders returning from Palestine in the late 1400s.[8]

No matter where written language sprang up, trust in institutions soon followed. After the Norman conquest of England in 1066, the written word gave birth to the *Domesday Book* in 1086, a grand survey of England's properties by William the Conqueror, written in Latin, resembling what we might now call a census; and then the Magna Carta in 1215.

These were among the beginnings of trust in the legal system, among the first laws in our Western culture to be established. The Napoleonic Code—*La Publication, des Effets et de l'Application des Lois en General*—and the German *Burgerliches Gesetzbuch* strongly influenced the laws of the lands as nationalism grew in the eighteenth and nineteenth centuries. The United States adopted English law rather than the European code, except for the State of Louisiana, which still follows the French system.

Trust in the Written Word

All this made it possible to invest one's trust in a system of law and religion based on communication through the written word.[9] As well, there was the beginning of a growing trust in the basic assumptions of a scientific culture as the written word could communicate the precision required for experimental research and scientifically derived conclusions.

The written word allowed for investing one's trust in an entity that could not be seen in any face-to-face manner. The dynamic of trust now has become much more complex. In the face-to-face context, through the spoken word, trust might be based on intuitive feelings and immediate transactions, such as a handshake or some exchange of payment or concrete product.

Trusting written words absent a human face required a transition to a greater focus on rational and abstract, left-brain thinking. Rather than relying on intuition about the character of the other person, one had to become more logical, causal, and time oriented. It made trust a more complex, challenging enterprise because it wasn't always possible to see the person(s) behind the words. One could more easily be exploited, in the absence of intuitive signals, such as the characteristics of communication discussed earlier, when one is not face-to-face with the other.

By the mid-fifteenth century, a tsunami of cultural change was taking place: the invention of the printing press by Johannes Gutenberg in Mainz, Germany, making mass production possible. This allowed for the printing of books that could now be sold to people all over the country, soon the continent, and then the world. This immense cultural shift changed how information was being conveyed along with raising the literacy rate among Europeans.

When the written word became the published word, after the Gutenberg Revolution, whatever was written in books was deemed trustworthy, because of the editing process and reputation of the publisher, at least until the advent of magazines and then self-published books. Then all bets were off since there was typically less editorial responsibility by either editor or publisher outside of the author.

Fast-forward to the present, as email allows for words without the facial expressions that humans have relied on for so much of our social history. Most of us have received messages asking for aid to assist some long-lost relative in dire straits, or to cooperate in the unloading of a vat of funds, in return for a 10 percent holding fee to be paid in advance, of course. Such familiar and even seductive requests can play havoc with our desire to trust in time of need, or for personal greed.

The frequency of scams on the internet gives us one type of mistrust that most of us have experienced at one time or another. And now, with the introduction of chatbots like ChatGPT and Bard, the issue of trust becomes exponentially magnified, especially when different chatbot applications can choose their own value systems to propagate whatever political influence they choose.

Virtual communication has its challenges that did not exist earlier in our history. But, even now, we still greet one another with our right hands (unless we bump fists or elbows to avoid contamination by some virus or other). We still produce documents that are much lighter than the original clay tablets, increasingly on an electronic basis. We still use letters but now mostly in English across the world on our cell phones rather than cuneiform. The form of communication has changed dramatically, but not the substance. And trust remains a challenge, even more so with electronic possibilities for fooling our senses.

I began this chapter by pointing to the advent of the printed book and its impact on our culture: transforming right-brain intuitive feeling into left-brain logical thinking. I shared how the history of trust was affected by the written word and its influence on the formation of institutions, starting in the land of the Canaanites in 3500 BC.

The written word allowed for trust in contractual documents that gave shape to codified law and religious dogma. The original Bible, the Old Testament, formed in about 539 BC, reaped the persistent trust of a growing mass of worshippers, leading to Christianity and other religions influencing many far and wide.

In the following chapter, we'll explore how trust in the legal system was enhanced by the early Greeks and Romans who spread their influence through conquest of other cultures. As the drive toward nationalism spread throughout Europe in the eighteenth and nineteenth centuries, trust in national codes increased, setting the stage for war among nations, some lasting decades, so strong was trust in the respective nations' codes.

I begin with my own experience of growing up in a highly bicultural city, Montreal, and then take the larger view of how the Renaissance transformed trust from the church to secular art and then to the world of science, thanks to the comprehensive efforts of artist/architect/innovator/scientist, the beloved Leonardo da Vinci.

6

How Leonardo da Vinci Influenced Trust in Science

"The greatest deception men suffer is from their own opinions."
—LEONARDO DA VINCI

For someone born and raised in the city of Montreal, Canada, as I was, where the Catholic church has a powerful place in history over the French-speaking population of the province, English- and French-speaking families lived side-by-side in much of the city. Education in that city was clearly divided between the French-speaking Catholic schools and the English-speaking Protestant School Board of Greater Montreal. Their high school curricula were quite different. An English-speaking person would attend the Protestant system, preparing for a professional career. The French Canadian Catholic system geared students along classical lines with little emphasis on professional career growth.

This resulted in a lopsided economy in which the Catholic students were unfairly limited in terms of middle-class career aspirations. As a youngster, I wondered why the Catholic system was so powerful in the seemingly unfair guidance of the students under their influence. That's part of what got me interested in the power of religious education and the source of that power. Let's pull the camera back a bit, way back to the pages of history before Christ.

How the Renaissance Transformed Trust—
From the Gutenberg Revolution to the Industrial Revolution
In this chapter, we'll explore the dynamic of trust between the church and its followers. We'll look at how the people were drawn away from

the limiting dogma of Christianity to the luring draw of sensuality in the new freedom of Renaissance art. The trust they felt in the church was threatened by the newfound liberal expression and growing personal power as they began to sense new possibilities in the emerging opportunities of capitalism.

Until the Renaissance, literacy was limited to the very few who were educated, and so common citizens had to rely on those who could read what was codified as law and religious ethics. Trust had to be invested in such individuals, and this gave them great power. Before the Gutenberg Revolution with the invention of movable type and the printing press when the published written word became more accessible, there was little choice but to put one's trust in the clergy and in the immediate governing bodies. Except for ancient Greece and the Roman Republic, there was no public forum of shared information for questioning the power of these bodies. That's why religion had such a strong influence then and trust in democracy had little chance of success.

To put it in the present context, that's why the Taliban in Afghanistan and even the Chinese and Russian governments in the present day try to control public media, so they can have more control over their countrymen and -women. Even though literacy exists, there is a damper on free public information.

Judaism and Christianity both began before the advent of public literacy. Both were based on the written word, but not the widely read word, as most people were illiterate. Judaism began to consolidate itself during King David's reign with the beginning of the compilation of the Old Testament Scriptures, the biblical Torah.

Books at this time, before the Renaissance, were kept away from the masses, sometimes locked away or chained to the shelves on which they lay, often encrusted with jewels, and embroidered with gold and silver threads. They dealt primarily with legal concerns, topics of medicine (as it was understood at the time), and religious doctrine, mostly written on parchment. Copies of books were painfully inscribed by hand, one slow page after another.

In the year AD 360, a temple of knowledge was commissioned by the ruler of the Byzantine Empire in what was then known as Constantinople. This exemplified the beginnings of the Age of Faith at the beginning of the Dark Ages when feudalism was the political norm and there was little advancement in knowledge as the focus was commitment to faith in religion. The temple was known as Hagia Sophia, or Church of the Divine Wisdom, otherwise known as the Great Church, or Megale Ekklesia. It served Greek Orthodox Christianity, the first denomination for Christians. For the most part, the battle for trust was persistently on the side of the church.

The Battle for Trust Between the Religious and the Secular

Then, from the sixth century AD to about 1200, the monasteries had an exclusive monopoly on the preservation of classical texts, copied from originals by scribes working in special spaces in the monasteries, known as scriptoria.

Even before the Gutenberg era of printing, books were popular, at least for the wealthy. The conquests of Alexander the Great helped disperse the ideas of Greek culture. The first great library was in Alexandria, Egypt, about 250 BC, then very much part of a vast Greek cultural empire. It functioned not only as a source of books, but also as a center of scientific research. It was here that astronomy, biology, geography, and geometry flourished and where it was proclaimed that the Earth was not the center of the universe, but rather the Sun.

By AD 1000, great castles were built along with cathedrals employing Romanesque lines of architecture with their thick walls and lofty towers. Most people were illiterate then and the religious symbolism in stained glass windows and sculpture made up the media of the day, capturing the trust of the surrounding populace. Saint Mark's Basilica in Venice; the Piazza dei Miracoli in Pisa, Italy; and the Durham Cathedral in England were exemplary of this trend.

By AD 1100, the Middle Ages were going strong, as Romanesque architecture was giving way to Gothic style. Two centuries later, the

Dark Ages began to yield to more secular values. The church's undisputed power was waning. People increased involvement in education, commerce, and community activities that were less formal than the religious rituals and more enjoyable to the masses.

Trust was shifting away from the church and toward more democratic forms of government. The shift in art along these lines was pioneered by such sculptors as Arnolfo di Cambio and Nicola Pisano and artists as Cimabue in Florence, breaking from the medieval to the more humanistic style in the early fourteenth century. Cambio, along with his better known student, Giotto di Bondone, brought forth, for the first time, the imaginative power of the human figure, allowing for dramatic tension in their paintings, as exemplified by the frescoes in chapels not only in Florence but in Rome, Padua, and Naples as well.

With the influence of Giotto's artworks and its emphasis on emotional expression and naturalism, the Renaissance was on its way. What St. Francis of Assisi had brought to Christianity in terms of humanizing the church, Giotto and his peers brought to art. And the power of trust followed right along. The shift in trust away from the Middle Ages and into the Renaissance was strongly influenced by the works of Giotto.

By 1500, religious devotion was very slowly shifting to more pleasurable social activities, especially in central Italy, revealing an additional option for their trust from religious dogma to more secular values. Trust solely in the clergy was giving way to the possibility of trusting one's own interpretation of the Bible and the surrounding world. The world of science began to find acceptance.

Florence, in particular, was a testing ground for the inexorable growth of the Renaissance. Here is where the wealth of the upper class began fostering the transformation from feudalism to capitalism. The wealthy Medici family competed for the talents of artists such as Lorenzo Ghiberti, Filippo Brunelleschi, and Donatello, using their talents to glorify such iconic structures as the Gates of Paradise, on the doors to the Baptistry of the cathedral that is commonly known as Il Duomo; designing its dome; and creating five statues for its campanile, respectively. One might argue that this was the birthplace of the

Renaissance, as the battle for trust turned slowly and gradually away from devotion to the church to the appreciation of the art that only incidentally supported the church.

In the Gates of Paradise, Ghiberti revolutionized door decorations by creating depictions of biblical scenes, using a background, middle ground, and foreground, creating a three-dimensional effect. In his bronze *David*, Brunelleschi was among the first to demonstrate an emotional realism that stood as a model for future artists. All this led to the High Renaissance beginning in the early 1500s, setting the stage for more secular artists as Michelangelo and da Vinci, bearing the transition of the battle for trust to art for the sake of art and not just for religious devotion.

Instead of glorification of the saints, artists began to focus on the human senses: depicting luscious fruit for the sense of taste; the performance of music for hearing; and the seductive, sensual bodies for the sense of touch. Slowly yet inexorably, religious worship began to yield to more realistic depictions of pleasure.

How da Vinci Affected Trust in the Realm of Science

Before Leonardo da Vinci became famous, he felt very much like an outsider. Born in Tuscany near the small town of Vinci, he was raised by his paternal grandfather. With the curious energy of what we might now call attention-deficit disorder, young Leonardo was always seeking more and more information. Yet, as he grew into an adult, he felt ostracized by the current intellectuals as he lacked the Latinate schooling of his peers. But this genius in the making had to get away and carve out a path for his ultimate creativity. In the spring of 1482, Leonardo wrote what could be argued to be the first résumé in history, listing talents he dreamed of but were not yet totally within his grasp, and set off for Milan, the most advanced city in Italy at the time.

What Leonardo promised in his résumé was the ability to build war machines, which were in great need because of the bellicose culture of Italy at the time, with Florence, Venice, Milan, and the papal states all fighting for dominance. Because of his natural curiosity, Leonardo found a book on war machines and pored over every page, becoming an expert in a field very few knew about. He was quickly hired by the Duke of Milan, Ludovico Sforza, and began his work on inventions.

The rest is history, just when the history of trust became highly influenced by the production of books, leading readers away from trusting Christian dogma as they warmed to the opportunities for self-determination. No longer bound to the church, they now turned to the benefits of nonreligious education, boundless career opportunities, and artistic expression that allowed for a brand new sensual awareness.

With the Gutenberg Revolution taking its place in Renaissance history, the cost of books was reduced significantly, thus considerably increasing their availability. The changes in typography and engraving led to greater dissemination of books and more precision for details drawn about new inventions.

When Leonardo arrived in Milan, he had absolutely no books. Within a decade, he owned thirty-five books and, a few years later, over 200. His intellect thrived because of his restless nature and need to learn everything he could put his hands on from all the books he could put his eyes to. With his interests in war-machine technology, the nature of life in the human body and mind, the mechanics of water flow and air dynamics, as well as art and sculpture, it could easily be argued that he had a great influence in carving out trust for the scientific method.

Trust in the church was being affected by the new "religion," the Renaissance. Loss of confidence in the church also meant losing trust in the individuals who made up the clergy of the church.

Trust in books was being influenced by Leonardo as he revealed the truth about physics, mechanics, human biology, and astronomy though his writings and illustrations. He was among the most influential messengers of truth about science at the time, and the battle for trust was being won by the written word at the cost of the church. Of course, Leonardo da Vinci didn't do it all alone, but he did contribute significantly, as Western culture was ready to transport its new knowledge of technology by exploring the rest of the world.

Trust Crosses the Atlantic

At this point, commerce was growing substantially. The Renaissance that resulted in the growth of the middle class spawned another era in the history of trust. Demand for expeditions grew. Trust in science, the rediscovery of the Greek philosophers like Plato and Aristotle, came to fruition. All this description of events underscored the world as trust made the quantum leap, so to speak, from the church to humanistic values. Trust is a dynamic concept that is difficult to make concrete. By considering the world as it existed at the time, and the art that transformed its culture, the changes in trust can be more readily comprehended.

The dawn of the Age of Discovery then found its home in Portugal where exploration, trade, and even slavery brought wealth that could now pay artists for richly adorned structures that emulated foreign discovery and a cosmopolitan attitude that gave birth to trusting exposure to foreign travel and the riches it brought home. That trust resulted in the decision of the Spanish monarchy to commission Christopher Columbus to set sail for what turned out to be the shores of America, setting the stage for the Age of Exploration, with ventures into South America, Central America, and, ultimately, North America. The rest, as they say, is history—in this case, literally.

The battle for trust between the church and the secular was now clearly moving away from the church and being replaced by a growing trust in exploration of the New World.

In this chapter, we took a tour through the consecutive transitions in trust across Europe, from the biblical era through the Middle Ages to the Age of Discovery. I told the story of Leonardo da Vinci whose overactive intellect and love of books enabled him to help strengthen society's trust in science. The history of trust was now ready to continue in the New World.

In the next chapter, I reveal the dramatic transition of trust occurring in Britain and the United States as the Industrial Revolution made its mark. The basis of trust traveled from the ear to the eye even as Shakespeare allowed his audiences to hear his plays being performed and read in printed copies of them as well. In a sense, his plays created a bridge across which the battle for trust could be followed clearly.

7

The Not-So-Dark Ages: From Steam to Electricity to Digital Qubits

"Society depends on trust. Trust is now seriously endangered by the replicative power of A.I. . . . . This is a grave danger."
—DANIEL C. DENNETT, author, *Science and Religion*

Although not as creative as the Greeks, according to Columbia University Professor Moses Hadas, the Romans were more responsible for making books available by using slaves as readers for the illiterate masses.[1] For the first time, there were books available on all topics. As more people learned to read, during this Golden Age, the prospect of trusting a select few—local clergy, feudal landlords—rather than one's own judgment became unnecessary.

People could now form their own judgments, beliefs, and opinions based on what they read. Their horizons expanded exponentially. The secrets of science were now revealed, disrupting blind faith in religion for some. The meaning of life could change dramatically for those interested in biology, astronomy, and other aspects of science.

Throughout Europe before this time, social trust was invested primarily in the church. However, with the fall of the Roman Empire, trust in the larger enterprises gave way to trust in the local, or at least regionalized, structures, such as the feudal manor. The Dark Ages saw a decrease in reading and interest in the written word.

But this period was not as dark as is commonly thought. Inventions such as the heavy plow, the modern harness, the nailed horseshoe, and the technology of rotation of crops gave way to increased agricultural yields and, consequently, to a new population growth. Democratic capitalism was on its way in and, with it, there was no need to subjugate one's trust to the upper class.

The Four Phases of the Industrial Revolution

All these changes sowed the seeds of the Industrial Revolution, which began in the late 1700s and continues to date.

- The first phase began with the production of hydroelectric and steam-powered technology, at the turn of the nineteenth century.
- The second phase began in 1900 with the advent of electricity.
- The third phase began in the mid-1960s with the beginning of computer technology, introduced by the IBM Series/360. (Truth be told, the first plans for computer technology came from Nazi Germany in the form of the Z4, invented by a man named Konrad Zuse. It first became operational in May 1941.)[2]
- The fourth phase, in which we're now immersed, is the rapid development of the combination of digital and physical resources with the biological, including smart watches reporting physiological functions, robots serving human needs, biological computer chips, artificial intelligence like chatbots such as ChatGPT using virtual reality, facial recognition, and more. It also includes the latest innovation in IT, namely quantum computing, introducing the qubit era. Instead of the states of 1 or 0, we now look forward to those two states being replaced by qubits that have the power to enhance processing of information by a factor approaching infinity.[3]

So, we can say goodbye to the privacy of encrypted communication. Prepare yourself for the challenging concept of pure random numbers replacing the no-longer-secure pseudo-random numbers used for encryption. (Not to worry, there will be no final exam on this.)

Just My Movable Type: Bronze Coins and Wine Presses

Now back to older, simpler innovations and their effect on trust. About two centuries before Johannes Gutenberg began working on his movable-print workshop in the 1440s, there was an experiment with a similar technique in what is now Korea. In 1234, a high-ranking government official, Choe Yun-ui, was commissioned by the Goryeo Dynasty to make copies of the fifty-volume work, *The Prescribed Ritual Text of the Past and Present* (*Sangjeong Gogeum Yemun*). He came up with the idea of using the technique for minting bronze coins and applying it to create movable type for characters. Then he was able to place these metal types in a frame to be run over by ink. This arduous project took a bit of time, like sixteen years, but, by 1250, it was completed. The result was the first book to be printed by movable type.

One big difference between this method and that of Gutenberg was that the latter had the advantage of using another technology available at the time, the oil or wine press, which he could use to quickly make copies. The earlier approach did not have that press, and the copies had to be pressed by hand, a much slower method. The other challenge was that English is limited to twenty-six characters while the oriental language used by Yun-ui involved thousands of characters.

It is possible that this earlier invention was carried through history by the Uyghurs, residing on the Old Silk Road, between Beijing and the Ilkhanate, in former Persia. The ruling Mongol Empire may then have had access to this invention, but there was little motivation to bring public printing to bear and so this invention, not so new by this time, lost its place in history. Whether or not it was available to Gutenberg, even as an idea, is mere speculation at this point.

In any case, unfortunately for us, this first book printed by movable type has not survived. The earliest book using this ancient form of movable metal type is *The Anthology of Great Buddhist Priests' Zen Teachings,* dating back to 1377. If nothing else, this helped to keep the ideas of early Buddhism alive in Korea over the years, keeping trust from transforming away from that form of religion.

How the Printing Press Transformed Trust

By 1300, books were becoming popular, even before the printing press. During this time, according to Sigfrid Steinberg in his book, *Five Hundred Years of Printing*, about 10,000 scribes made their living in Europe by copying manuscripts in order to meet the growing demand for books.[4] The precursors of the Industrial Revolution gave birth to the printing press, and that is one of the great turning points in how the process of trust was transformed from a collective, hierarchical structure with less personal power to one involving more egalitarian relationships. This led to a greater sense of power with the prospect of making personal choices more readily available.

Though people trusted each other till this time, trust was somewhat less of a personal choice, but rather a social process by which individuals survived only with the support and consent of the wealthier, more powerful, more literate classes. After the Gutenberg Revolution in 1450, the country-bred and journeymen need no longer fear the whims of the courtiers and court dwellers as much.

Though many of them could not yet read, the distribution of codes of law and mores offered guides to enhanced personal power heretofore unknown to most. The stubborn hierarchical social system, where obedience to the more powerful was essential for survival, could give way to a new structure in which egalitarian relationships could more likely be based on mutual trust.

According to literary critic Andrew Marantz, "After Gutenberg, books became widely available, setting off a cascade of salutary [helpful and wholesome] movements and innovations, including but not limited to the Reformation, the Enlightenment, the steam engine, journalism, modern literature, modern medicine, and modern democracy."[5]

Capitalism was not far behind, as a new middle class emerged. Merchants could now enter business relationships, based on a new form of interpersonal trust involving contracts and the beginnings of accounting. Manufacturing and commerce could now flourish as never before.

Finally, with the printing press and the commercialization of the book, literacy became increasingly universal, and trust once again became a process between individuals at the local level. With fewer hierarchically based power structures, there was more freedom to choose whom to trust and individuals could more easily make such decisions. Self-reliance and independence were now possible as never before.

From Ear to Eye, So We Could See How "All the World Will Be in Love with Night"

As Marshal McLuhan put it, the printing press was the first large-scale mass-production manufacturing operation.[6] Large-scale commerce could now transcend long distance as well as time. "Printing marked the first stage in the spread of the industrial revolution," concurred political economist Harold Innis, author of *The Bias of Communication*.[7]

According to historian George Sarton, the discovery of printing was one of the great turning points in the history of mankind.[8] It changed the very warp and woof of history, for it replaced precarious forms of tradition (oral and handwritten manuscript) by one that was stable, secure, and lasting, and, therefore, more trustworthy, I would add. The wide distribution of books made all this possible.

And so, the printing press transformed the basis of trust in Western culture. Before, trust between individuals was based on hearing the other person—an aural process. After the printing press, trust became centered on the eye—a visual process. As anthropologist J. C. Carothers put it, the discovery of printing in the middle of the fifteenth century implied the beginning of a turn to a type of civilization dominated by the eye rather than the ear.[9]

This transition of trust from ear to eye took place in the days of Shakespeare, as his writing became available in the written word along with his theatrical performances. Now people could have the luxury of seeing Shakespeare's words on the page of a widely published book through eyes, in addition to hearing them performed, through ears, and enjoy, either way, such delicacies at the ending of *Romeo and Juliet*, as she wishes for Romeo's fate after death:

> and cut him out in little stars
> And he will make the face of heaven so fine
> That all the world will be in love with night. (III.ii.22–24)

In the next section, we'll explore the institutions of government, religion, law, science, and commerce. Then we'll look at the ramifications of the four phases of the Industrial Revolution, sparked by the invention of the printing press, the Gutenberg Revolution. We'll explore how our need for trust was affected by this growing technology. Finally, we'll see how all this has affected our need to trust, for better or worse, and the challenges of how our culture may have gone too far in the modern age of technology, contributing to the current Age of Mistrust.

PART IV

Institutional Trust: The Medicis, Marshal McLuhan, and Justice Ruth Bader Ginsburg

Institutional trust: The extent to which we perceive and accept the institutions in our lives to be reliable, responsible, and benevolent. In a free society, an institution is only as strong as those involved make it to be. We'll explore how governmental institutions were able to develop once documents could be written and shared.

"Institutions don't defend themselves. People do that."

—LIZ CHENEY, during broadcast of Select Committee on January 6

8

The Revolution of Trust in Institutions

"Every kind of peaceful cooperation among men is
primarily based on mutual trust and only secondarily
on institutions such as courts of justice and police."
—ALBERT EINSTEIN

Several years ago, I spent a few wonderful months teaching at a military base in Livorno, Italy, about an hour and a half west of Florence. I spent most of my weekends in Florence, of course, where I could see the gorgeous dome with its neo-Gothic facade at the Piazza del Duomo, constructed by Brunelleschi in the fifteenth century, from wherever I lodged for the night. I learned about the powerful, rich Medici family and how it became an institution for developing arts of the Renaissance in Italy.

It was then that I began to appreciate more deeply how institutions can affect values and beliefs. They're not just based on government or on professional practices; they can also affect what people trust.

Institutions are defined as societies or organizations founded for religious, educational, social, or other purposes, such as establishing a system of law, medicine, or science. Other examples include the military, police and firefighter unions, the stock market, and even social groups comprised of wealthy individuals patronizing the arts and sciences as, for example, Italian families like the Medicis. An institution forms an organized system of social relationships that embodies a set of common values and procedures to meet basic social needs.[1]

Plato formed his own institution, the well-trusted Greek Academia in ancient Greece just outside of Athens. Here he advocated the ideal state in which the leaders were well educated and free of corruption.

Although he was initially against the written word as a source of pre-sentation, using the Socratic method of intellectual give-and-take interaction, he did ultimately take notes on his own teachings, unlike his predecessor, Socrates, and so his philosophy is more readily available to us in the twenty-first century.

Written language has made institutions easier to build and maintain. It allowed for the content of their focus (whether that was medicine, law, or science) and their values and procedures to be shared uniformly, among the respective institutional entities, progressing into the future, making them more reliable and trustworthy. People could then put their trust into these organizations more comfortably. But recording all this also gave people a chance to question these same institutions—a double-edged sword.

Now we have social media, including chatbots, and a new mentality of crowdsourcing, which, we guess, Plato might have abhorred. Trust, for some, in this Age of Mistrust, has pivoted in a direction we never expected.

More on that later.

Cosmographia: A Forerunner of Wikipedia

Books, now written in local languages, became widely available, in part because they were significantly less expensive due to the mass production made possible by the new printing press. People could then overcome the tyranny of trust in the power of the church, with its monopoly of handwritten manuscripts (in the literal sense) of the Bible in Latin. Priests could no longer as easily interpret the scriptures to the less literate. Along with this, the ruling class at the time, including royalty and the landed gentry, who gladly allied themselves with the church to justify their dominant positions, were losing power.

Now, many could place their trust in the collective human process that became available because of the spread of knowledge in popular books. The monopoly of the select few who hoarded the power of the spoken word in the church was now broken. The masses could trust their own thinking more easily. Their ideas were now more likely to be self-generated rather than coming from above, interpreted by the church and supported by the wealthy and powerful. Individuals could communicate with one another through the printed word, using their own eyes to read, and understand and interpret for themselves, rather being told what others had to say. The former dependency on the church gave way to a sense of independence and greater self-reliance and confidence.

One of the outcomes of this new communication opportunity was something akin to Wikipedia—its sixteenth-century predecessor, Sebastian Munster's *Cosmographia*, a compendium of knowledge and information printed all over Europe. From 1544 to 1628, this collection of consensual wisdom grew from 650 to over 4,000 pages over its forty editions.[2] Now there was another dimension of trust, one that could reach an unlimited number of individuals in far-flung places through the written and printed word.

This document may have had its errors, just as any communal enterprise might have, but that's not very different from today's Wikipedia with its frequent editorial changes. Now we argue about the difference between the validity of evolutionary genetics and that of intelligent design. In Wikipedia we can "think out loud" about changes in understanding COVID-19, allowing us to see research publications prior to peer reviews, with research results about potential treatments being disseminated more quickly and more broadly, with the possibility, therefore, of saving some lives.

There were probably similar debates among the readers of Munster's *Cosmographia* about the different values of emerging science and long-standing religion, as well as different cures for prevailing medical ills. The more things change, the more they stay the same, at least for the basics. But both the historical *Cosmographia* and the current Wikipedia did and do create challenges for our decisions about what to trust in emerging value systems.[3]

From Ear to Eye—Revolutions of Trust in Nationalism, Religion, Commerce, and Education

Though historians attribute many reasons for the transformation into the Industrial Age, my contention is that the printed word played a major role. Let's look at how this influenced the great institutions of our culture and the effect it had on our need to trust. First, we'll look at how the printed word slowed down the evolution of languages, consolidating and stabilizing languages formerly used by neighboring regions, then how it made possible challenges to Catholic dogma and enabled a new movement away from the power of the Pope and to the formation of new religions. This changed the history of trust in Western civilization forever.

As the printed word and the proliferation of affordable books encouraged languages to become more complex in terms of fixed grammar, it also allowed for the opportunity to concentrate ideas from many sources into greater concepts. Culture was no longer dependent on a select few who wrote in classical languages and who could read, and thus interpret for others less literate. Nation-states weren't built on dialects of language but rather on standard languages understood by many and capable of recording laws, contracts, science, and math, for example. As the Renaissance progressed, greater and greater numbers of people had their sense of trust liberated. Finally, we'll see more clearly how it contributed to Western capitalism and the growth of the middle class and, unfortunately, to the Thirty Years War as well.

This transformed the majority of people from dependence on the ear to the eye—from being told "what is written" as the primary mode of communication to seeing what others wrote in books that they could trust with their own eyes. All this resulted in five milestones of cultural transformation:

1. The increase of movement toward political institutions
2. The Protestant Reformation
3. The transformation of trust in trade practices so that capitalism could begin with the laissez-faire dynamic of free trade

4. The emergence of a new middle class, which was now receptive to a more standard form of education

5. The consolidation of a culture of science that allowed for trust in the importance and validity of experimentation

Let's take a look at each one of these.

The Increase of Movement Toward Political Institutions

The advent of printing in local dialects (rather than Greek or Latin) slowed the natural evolution of language.[4] Once a local dialect found its way into popular print, there was then a record of the language as a reference for further use. So, although languages still evolved, the rate was nothing like the changes that had taken place before the advent of the Gutenberg Revolution. With the standardization of such languages in Europe, institutions took on a new form as well.

With printed language, along with the concentration of population and wealth in the growing cities, regional power became consolidated toward national institutions. People in large cities could now identify as part of a larger entity more easily (the beginning of nation-states) because they were exposed to newspapers and published essays that described cultural commonalities, using a common language that characterized their emerging national values.[5] In addition, larger cities led to more centralized institutions because urban development meant common urban issues that necessitated more organized maintenance.

The printing press, according to Marshal McLuhan, a Canadian philosopher, encouraged the idea of equal rights of individuals to determine the state and government to which they belonged, including the rights of self-determination. Even the cry of "Liberty! Equality! Fraternity!" characterizing the French Revolution, and the American Declaration of Independence calling for equality among men, both a couple hundred years after the invention of the printing press, still owe their premise to the focus on trust that citizens could govern themselves rather than being regulated solely by a higher authority such as the church or prince-bishops.[6]

But now, in modern times, the turn to trust has reversed itself. The trust in fellow citizens, in this current Age of Mistrust with its social media, has transformed into a trust in "tribalized" individuals, and against the larger collective domain of fellow citizenry. For reasons to be fully explained in the following chapters of this book, the divide between classes has been sharpened and even exaggerated by social media, creating a greater gap between the haves and have-nots.

This current revolution of Republicans is against what is seen as the old order, what candidate Hillary Clinton represented as a partner to prior administrations, what President Obama represented in his aim to bring America into a more centralized community.

These "rebels" wanted a new order, where they could exert more power; claim their own territory to air their beliefs in alternate realities, long ignored by the existing powers; where they could enjoy their new middle-class status, removing their COVID-19 masks and placing large Trump signs on their boats so they could begin to enjoy a life they've worked hard to achieve.[7]

Even as Trump was hauled into one court after another, both federal and state, for his alleged misdeeds, they were drawn to him even more strongly. It was what fed their fury against the established order of institutions and into the modern age of Trump.[8]

The Protestant Reformation

Though Martin Luther is best known for the posting of his Ninety-Five Theses (in German) to the door of the All-Saints' Church (also known as Wittenberg Cathedral) in 1517, it really was the wide publication of his ideas that all people could have a direct relationship with their divine master, one-on-one, rather than being required to channel that relationship through an agent of the Catholic church. The printing press spread his message throughout Germany in a fortnight and through Europe in a month, according to British historian, Margaret Aston.[9]

Trust in Christ was now more easily validated by fellow church members, guided by biblical text that they could read in their own language, rather than through the hierarchy of Roman theology.

The printing press then had a similar effect in earlier times that the cell phone has had in our time, resulting, for example, in the Arab Spring (leading to a democratic uprising among Arab states) and in the speedy dynamic of present-day protests,[10] including the subsequent women's courageous protests in Iran and the unheard-of public protests across China against its authoritarian leadership, about the COVID-19 lockdowns.

Speed in communication, where individuals can come to trust a new medium, changes history. Trust in a new medium to communicate new ideas in a more accessible way, in the sixteenth century and in our own twenty-first century, respectively, had a similar effect—transforming our culture of trust, or at least to a larger range of opinions. In the sixteenth century, it was away from the centralized power of Catholicism. Today, it's away from the "old" order of politics. More on that later.

It's interesting to note that familiarity with the original language of Catholicism—Latin—had its effect on which nations chose to remain Catholic. Though there was a political divide going back to Roman times, the countries with the Romance languages, namely, France, Spain, and Italy, remained Catholic likely in part because they could better relate to the Latin language, and therefore had greater trust in that religion; while those with Germanic language roots, such as the Germans, English, and Scandinavians, chose to go with the Reformation for similar reasons—the default of familiarity with a language.[11] Such trust, based partly on language, allowed for greater influence of the respective religions.

Of course, there were other mitigating factors as well. Henry VIII decided to form the Anglican Church in 1534 so that he could break away from the Roman Catholic church and create his own religion to enable his divorce from Catherine to marry Anne Boleyn. In the case of the strong Lutheran countries, such as Germany and Scandinavia, history suggests that it was mainly the selection and imposition of an official religion by the rulers of these countries and territories that resulted in their breaking from Rome.[12]

The other Protestant strain, Calvinism, triumphed for similar reasons in Holland, Switzerland, and Scotland.[13] England involved an entirely different political issue, as mentioned earlier, and the Church of England (a compromise between the two factions, influenced strongly by Elizabeth I) even today remains with liturgical rituals very close to Catholic practice.

Not to be overlooked is one of the less fortunate aspects of the Reformation—the Thirty Years War, from 1618 to 1648. It began primarily as a conflict between the Roman Catholics and Protestants in Germany but eventually involved the Danish, Swedish, French, and Austrians. The end result was the recognition of Calvinism and Lutheranism along with Catholicism as established churches, as well as the development and foundation of the modern state system in Europe.

Hence, we see how the printed word transformed the power of trust in the overarching Catholic church to a multitude of competing denominations, which dramatically impacted the nature of trust in religious factions that continues to exist in modern times.

The Transformation of Trust in Trade Practices So That Capitalism Could Begin with the Laissez-Faire Dynamic of Free Trade

The terms *free trade* and *laissez-faire* are synonymous, meaning allowing international trade with minimal interference by government, in other words, without the strictures of tariffs.

Books, according to McLuhan, created the price system.[14] For, until commodities are uniform and repeatable, the price of an article is subject to haggle and adjustment (as is still the case in the tourist areas of countries in the Mideast). The uniformity and repeatability of the book created the necessity for, and trust in, the modern system of prices, allowing for international trade based on a fixed price system.

So, books played a dual role in the power of trust to embracing capitalism, first, by becoming a prototype of sorts for a commodity with a fixed price that transcended borders and, second, by offering information about services and products that could now be put on the international market, thereby creating a demand that had never been so easily circulated. There was now sufficient trust in an economic system that could transcend the boundaries of diverse cultures.

The Emergence of a New Middle Class, Which Was Now Receptive to a More Standard Form of Education

This would allow for career growth and professional affiliation with newly learned crafts. The power of trust in one's own potential for career success was a seminal shift in trusting one's own personal power and independence.

Prior to the printing press, education was limited to private tutoring among royalty and the upper classes. When books became inexpensive and readily available, there was a revolution in education, allowing the working-class children to learn in groups with books on their desks, opening the gate to the prospect of universal public education.[15]

A sense of freedom replaced the resignation to one's station in life, previously self-limiting and unchanging. One could now imagine and aspire to accumulate money and, with dedicated effort, become financially self-reliant. With time, they earned the potential to enjoy some degree of wealth.

Over time, there developed a clear division between education aimed at practical skills and crafts, on the one hand, and a more humanistic and classical education, on the other. The first formal public school in North America along classical lines was the Boston Latin School, established in 1635, under the tutelage of the Puritan settler, Philemon Pormont.[16] At that point, Latin was still considered the lingua franca of intellectual and theological pursuits.

Lasting into the 1950s and '60s, many public schools continued the teaching of Latin as a main course in high school. At that point, students at many schools could choose between two tracks: the humanities, including law, which necessitated taking Latin; and the sciences, which replaced Latin with calculus.[17]

This development of education starting with the printed book led to an increasing sense of the power of trust in one's own ability to choose one's future, rather than relying on the existing hierarchy of status from which one could barely escape.[18]

This sea change in education was instrumental in the growth of the middle class. Graduating students could then enter livelihoods that enabled them to earn and save money that could propel them into levels of power heretofore denied them. It opened the door to higher levels of learning and therefore more earning power. This critical transformation cultivated a change of trust in their own control of their destinies.

The Consolidation of a Culture of Science That Allowed for Trust in the Importance and Validity of Experimentation

Once the technology of scientific experimentation could be communicated clearly through published articles and books, then a whole society of people could entertain the same value system of working out the truth of scientific reality, no matter how far apart they were in terms of geography or time.[19]

Now society could grow a mutual trust in science based on one another's works. The requirement for replication of results replaced opinion and dogma. Whatever the specialty, whether engineering, physics, chemistry, medicine, even business practices, all results would depend on the consensus of replicated results in published form. There was no place for "alternate realities." Trust in scientific method became widely accepted.

In this chapter, we began with how the written (but not yet printed) word led to the early institutions, such as Plato's Greek Academia. Then we compared Sebastian Munster's *Cosmographia* from the sixteenth century to today's Wikipedia and noted their similarities. We then followed up with how the printed word influenced the history of trust in terms of nationalism, religion, commerce, education, and science.

In the next chapter, we'll see how a case is made for the printed word transforming an ear-based aural holistic female culture into an eye-based linear male one and from egalitarian to male-dominated. We'll also see how and why trust in institutions began to decline, including the currently shifting institution of marriage. Some children can have two fathers, and some fathers can have many, many children. One math professor has over one hundred children, as he offers himself to single women who want to avoid costly medical involvement to have children as single adults. Love and trust in family building take many forms.

9

WEIRD People and Subjugated Women

*"Polarization affects families and groups of friends.
It's a paralyzing situation. A civil war of opinion."*
—MICK JAGGER

As fellow citizens dealing with common challenges, as colleagues working to bring sanity back to our politics, as neighbors supporting one another in these challengingly divisive times, as family members wresting ourselves away from our smartphones, how do we deal with the fact that half of voting Americans voted for the "wrong" candidate—the one you earnestly voted *against*?

There is a need for critical thinking, gathering evidence before we choose. But half of the voting public seems to be incapable of doing so. Radical right-wing voters see their left-wing enemies as "dirty commies," who are ruining our country by spending much too much money, while the latter see the former as extremely shortsighted and heartless chauvinists.

Some maintain that rampant individualism is the hallmark of American society, overtaking the sense of community and communal solutions we seek. Hopefully, the passage of time will see us transcend the division manifested by social media over the past few decades and come together once again.

That's why finding meaning and trust at home is more challenging these days, yet quite crucial to our ultimate satisfaction. Our happiness also includes finding meaning in our work with coworkers-workers, bosses, and direct reports. It means taking responsibility to be true to ourselves, so that fulfillment is a daily outcome, not easily achieved. It means putting in the work and selflessness necessary to make close relationships more satisfying.

Our capability to trust our current society seems more challenging now than ever before. We need to feel satisfied with our communities, both large and small, despite the sense of disenfranchisement so many are feeling in this Age of Mistrust. So many feel cynical. We've learned what sheltering at home can do—making us feel out of the loop, losing touch with one another, feeling insignificant over time. We have learned to use electronic communication to mitigate that challenge, and we can learn to do that in more meaningful ways, with groups that inspire us, stimulate our thinking, and enrich our souls, with groups in which we can invest our trust.

Trusting institutions, these days, is not an easy choice. But history tells us that it is totally necessary if we are to survive, both as a nation and as a culture.

Leonard Shlain, author of *The Alphabet Versus the Goddess*, proposed that the written word transformed trust in humanity from a feminine-based outlook, "holistic, simultaneous, synthetic, and concrete view of the world," to a male-based outlook, "linear, sequential, reductionistic, and abstract thinking."[1]

Trustworthy decisions can be made on either basis—with linear logic or intuitive feelings.

Our crisis with the COVID-19 pandemic and its variants offered interesting challenges along these lines, on both the holistic and linear sides. Parents were required to make decisions about their children's school attendance. At work—where remote roles replaced at-work attendance—we were reminded, during this pandemic, how vulnerable the whole structure of work society is. Decisions that were quite clear and logical before the pandemic now became blurred and complex, dependent on subjective, less logical conclusions.

So, the best solutions had to encompass both the linear "alphabet" and the holistic "Goddess." The decisions were never easy, coming to some resolution only as the pandemic began to subside with the delivery of vaccines across the country.

Whether our children went to school or stayed home depended on many factors, most of them impossible to measure accurately in the moment, without help from some form of leadership by public health scientists and the leaders who appoint them. How could we measure the need to learn at school with the need to be safe from the pandemic?

Logic suffered here, because of the complexity of the measurements. Might we need a more intuitive-based type of decision-making? Yet we hoped for scientifically based guidance. We remained stuck in that dark area of uncertainty, despite the life-threatening aspects of our decision. In this daunting Age of Mistrust, it is hard to know which sources of information to trust.

How Cultural Institutions Subjugated Women

Before the written word, men and women, according to most anthropologists, were equal in power—for example, the Hopi and Iroquois in North America, the African !Kung, the inhabitants of Polynesia. Trustworthiness was equally shared between the genders. But, with the advent of literacy, according to French anthropologist Claude Levi-Strauss, we get the establishment of hierarchical societies, where one part of the population is made to work for the other part, including the subjugation of women and people of color, who continue to struggle with this inequality.[2]

The first major written work was the Old Testament, creating the basis for trust in three major religions, Judaism, Christianity, and Islam. All of these portray spiritual power invested in masculine figures, except for Mary in the New Testament, stalwart of divine feminine nurturing. Prior to those written documents, the feminine played a much larger role in religion in terms of goddesses and their spiritual powers. Goddesses, according to Shlain, were well accepted prior to 1500 BC but slowly lost their place by AD 500.[3]

We Are WEIRD People

Some time ago, Joseph Henrich, a cultural anthropologist, came out with an interesting theory that corroborates much of what we've discussed till now. We explored how the printing press changed the nature of trust in our culture, broadly speaking, from intuitive, ear-based, female-oriented communication, as Shlain put it, to eye-based, male-oriented communication. Now Henrich explains, in his book, *The WEIRDest People in the World*, that the transition we've described in this section was characterized by the transformation from tribes to states, from lore to science, and from custom to law.[4]

These transitions evolved in their own course, but their main turning point was the printing press. Let's look at each one. Tribes became states long before written language, but the formalization of laws and contracts could only happen after that. Lore became science slowly as well but did not take off as a shared enterprise until printing took place. And custom could only become law once the written word could record contractual agreements. So the printing press just accelerated transitions in these institutions and gave us a reference point for this process, just like a milestone on a long road on which change takes place slowly.

To make sense of the title of Henrich's book, you need to know that WEIRD is an acronym for **W**estern, **E**ducated, **I**ndustrialized, **R**ich, **D**emocratic people. Henrich feels that we WEIRD ones are the outliers of the world, that our culture, the one we are most familiar with, of course, is at the center of the world, at least our world. Henrich and his colleagues believe that the world is made up of many societies, and our Western culture is only one small, but powerful, part.

Based on measurements of such variables as visual perception, fairness cooperation, spatial reasoning, categorization and inferential induction, and moral reasoning, Henrich concludes that we WEIRD ones are the unusual ones. In any case, we are WEIRD mostly because of our technological advances, primarily a result of the Industrial Revolution, marked most clearly by the invention of the printing press and its effect on the institutions in our culture. Without it, we would not have advanced as far as quickly.

Trust in Our Future

How do social media affect our need to trust modern-day enterprises? As Tom Friedman has put it, our world is now hot, flat, and crowded, requiring more innovation to overcome climate change and economic and other social issues.[5] Our current society is running wild with new inventions on a weekly, if not daily, basis, one displacing another. Institutions in corporations, governments, and entertainment are all affected by this. Add to the mix the advent and pervasiveness of the recent pandemic.

With all this disruption and constant change, what dare we trust? Will all these innovations save the day? But this has been going on for generations, with robots promising to relieve us with their limitless energy and low cost.

We fear that robots are taking over, as was predicted long ago. *Frankenstein*, written by a teenaged Mary Shelley[6] in 1831 about taking parts of dead people and animating the result with electricity, predicted robots resembling humans and programmed with emotions and the facial expressions to express them. Jules Verne[7] predicted flying machines before airplanes were known, and who would have thought of drones at that time? Arthur C. Clarke[8] predicted electronic communication, and Chester Gould,[9] who depicted Dick Tracy in cartoon format, clearly predicted the smart watch, over a half century before they arrived on the scene. In 1903, the Wright brothers flew the first sustained plane ride at about 25 mph. Sixty-six years later, the Concorde flew at a speed of 1,400 mph. Millennials today would ask, what took them so long?

By 1971, we knew we had a problem. *The Limits to Growth*, originally reporting on the exponential growth of the Industrial Revolution to international groups in Moscow and Rio de Janeiro, made us realize we had to be more responsible about our impact of development on humanity. At the beginning of the published report, the following document, signed by over 1,600 scientists, including 102 Nobel laureates from seventy countries, reported in 2004:

Human beings and the natural world are on a collision course. Human activities inflict harsh and often irreversible damage on the environment and on critical resources. If not checked many of our current practices put at serious risk the future that we wish for human society and the plant and animal kingdoms and may so alter the living world that it will be unable to sustain life in the manner that we know. Fundamental changes are urgent if we are to avoid the collision our present course will bring about.[10]

It's interesting that Paul Ehrlich, along with his wife, Anne, predicted, in their 1968 book, *The Population Bomb*, that, by the 1970s, "hundreds of millions of people are going to starve to death."[11] That didn't happen because of the green revolution in intense agriculture. No wonder it's difficult for many to trust those calling out about climate change. Humans are very resilient and respond to crises by creative innovations that were not predicted earlier.

The human population has grown exponentially over the past 500 years, yet humanity has, for the most part, survived in good order. However, during this Age of Mistrust, we may see some crises that may be more difficult to manage, not the least of which are chatbots like ChatGPT.

Losing Trust in Current Institutions

During the Middle Ages, the primary institution was the Catholic church, which totally ruled all aspects of education, about language acquisition and religious doctrine. Education began to become an institution of its own with the great universities separating from the church about the eleventh and twelfth centuries.[12]

Both of those institutions were stable enough for people to trust. They were the only institutions they could trust for the time. The church offered stability, and the universities offered education for the elite to further their enterprises of government and commerce. All this came together in the form of prince-bishops who led semi-independent states in Germany, the first of whom was Bishop William Walcher. He and his successors ruled by divine right, spanning the secular and the religious, as did the most famous king to do so, Louis XIV of France. These leaders ruled with absolute power, without accountability to any parliament or any other institution. Trust in such powerful leaders was absolute. At least until the rebellious events like the French Revolution.

Fast-forward to today's society. What do we do with our need to trust in current institutions? According to a Pew Research Center study looking at the past generation, trust in our government is suffering as we see it battered by political uncertainty, an unstable economy, inner conflict, and truth obscured by competing.[13]

And what about the effects of climate change, with the forest fires on the West Coast, failed crops in the Midwest, and flooding on both coasts?[14] No wonder there's a movement that appeals to a fantasy for alternate realities.

We live in a highly productive world, but here's the irony: Trust in institutions is not as dependable as it used to be. I don't know about you, but I am concerned about this Age of Mistrust—concerned that our government is no longer functioning in the democratic fashion it was meant to do; concerned that every new innovation will soon be replaced by a better mouse trap; concerned that our jobs are disappearing with the advent of more sophisticated robotry like ChatGPT and DeepSeek; concerned that our savings and investments will be destroyed with inevitable inflation caused by the excessive spending by our government leaders; concerned that the Chinese or Russians have hacked into our election process, making it invalid; concerned that never-ending pandemics and their variants will come back to haunt us.

Trust in Ourselves

We must consider the option of beginning to invest trust in our own decisions. We are responsible for electing our leaders. We are the ones doing the innovation. We are the ones deciding how to live out our chosen careers. We are the ones asking for financial help from the government. We are the ones putting our heads in the sand when it comes to dealing with foreign governments attempting to influence our systems of election. In other words, only we are to blame and, to use the cartoon character Pogo's words, "We have met the enemy, and he is us."[15]

We no longer have many places to trust—unless we change our ways, create new opportunities for ourselves, and choose different habits of establishing trust within our social circles, within our career environments. And that we can do, both at home and at work. That is, in part, what this book is about.

In this modern society in the Age of Mistrust, we may be more advanced, but we're also more separated, even before the pandemic forced us to increase that separation. COVID-19 aside, we interact much less at the interpersonal level. For some, sheltering at home was not much different from how it was before. For many, working from home did not begin with COVID-19.

Now, more than ever, we need to learn to communicate more openly with one another, be more emotionally available to one another. With our expectations for our institutions in flux, we need to relearn how to trust one another, yet our society is fractured, angrily split.

In this chapter, we began with the transition from trust in women's power to trust in men's power as the Gutenberg Revolution changed our culture. This "competition" was recently revisited when parents had to make decisions as to whether or not to keep their children at home at the height of the pandemic—a "female, intuitive" decision or a "male logical" decision?

Even the Bible shifted trust in women goddesses to the masculine divine entities, leaving Mary to bear the burden of feminine nurturing for Christians. Of course, this was occurring in the Western world primarily with us WEIRD people. We looked at all this through the prisms of religion, population growth, predictions of inventions affecting society, and the challenges of trusting the changing institutions over time.

The history of trust changed significantly with the advent of the printed word, transforming the genders of our gods, the structure of power between men and women, the rapid growth of new discoveries, and even the sacred institution of marriage.

In the next chapter, we'll take a look at how our sense of trust had to change, from intuitive to analytical, from automatic to calculated, and from casual to thoughtful, as we traveled from the Gutenberg Revolution to the Chatbot Revolution. We look at the dramatic divisions of trust in the government and the institution of law, including the significant loss of trust in the Supreme Court.

10
Losing the Battle for Trust in Social Media

"Television is a deadly sedative: hundreds of channels are streaming thousands of shows, and a person glued to it loses cranial sensation."
—GARRISON KEILLOR, on television as an institution

The primary definition of the term *institution*, according to the Merriam-Webster dictionary, is "an established organization or corporation . . . especially of a public character." But it goes on to include "something or someone firmly associated with a place or thing."

One such someone is the late Justice Ruth Bader Ginsburg. The place is the Supreme Court, and the thing is a rare combination of dedication, focus, and trustworthiness—dedication to a humane interpretation of the law, focus on women's (and men's) rights, and trustworthiness through creating a legacy of working diligently and persistently over the years despite personal hardships.

Born Joan Ruth Bader, the daughter of Russian immigrants in Depression-era Brooklyn, she attended law school at Harvard University. This shy, very reserved hard worker met and married the very outgoing and jovial Martin Ginsburg whom she wed in 1954. Still in her early twenties, Ruth cared for her husband who was going through treatment for testicular cancer, attended her classes, made notes for Martin, raised their first child, and had an active role in the *Harvard Law Review*, getting along on very little sleep.

Upon graduation, no one would hire her, she later explained, because of three counts: She was female, a mother, and of the Jewish faith. Through the efforts of a determined former professor, she finally landed a clerkship at a federal district court and then Rutgers University hired her to teach law. Later, as counsel for the ACLU, she focused on gender bias, building a sterling reputation for all her successes. In 1980, President Carter appointed her to the US Court of Appeals and, in 1993, President Clinton appointed her to the Supreme Court.

Everyone close to her had unqualified trust for Justice Ginsburg— her husband for whom she cared while he suffered from cancer, as she herself was a mother and going to law school; her clerks whom she mentored with nurturing warmth; and her colleagues at the Supreme Court who respected her thoughtful and incisive opinions. Of course, conservatives may have thought she was too liberal, especially on issues relating to abortion and gay marriage, but her trust by them was hard won over the years, because no one questioned her integrity.

The Challenge of Trust in the Age of Mistrust

Let's admit it. Trusting isn't easy these days in the Age of Mistrust. It's scary to open a discussion of politics with someone you've just met, whether electronically or in person. It's been scary to go shopping for groceries, let alone an occasional trip to the restaurant of your choice. We're so much more reluctant about opening our hearts and trusting, yet we need to trust. We can't live without it in large part because we're hardwired to trust. So we must learn how and where to do it, even though we've spent a couple of years sheltering at home and may be forced to do so for a while in case the variants of COVID-19 or some form of bird flu create even greater medical problems.

It's as if we were back to living in caves, far away from our neighbors, isolated and on the lookout for the next visitor, hoping for a friendly smile rather than a spear thrown our way (or a bullet). But we had our technology to be used wisely in the interim of the pandemic.

The written word changed our culture, especially when that written word became public and easily available after the printing press. Now we have electronic communication available that has become so essential currently. It makes trust more challenging, but not unattainable. We just need to work harder and smarter, gaining the necessary skills for managing the social media technology available to us.

And that's what we can do as we also explore our personal and work relationships.

From this vantage point, we can see how the medium became the message. Once we had written language that could be distributed quite readily through the published book, then our sense of trust had to change, from intuitive to analytical, from automatic to calculated, from casual to thoughtful. Now we need to be both thoughtful and analytical as well as intuitive in this cognitive technology revolution.

Seeing Is No Longer Believing

During that period between the Gutenberg Revolution and what I refer to as the Chatbot Revolution, much of our trust in institutions was affected by what we read in newspapers, magazines, and books. But, with the advent of social media, trust in institutions began to suffer.[1,2] For example, was it true that Justice Clarence Thomas acted unethically as the mainstream media portrayed him, or was it just a leftist campaign to harm the Supreme Court as the right-wing press claimed? And what about Justice Alito? We can't trust social media the way we were content to trust books before the advent of self-published works. We used to be able to say: seeing is believing, but no more, as photos and videos can be photoshopped, especially with deepfakes, to create total fabrications, making people appear to say things they never said. Social media and chatbots have poisoned our ability to trust. We just need to work harder to regain that privilege.

Even our reading habits have changed drastically. Books written in past centuries were longer—not only books, but paragraphs and sentences as well. Personal letters were much longer and emotionally more open. The typewriter, first sold in 1874 by Remington—introducing the QWERTY keyboard layout—changed writing as well, to become less personal and more businesslike.[3]

Now we've become habituated with snippets on our screens, all the better if in PowerPoint format. We've become accustomed to plowing through emails, most often just glancing at subject lines.

Instead of reading news articles, we skip over headlines. Our brains have changed back to pattern-recognition mode, more common before the printed word. We've regressed, perhaps back to preindustrial times. But it feels more like survival mode (killing time) than interpersonal engagement.

Since we can't believe our eyes any more on social media—seeing is no longer believing—trust has become more of a challenge. We need to become much more discerning. It may take more time, but it is doable. It needs to be doable because we need to trust—someone, something out there that earns our trust, one person at a time.

Another obstacle to trusting institutions is the presence of algorithms, for example, as Big Social media look to increase viewership with almost no human interface. Algorithms that make up computer programs are not innately bad, evil, or harmful, but their use to replace human interface as a way of economizing can lead to frustration and abuse. They are simply devices used to make decisions easily and automatically.

When such algorithms prevail, there is no negotiation, except with the individuals who control the algorithms. Most often, in such situations, it feels impossible to gain access to the appropriate individuals in charge, and what is meant to solve problems more easily ends up creating more frustration when our issues are not routine but may require some explanation.[4]

Misplaced Trust

One more challenge to trust in the institution of government is the deeply ingrained belief in the reality that a sufficient number of people are confident that President Trump did win the 2020 election and that it was stolen from him—rigged, in the parlance of many of the 74 million who voted for him.[5] Here is a case of the battle for trust that was clearly influenced by the social media.

Many accounts of those speaking with the protesters/insurgents revealed that they sincerely believed that they were acting morally and appropriately, fighting as patriots against the evil agents who had stolen the election. Here's an excellent case of a battle for trust gone awry, because of the power of social media to successfully influence half the voters with faulty information.

The greatest challenges for building trust lie in working with larger institutions. These tend to be set in their procedures and values, particularly the larger ones, with everything fixed in place over time. But, at the end of the day, humans need institutions that are led by humans and those humans have the power to negotiate, if they allow themselves to.

The Institution of Law: Why Justice Wears a Blindfold

For example, if you're involved in a court case, the rules, or laws, are already set. So, negotiations take place between the two parties in front of a judge who is committed to impartial judgments, according to the law. At the highest level, the Supreme Court, it is possible to argue a case and change the legal system in a comprehensive manner relatively quickly. This is precisely what Justice Ginsburg did prior to her appointment at the Supreme Court. She pled on behalf of human rights for both women and men before her Obama appointment and typically won.[6] Even in the largest of institutions, there are individuals with whom to negotiate.

Since the passing of Justice Ginsburg, we don't want to ignore the latest consequences of that event to one of our greatest institutions. The option to trust the new Supreme Court may be challenging for those who appreciated the formerly more balanced court. Now, with the appointment of a relatively young and much more conservative Justice Amy Coney Barrett, along with Justices Gorsuch and Kavanaugh, we must adjust. Fortunately, those who know Barrett well see her as highly intelligent and less political than Justice Scalia. According to Brian Fitzpatrick, law professor at Vanderbilt University, "She is sympathetic to Justice Scalia's methods, but I don't get the sense that she is going to be a philosophical leader on how those methods should be executed."[7]

"Judges are not policymakers," Justice Barrett proclaimed, putting forth her own philosophy, "and they must be resolute in setting aside any policy views they might hold."[8]

With President Trump's second administration, we're faced with the possibility of more conservative judges being appointed to the Supreme Court. The 6–3 conservative supermajority will likely be even more skewed before the end of that administration. Both Clarence Thomas and Samuel Alito are at least seventy-five years old at the time of this writing. They're ripe for retirement if Trump wants to bake in some younger conservatives that might last for the next twenty years. This new "updated" court might even bring up and enforce the Comstock Act of 1873, banning abortion medication through the US mail.

The current Supreme Court will likely be an adjustment for those left of center. These are tough times for trust, especially in our institutions. So, we need to dig deep and explore where we feel most comfortable placing our trust and allowing ourselves to become trustworthy, by taking more responsibility to become more educated about the issues that matter to us and by voting in more elections at the county and state levels.

Information technology is getting more sophisticated. There's a sweet spot between being too careful and being naively open. We're approaching a quantum leap in that area, literally speaking.[9] More information is becoming available, with more options for openness and discovery. Somewhere between alternate realities lies the truth. Trust what feels right but verify with discerning research. Explore and learn what's real for you.

Adieu to Justice Ginsburg and to Trusting the Legal System

The Age of Mistrust, as mentioned, relates to misplaced trust in entities that don't deserve our trust. But when we come across an institution that has proven its trustworthiness thoroughly over time, then that is indeed a privilege to be honored. Sometimes that trust can be embodied in a single person of unquestionable integrity and devotion to the public weal. Such an individual was Justice Ginsburg.

Toward the end of her life, she became an icon of trust, as her personality took on unprecedented attention for that quality, even parodied on *Saturday Night Live*. I dedicate this chapter—on trust in institutions—to her.

In these last two sections, I looked at the history of trust as we know it from the framework of the growth of communication through the written word, then books, then electronics. I took a close look at a brief history of trust, starting before written language, through the burgeoning interest in books, especially after the Gutenberg Revolution made them widely available, and ending with the internet and how social media damaged trust as we know it, especially with the advent of generative AI such as ChatGPT, R1 and Bard. We explored how trust in institutions developed from a historical, social point of view.

False Beliefs

On the Field of Battle
for Political Trust

PART V

Political Trust:
The Need to Belong

Political trust: What people feel toward their governing bodies. In democratic countries, there are at least two political parties, whose beliefs range along a spectrum from liberal to conservative values. Loyalty to one party or another makes up the dynamic of political trust. Information disseminated by any party is sometimes characterized as propaganda if it veers too far from common perceptions. In the US, there is currently a big divide between Democrats and President Trump's Republicans, creating a big split in political trust.

"The propagandist's purpose is to make one set of people forget that certain other sets of people are human."

—ALDOUS HUXLEY

11

Our Need for Tribal Trust

*"It is impossible to go through life without trust:
that is to be imprisoned in the worst cell of all, oneself."*
—GRAHAM GREENE

What groups do you trust? Close friends? Neighbors? Fellow employees? What institutions do you trust? The government? Your bank? The post office? Whom do you trust at this moment? Consider this for a minute or two before reading on. And an equally important question: Who trusts you?

The answers to these simple questions can define your emotional life. And here's an even more critical question: Are you aware of your deep need to trust—someone or something? Could this dearth of trust so many of us are experiencing in our day-to-day lives be a common feature in our present-day culture?

Without such trust, you can be a very lonely individual, quite unhappy and unfulfilled. In this book, we're learning what it takes to avoid such unhappiness and create a richer, more fulfilling life with the skills necessary to trust the right people—in the right settings.

Trust in a Divided Society

When trust is present and strong, all things are possible. Without it, dishonesty, dysfunction, and the potential for destruction prevail. Trust is the essential web of connection between and among individuals, groups, organizations, and nations. Therefore, trust is a universally essential element in our individual lives and among groups and cultures that make up our world—the thread that holds every society together, as Scott Pelley put it in characterizing this book.[1]

Our Need to Trust—and Distrust

Animals that live in packs need to trust one another for their survival. If one of them remains behind, whether due to carelessness or injury, that lone figure loses the protection of the pack, and that vulnerability may result in death. Should a predator attack, there will be no group to defend it. Any documentary on animal behavior, such as *Nature* on public TV, illustrates that over and over. So, the need to trust the others in the pack became hardwired through evolution.

Similarly, with early humans. A lone person, apart from the pack or tribe, becomes vulnerable to predators and is much more likely to die alone. Over time, that ongoing togetherness results in a collective belief system. Tribal experiences that are shared transform into tribal values that become that group's mythology, about creation, about spirituality, about attitudes toward critical life choices. The need to trust fellow tribal members becomes strongly ingrained, not only because it's physiologically hardwired, but also socially learned through shared group experience over time.[2]

This tribal experience satisfies the need for feelings of safety and self-validation through social and emotional interaction with others and leaves us feeling more secure and less anxious.[3] When society becomes much larger than individual tribes or villages, then the need to trust leads to the formation of grouping fragments of the larger society. It's almost as if there's a primal need to revert to the size of the tribe or, at least, to a less overwhelming group than the entire nation or city in which one dwells. The values or mythology of the large group becomes too complex, too heterogeneous. There is an undeniable need to trust something simpler, more easily defined and understood. The need for trust within a smaller group now has the counterpart of distrust of the outside group—which brings us to the current battle for trust.[4]

Sometimes the need to trust a smaller group goes underground. And sometimes that something simpler goes awry and becomes something very complex, such as the conspiracy theories that challenge the minds of nonbelievers. But the tradeoff is a highly dramatic narrative that builds on itself and promises redemption when a "savior" of some sort is hoped for—a savior who will magically turn the world upside-down and right all the wrongs that are responsible for one's disappointments in life with all its daunting challenge.[5] And sometimes that hope is projected onto a leader who welcomes it, enjoying the mantle of worship that comes without any effort on his or her part.

When and where does our need to trust meet its point of crisis? How do the emotional diatribes based on our us-versus-them mentality, with the driving principle of motivation attribution, make us believe that we are the loving ones and that they are hateful? Have social media finally driven us to completely reject those who don't share our beliefs? This divide was literally killing us when the prospect of pandemics hovered over our heads.[6] For those who avoided vaccines and masks for political reasons, severe illness and possible death were more likely.

The Battle for Trust in American History

How has social trust evolved over the eons? What was it like before Zoom meetings and discussions, before TV, before radio, before the telegraph, before the US mail was initiated?

In the larger view, the United States has a long history of internal conflict based on mistrust. Our very existence stems from the decision to defy the British authorities because of what was considered unjustified taxation against tea. We decided to go to war with Great Britain to fight for our independence instead of resolving the conflict. Those who decided the war wasn't justified decided not to get involved. They were the monarchy-loving Tories, some of whom are now called Canadians. They moved north of the American colonies to join the French "habitants" (who remained after the French Army lost to the British in the battle for the New World in 1759) in what became Canada about a hundred years later. Were those future Canadian individuals more trusting of their British monarch than were their southern counterparts?

Even now, there is a clear distinction between those above and those below our northern border. Just as Canadians are often seen as polite and reserved, though caring (is that why they didn't want to fight?), Americans are, in contrast, often typified by Europeans as more direct and libertarian, more apt to fight for their rights. Even when the pandemic was raging in the US and across Europe in the fall of 2020, Canada was still in the low figures. Some thought it was because Canadians were more obedient to authority.[7]

So, the difference in national characteristics can be better understood in this historical context, in addition to the fact that Canada doesn't have a gun culture, nor does it have to deal with illicit drugs coming from South America as much. As well, the American attitude of struggling for independence from British authority by armed citizenry is a part of its history. The Second Amendment attests to that. Perhaps this helps put more texture to understanding the lower level of political trust in the USA.

To begin with, there was distrust between the larger states and the smaller states, as well as between the states-rights proponents, such as Jefferson, and the pro-Federalists, such as Hamilton, even as independence was being formalized. The Founding Fathers were concerned about protecting the government from being chosen by the "rabble," so they insisted that only those "honorable" White male property owners, with a "claim to the land," would be able to vote. To form a proper democracy, the House of Representatives would be based on the popular vote.

But to get the smaller states to sign up, a decision was made at the Constitutional Convention to form a bicameral government, with a Senate represented by two members per state. This was referred to as the Great Compromise, resolving the lack of trust between the big states and the smaller states, as well as between the power of the states and that of the central government. That's precisely what led to the formation of the Electoral College.[8]

Now, to become a law of the land, a bill had to be passed by the House of Representatives, then the Senate, where smaller states could protect themselves against the desires of the more populated states. Following that, the president can veto the bill, but that can, in turn, be overturned by a two-thirds vote in both houses. As a final check to balance the legislative process from undue power, the Supreme Court can judge the bill as counter to the principles of the Constitution.

The Ongoing Battle for Trust

Thus, the battle for trust, in the complex system of government of our republic, is resolved by this intricate process in which the larger states, the smaller states, the president, and the Justices of the Supreme Court all play their parts, hopefully with sincerity and integrity, taking into consideration what the Founding Fathers intended as they formed the Constitution as a basis for mutual trust across our nation.

But conflicts testing these political structures arose, nonetheless. After the US entered World War I, under Woodrow Wilson's administration, the conservatives were at an internal war against the progressives and minorities. There was a growing number of lynchings against Blacks, including the raiding and burning down of Black neighborhoods. Worker unions' efforts were attacked by vigilantes, while the government looked the other way.

Made up of a force of a quarter of a million vigilantes, the American Protective League, acting on behalf of the Department of Justice, attacked thousands of immigrants because they were accused of being subversive. Employing the recently legislated Espionage Act of 1917 and the Sedition Act of 1918, the government harassed any progressive publications that had any leftist leanings. It even succeeded in having presidential candidate Eugene Debs put in jail for his socialist agenda.

Fast-forward a century and we have a somewhat similar dynamic as a number of patriots attacked the liberal agenda and attempted a takeover of government. Without the government's support, much of this antiliberal movement went underground, at least initially, in the form of a growing group known as QAnon.

QAnon's Origins

The group known as QAnon may owe its ideological origins to the Know Nothing Party, arising in the mid-1800s out of fear that there might be a conspiracy to subvert civil liberties in the country. Just like QAnon, it began as a semisecret organization. The name was derived from the secret agreement to reply "I know nothing" to the question from outsiders regarding what the movement was all about. The original Know Nothing Party was initially formed as a reaction to those not to be trusted, primarily Catholics of Irish and German origin. The party feared the outside political influence of the Catholic priests and bishops, a stronger persuasive force at the time than they are currently.[9]

By 1856, the party was sufficiently powerful to enter the government as the American Party, which later morphed into the Republican Party. The Know Nothings were concerned with the surge of immigration in the 1840s,[10] just as those in QAnon were concerned about the wall excluding immigrants in our time, and even had very similar conspiracy-theory beliefs, accusing Catholic priests and nuns of holding young women hostage and strangling infants. In both instances, instability in the country—a deeply divided government prior to the Civil War, dealing with the question of slavery then and the issue of racial injustice now—created an opportunity for such alternate realities.[11]

The initially obscure Know Nothing Party eventually won forty seats in Congress.[12] So deep distrust of the "others" in American politics has had its adherents early in history.

Getting back to tracking the history of trust, in the early 1950s, there was a conspiracy theory against "others," that the army and film industry were infiltrated by hidden communists. Senator Joe McCarthy took it upon himself (along with Roy Cohn, later a mentor to Trump) to wage a war against anyone who would refuse to name friends and colleagues who had ever had affiliations with communist organizations, even though that was common, even stylish, for the intellectual crowd during the post-war years in the late 1940s.

This witch-hunt finally ended mercifully when Army counsel Joseph Welch, defending a young, innocent lawyer egregiously attacked by McCarthy, asked of the Senator in one of the last public hearings, "Senator, may we not drop this? We know he belonged to the Lawyers Guild . . . Let us not assassinate this lad further, Senator; you've done enough. Have you no sense of decency, sir? At long last, have you left no sense of decency?"[13]

That ended McCarthy's reign based on the public's distrust of the government. The deep-state conspiracy theory, conjured up by McCarthy, was finally rebuked when he was censured by the Senate soon afterward.

In the next chapter, we'll continue to look at what is trustworthy and what is not. We'll begin by exploring how social media have bifurcated our culture into us versus them as never before. Our society has been transformed from a time of interpersonal dialogue to the Digital Age. Let's see how that came about.

12

The Slow Strangulation of Trust

"You can't trust someone if you don't understand 'em."
—MARK ZUCKERBERG, interviewed on *Axios*

*"We're the product. Our attention is the
product being sold to advertisers."*
—JUSTIN ROSENSTEIN, former engineer for Facebook

Hitler came to power in the early 1930s, just as technology was taking off. He was able to use radio as a way of reaching the entire country with his highly emotionally charged speeches, giving free radio sets to German citizenry. He was able to use film to popularize his annual highly staged rallies in Nuremberg where Leni Riefenstahl directed and produced the iconic film, *Triumph of the Will*, a powerful propaganda piece on the glories of the Third Reich. He was able to use a private plane, his own Junkers Ju 52, to visit one city after another—twenty cities in six days—to make himself more popular, descending from the sky like an omnipotent savior.

And now we have social media, reflecting the power of another omnipotent savior, in part what got President Trump his second mandate.

A major factor in the breakdown of trust is the role of social media, from where we get much of our information.[1] One-on-one communication has largely been replaced by crowd consensus, an outgrowth of the digital revolution, where multiple voices reinforce one another to echo and amplify a given perception, often false to begin with, and then exaggerated to include imaginative and dramatic variations.[2]

Result? CONFIRMATION BIAS → LACK OF CRITICAL THINKING

Democracy is based on the vote of a nation's citizens. However, with the advent of social media, and its incredible efficiency in transmitting information—or misinformation—the voting process is no longer as trustworthy as it was in years prior. Some people are now more easily brainwashed into believing radicalized theories that can make them zealots for a new religion of politics.

Blame it on a system of algorithms that are designed to keep our eyes on the screen by creating a dramatic conflict between us and them. This "drama" seduces our attention, and the algorithms keep pulling us in, further and further, until we begin hating the other side, because we're so right and they're so wrong.

"What keeps us trolling?" asks journalist Maria Ressa, winner of the Nobel Peace Prize. "Fear, anger, hate!" she replies. And Trump knows how to use this. He said, while being interviewed by Bob Woodward and Robert Costa in 2016, "Real power is—I don't even want to use the word—fear." The current administration uses this fear factor well in its attempts to deconstruct our institutions to weaken their power and strengthen its own. Jeffrey A. Sonnenfeld, a Yale School of Management professor, told this to *The Atlantic* reporter, Isaac Stanley-Becker, "he's at war with the country, and they know it."

"The longer you scroll, the more you get," reveals Tristan Harris, former ethicist at Google.

Now we have a country besieged by hyper-individualism. Our nation used to get its information from three major TV channels—ABC, CBS, and NBC. Now, according to *Statistica*, there are more than 1,758 options from which to choose. Over fifty of them are national, free-to-air networks, and there are over 5,200 cable networks run by 660 operators.

Currently, with social media at our fingertips, there's no need to watch TV or read newspapers to find out what's happening. This creates two challenges: The news we seek is as diverse as the number of sources at our disposal; and what ends up on our screens, whether cell phones, iPads, or computers, is quite likely to be misinformation. The one thing that most of these sources have in common is the effect of having us believe strongly in either the right or left slants in interpreting the news events of the day—one of two alternate realities.

Here's why: The intersection of owners', advertisers', and viewers' interests used to be managed by editors and producers who were classically trained in journalism. Today's replacement for political insight is a conglomeration of algorithms, financial models, and popularity tote boards. That no longer works, and maybe that's why CNN and other venues such as Meta and Twitter are on the ropes, financially speaking—too much confusion in too competitive a market.

Many news outlets, whether Right or Left, gear their reporting on subject matter that appeals to their existing base. That's what increases their audience, and consequently their bottom-line revenues—very different from what we expected from old-time reliable and highly respected reporters such as Walter Cronkite.

Reports that favor either side are primarily consumed by the side that comes with their beliefs already in place. Without an editorial mandate to include diverse opinions toward deeper understanding, these reports have little power to inform or influence the other perspective.

Not ever before in this past century has there been so much distrust of our national government.[3] The prospect of fake news and disinformation, largely dispensed by conspiracy theorists,[4] continues to haunt us. Somehow, these individuals—the "silent majority," as Nixon referred to them, appear to get a sense of control by feeling, "We have some knowledge that others don't." They enjoy a sense of belonging with one another by committing themselves to a large group that otherwise feels left out of the body politic, driven by the need to trust, in other words.

Jack Burton, who tried to create a fake accusation of sexual assault against Robert Mueller, has admitted on the Andrew Ross documentary, *After Truth*: "Fake news is a weapon . . . and people believe it. It's become a tool of war . . . if others are using it, I'm going to use it."[4] Devoted advocates to their cause, such people feel a moral imperative to use these techniques to further the success of their party of choice.

Remember that all these conspiracies don't exist in a vacuum. Such disinformation is sucked into social media, and its impact is forwarded into public awareness at an accelerated rate. The surprising speed of dissemination is what makes these conspiracy theories so dangerous.

Understanding Trump's Successful Battle for Trust

Those who trusted Trump in his first administration saw his accomplishments overcoming his personal foibles. They pointed to his contributions to the growth of the economy; the lowest unemployment rate in years; a favorable stock market; attempts at some type of understanding with North Korea that no other president dared try; greater support of Israel, even moving the American consulate to Jerusalem; and then creating peaceful negotiations with the United Arab Emirates and Bahrain; and supporting the principles of right to life.[5] When asked about COVID-19, instead of acknowledging his delayed response, Trump supporters would say that both China and the World Health Organization denied the significance at first, so Trump was not to blame for that.[6]

Those who try to understand Trump's motivations are often stymied. One approach to understanding him—the best we can come up with—is to understand his motivational system resting on three components: emotional, based on his being reared by his father as the favorite son; spiritual, based on the influence of Norman Vincent Peale, the pastor at the church his family attended; and moral, based on the values of his former attorney and mentor, Roy Cohn.

- Trump's father taught him to see himself as a winner at all costs, to succeed no matter what.[7]
- Norman Vincent Peale taught him that life is to be enjoyed by focusing the mind to see oneself as deserving success through the discipline of positive thinking.[8]
- Finally, Roy Cohn taught Trump the principles of protecting himself.[9]

These three influential factors do not always garner a sense of trust. Instead, they result in one of two reactions: either worship of a man who never gives up and fights his way to the top or, in the alternative, comfortably successful.

Trust had become the victim of all this, both nationally and internationally. Europeans were scratching their heads wondering how we Americans had blundered so badly managing the pandemic, how oblivious we seem to be about climate change. They wondered what had happened to American values, while China, offering a new ideological alternative, slips into the role of international leadership to fill the vacuum left by us on the world stage. Their leaders don't trust our government and are waiting for better times with us, desiring a better relationship with us than we seem to want with them.[10]

What has happened to America's values of openness and tolerance? Why, instead, does it appear selfish and isolated, even dysfunctional? To some, we've become an international laughingstock, both polarized and paralyzed, unable to fix our overspent economy, or even manage our elections.

Meanwhile, driven by computer algorithms designed to accelerate the frequency of the storytelling, some politicians continued to weave the web of a completely imaginary universe,[11] most obvious in Trump's acceptance speech at the 2020 Republican National Convention, claiming that the pandemic had been taken care of and that our economy was booming.[12]

How ironic that he, along with some of his staff and associates, became infected with the virus at the beginning of October 2020. And then, after returning to the White House, advising people not to be dominated by the pandemic, removing his mask in grand style. He had "beat" the pandemic and that it made him feel twenty years younger.[13]

What direction does our need to trust take in all this craziness?

One group, the Lincoln Project, founded by eight Republicans who in their past had worked for such Republican leaders as President George W. Bush, Dick Cheney, Rudolph Giuliani, Newt Gingrich, and Mitt Romney, was now ready to take the battle to Trump.[14]

At one time, not too long ago, there was a stronger bond of trust between American government and its citizens. But in the last eighty years or so, this dynamic of trust changed drastically.[15] Presidents, such as the Roosevelts, Dwight D. Eisenhower, and John F. Kennedy, were held in high esteem by most citizens. Then came the more controversial presidents like Nixon, who lied about his infamous tapes; like Johnson, who misled the country about the war in Vietnam; like Bill Clinton, who lied about his sex life; and the most controversial of all, Trump, who promoted the greatest divide between the two parties.[16]

How Trump Continued to Win His Battle for Trust

Our need to trust, in this Trump II era, has never been greater, but our ability to do so is as frail as it ever has been despite advances in information gathering opportunities with electronic communication and even Zoom-based learning through group discussion. According to Tom Nichols, author of *The Death of Expertise*, we trust experts less and less over time.[17] There appears to be a lack of trust between the general laypeople and those who know best due to their training and expertise.

One of the problems is that many people are ignorant of the important facts so they don't choose to respect the advice of experts. There's a name for this—the Dunning-Kruger effect—which points to the fact that uninformed individuals are unaware of the degree of their lack of knowledge.[18]

This helps account, according to Trump's detractors, for his success in winning the presidency not once, but twice. He accurately answered the tough questions coming his way with a bravado and confidence that were impressive in and of themselves.

As Nichols points out in his book, more and more, people are valuing their own opinions over those of experts. You, as you follow the latest events, need to learn the facts, judge for yourself, and then decide whom you trust.[19]

It was perhaps precisely a widespread lack of trust that got Trump his two victories, and why many refused to hold him accountable. According to Dunning, "Some voters, especially those facing significant stress in their life, might like some of what they hear from Trump."[20] This was especially true in the challenging times of COVID-19.

On the other hand, some—typically conservative Christians who support Israel and the Bill of Rights—may know enough about his gaffes but chose to accept him for his achievements despite this. They typically would say, "I don't like the way he speaks, his rude comments, his attitude, but I like his policies," or "I don't like Trump's personality, but I like what he's done for the economy." Others pointed to his advocacy of personal freedom above all. That accounts, in part, for the fierce reaction by some against face masks, especially when they were mandated by local government or recommended by experts in public health.[21]

Each party follower had their own internal point of view, feeling that their respective decisions were being made with full and accurate knowledge and even more important to them, full freedom of action. Like victors of international wars shaping future history books (as Churchill is known to have said), who's to say which group is suffering from the Dunning-Kruger effect? In other words, the victorious group would be expected to write history in its favor, despite what they didn't know about what they didn't know and their high confidence despite their lack of accurate knowledge, if that were indeed the case. And, according to the theory, the more they didn't know, the greater their level of confidence. Followers of such victorious groups would then see their own point of view as being the right one. And they would expect their leaders to write history along those lines.

The original research on the Dunning-Kruger effect involved eighty-four Cornell undergraduate students who were given a test measuring their grammar skills. Those who scored at the lowest 10th percentile overestimated their ability at the 67th percentile. On the other hand, those who scored highest underestimated their own abilities. This finding was replicated many times over the following years, including a test of emotional intelligence, in which high scorers sought to increase their emotional skills while low scorers "had limited insight into the deficits of their performance" and "expressed more reluctance than top performers to pursue various paths to self-improvement, including purchasing a book on EI or paying for professional coaching."[22]

How Trump Won with the Promise of Simple Solutions

The battle for trust appears to emerge when many people share a common source of values. The more common values can be consolidated in some simple understanding, the greater the pull of trust toward the group. And the more the leader can simplify and emotionalize the set of values, the greater the trust grows.[23]

There is a time in any culture that makes it ripe for simple solutions to seduce a populace into submission because of a tendency to trust. The 1919 Treaty of Versailles demanded that Germans pay reparations as the losers of the world war.[24] Unemployment was high and soaring inflation rates made their currency so worthless it had to be carried in large bundles to make purchases. The German economy was in free fall. There was no social trust at all. Their society was falling apart.

So, who were the Germans of the day to trust with all their problems?

Goebbels used the phrase "The Führer Over Germany" as great propaganda. Using all the emerging technology of his time, he was able to build an incredible relationship of trust with the German populace.[25]

In politics, trust can be built by a leader who can reach into the hearts of the citizenry and offer them solutions, the simpler the better, to the problems of their time. (Ronald Reagan was a great example.) But this was not as easily accomplished before the advent of technology. When our Founding Fathers created the Constitution, they had no idea that radio, TV, or the internet could affect the dynamic of trust in leaders. They had no idea that a telegenic Kennedy would succeed over a poorly televised Nixon, or that years of highlighting a popular TV series such as *The Apprentice* would add to the popularity of a New York real estate mogul who would later run for president.

Nor did they realize how a savvy network like CNN could still be hoodwinked by Trump when it allowed him to broadcast all his conspiracy theories and deride the woman, E. Jean Carroll, who had the night before been awarded a $5 million judgment against him, by calling her a "whack job" on live TV on May 11, 2023.

In his inaugural address on January 20, 2025, Trump announced that his election was a mandate "to completely and totally reverse a horrible betrayal, and all these many betrayals that have taken place, and to give the people back their faith, their wealth, their democracy, and indeed their freedom." This total denial of President Biden's proven contributions to the national economy, to reaching across the aisle to produce legislation that improved the national well-being, and to accommodating to the transfer of power in a manner unlike President Trump's, gave proof to the case that this was not a fair assessment of the preceding administration. And Biden was sitting just a few seats away as Trump made this declaration. Later in the day, as Trump was offering his gratitude to all who had helped him win, he characterized Biden's reign as "the worst administration in history."

In this chapter, I began by pointing out how social media have replaced the three standard TV channels that informed a previous generation of the latest news. Now we have a large selection from which to choose the slant of news that fits our political values. These formats are selected not by traditionally trained journalists but rather by a conglomeration of algorithms, financial models, and popularity tote boards.

I revealed how Trump's values were greatly influenced by his lawyer, Roy Cohn, who taught him never to admit fault and, instead, to fight back by doubling or tripling the original accusation back toward the accuser. Finally, I pointed out how seductively simple solutions can replace the workable solutions to complex issues. Historically, that's how Mussolini and Hitler were able to attain the power they did in difficult times.

In the next chapter, we'll explore the history and rapid growth of both TikTok and QAnon.

13

TikTok, Time Is Flying

"If the people of Arizona elect me,
I'll make sure they never have to vote ever again."
—Cecily Strong of *SNL* impersonating Kari Lake, Oct. 30, 2022

"[F]acts still don't slow down conspiracy theories."
—John Green

A relatively controversial site, TikTok, began with the concept of awake versus asleep, and I'll explain that shortly. This site offers very brief contributions, many less than a minute, about any topic under the sun. At one early point, it was famous for the caper in which young people registered for one of Trump's early rallies and claimed seats for the event. Their purpose, however, was not to attend but rather to make Trump think that the event was all filled up even though these reservations were bogus. There was no intent to attend, but merely to raise the expectation to make Trump look bad.[1]

This may have been one of the seeds of motivation for Trump to create his own social media platform, *Truth Social*, in October 2021 so he could have complete control.

TikTok allows for brief contributions on any topic. One that had caught on is virtually impossible to label. It had to do with questioning reality as we know it and to mix conspiracy theory with both political philosophy and spiritualism.[2] It caused many a young person to question reality and to lose trust in their formerly well-structured world. As it continued, those who were awakened to this mode of questioning reality—referred to as awake (more casually as woke)—differed strongly from those who didn't question their reality—referred to as asleep. Of course, most adherents to TikTok would choose being woke—that is, aware of the dynamics of society and the great influence that modern institutions have, and what spiritual options are available, as opposed to remaining asleep.[3]

TikTok has captured the youth culture's attention as no other, now in forty languages. Since its inception in 2016, it has become the most technologically driven source of culture change in social media with its sublinear computational complexity, and a lightning point of the trust/mistrust issue. Overriding Google, TikTok has a global following of about 1.12 billion monthly users, 170 million of them in the US. Its algorithms hook on to users to discover what appeals to each of them and serves back what they like, to create an ongoing stream of "captured" viewers. Some of the constant viewers are so enthralled that they're unable to look away, so to speak. Its motto might as well be launch, look, consume, all this with the greatest passive pleasure. In discussions of books, TikTok has created best-sellers. One video, #Book Tok, had created surprising best-sellers like author Colleen Hoover, selling more copies of her books than the Bible in 2022.

TikTok had become the prominent app among high school students, but had also captured a significant adult audience, with a plethora of categories, like one for neatniks (#cleanatok) and one for clutterers (#cluttercore), also serving 7 million farmers on #farmtok and 14 million fishermen and -women on #fishertok.

But the issue of trust raises its head when one looks at its Chinese leadership. The Chinese government has become intent on surveillance and propaganda. Is it possible, some wonder, that TikTok is being used for such purposes, even gaining influence over its international audiences? Is its ability to influence the youth culture unabated? Well, we all know how the TikTok situation turned out.

In 2025, Congress voted to ban TikTok unless the owner, ByteDance, were to sell it to an American owner. There was concern about the pro-Chinese government bias. But President Trump issued an order to delay that event for at least 75 days while attempting to get ByteDance to sell 50% of its $50 billion value to some American company such as Oracle or Microsoft.

So, both TikTok and QAnon were contributing to the level of trust across the nation. QAnon has a following of millions, as many as one in five Americans,[4] involving over 9 million contacts over a six-month period, with close to a million coming from Canada and Great Britain; and TikTok in even much greater numbers, "over 800 million active monthly, up 300 million" over a year's time, according to Ryan Donovan, CTO of Hootsuites.[5]

In Europe, Germany in particular, QAnon caught on like wildfire.[6] In the US, according to *New York Times* reporter, Katrin Bennhold, QAnon had already evolved from a fringe internet subculture into a mass movement veering full force into the mainstream. But the pandemic was supercharging conspiracy theories far beyond American shores, and QAnon was metastasizing in Europe as well. As a matter of fact, stories about QAnon had tripled from 2016 to 2020.[7]

How to Manage Conspiracy Theories

What keeps the conspiracy theories going stronger over time, and what makes them so difficult to debunk? They are facilitated by four factors:

1. The mind looks for meaningful relationships between big events rather than the accidental or natural complexity of causal events such as the Kennedy assassination. This is commonly known as proportionality bias. The cause of a highly significant event needs to be as significant as the event itself, and this is referred to as proportionality. How could one man, like Lee Harvey Oswald, be solely responsible for such a gigantic, historical event?[8]

2. Conspiracy theories are self-sealing. They cannot be debunked because of the logical consistency within the theory. The emotional factors seem to make more sense than the more complex reality. Since there is no hard evidence to begin with, new evidence from reality is rejected as lies from the other side, not to be trusted at all.[9]

3. The ease with which the internet spreads the theories and repeats them exponentially serves to make them more credible. Repetition leads to credibility in general, the louder the better. This is how the

human mind works.[10] This is especially true on the internet, where most people get the stories for their political beliefs. One example of this is Facebook, which is visited by almost 3 billion active visitors a month, earning over $29 billion a year.[11]

4. And then there is Fox News, with its primary conspiracy tenders, Sean Hannity and, formerly, Tucker Carlson. According to author and journalist Brian Stelter, Hannity achieved this close affiliation with the president after years of acting as his sounding board and then became a megaphone for conspiracy theories supporting Trump's drive to get reelected.[12] With the main media sites having shut Trump out, conspiracy-theory advocates moved to smaller sites such as Gab, CloutHub, MeWe (also known as Sgrouples), Telegram, and far-right message boards such as 8kun, along with former president Trump's Truth Social.

Finding the Truth

So how do you separate false conspiracies from truth? There are five simple considerations:

1. Is there a more logical rationale involving critical thinking for understanding and explaining the event?
2. How does the theory fare under the scrutiny of experts who have already won your trust?
3. How plausible is the theory as a practical matter?
4. These theories have much more to do with emotions than they do with facts, so repetition of facts will not convince the conspiracy-theory believer.
5. The only way to convince the believer that the theorists are wrong is to, first, invest some time in understanding their basic values, which all humans share. Then, when they feel understood, reveal how their own theories contradict their basic values. This is not easy and takes much time and energy and, in all candor, won't always work, but it's your best shot.

The more these organizations grow, the more vulnerable is the level of trust in our nation. Many mothers are drawn to QAnon, motivated to protect their vulnerable children from the horrid individuals purported to be practicing sexual abuse, according to the wild speculations of these conspiracy theories.[13] What will all this negativity do to our collective psyches over the years? Where will it all end?

In this chapter, we looked at the origins, memberships, and rapid growth of TikTok and QAnon and their influence on trust, especially in politics.

PART VI

Tribal Trust:
How We Form Our Society

Tribal trust: A sense of community among those who feel outside the domain of conventional culture and therefore have a need to connect strongly with others who share a set of values unique to the group. As with American indigenous cultures, tribal trust allows members to share certain rituals and symbols to strengthen the sense of community that derives from a particular set of cultural values—"togetherness" to form sufficient strength to fight against potential enemies. This form of trust can become emotionally visceral in its view of outside influence, leading to mythologies that depart far from conventional social norms. This is what the extreme right was subject to and how they won the 2024 elections.

"There's so much active misinformation
and it's packaged so well."
—BARACK OBAMA

14

How We Build Trust among Ourselves

*"Conspiracy theories are an irresistible
labor-saving device in the face of complexity."*
—HENRY LOUIS GATES

In this section, we'll go back to history to discover the evolution of conspiracy theories, observing their birth among our primate ancestors. We'll start with observing Hitler as he used a conspiracy theory to justify the onset of World War II, then examine the characteristics of conspiracy theories, before going into the evolutionary history. Conspiracy theories can have powerful effects. We need to study them thoroughly and that's what we'll do in this section.

The Conspiracy Theory That Started a World War

One case of a narcissistic conspiracy theory leading to war took place over a hundred years ago. When World War I ended at the eleventh hour on Nov. 11, 1918, the last country to give up was Germany, with the Germans fighting the French from both of their muddy, stinky trenches until the very last minute. This ugly and frustrating experience of trench warfare with little success by either side as infantrymen slaughtered one another in utterly sickening conditions of horrific one-on-one combat would only end with unreasonable demands that would lead inexorably to the next world war.

Even as that country signed the Versailles Treaty about six months later, its countrymen felt that they really could have continued to fight but it was the Jews and republicans—Socialists and Bolsheviks—in Germany that manipulated the surrender. And there really was no surrender, according to many in the high German command, but it was an armistice, ending a conflict resulting in 8.5 million military casualties, all to no avail, an utter waste of human life.

This broadly held belief among the German population helps explain why its country's surrender contributed to the ascendancy of Adolf Hitler, one of history's most narcissistic and destructive national leaders, and the tragic destruction of many millions of lives.

The right-wing circles adopted this conspiracy theory known at the time as the stab-in-the-back myth, literally from the German as the "dagger stab legend." They couldn't imagine being losers, so they named those who signed the armistice as the "November criminals." As the German soldiers returned from battle, they were told they were undefeated in the field: "No enemy has vanquished you," and the unofficial term, "undefeated on the battlefield," was given to the *Reichswehr*, the defeated German Army.

When Hitler came to power in 1933, he continued this conspiracy theory as an important part of his campaign to justify the removal and execution of many communists and subsequently Jews. This dangerously divisive conspiracy theory lived on, and Hitler used it to justify breaking the terms of the Versailles Treaty and initiating World War II.

Pssst! Here's Exactly How Conspiracy Theories Destroy Trust

A conspiracy theory is a belief, typically false, that some covert but influential group is responsible for an event or set of circumstances that affects others.

I've often wondered what makes conspiracy theories so appealing to so many. Certainly, the theories are much more imaginative than good old reliable facts. And then there's the mystique of knowing what other people don't. There are so many examples: That the moon landing was faked and filmed in Hollywood, that JFK was murdered by factions in the government, that Trump won the 2020 election. Why would such a large portion of our population find it hard to give up their erroneous take on reality? Social scientists seem to have some of the answers.

There's something about the role of these theories in our cultural evolution that makes them so powerful, particularly in current times when anyone can make themselves heard online and easily become impactful.

Let's look at the factors that make this easier to understand. To begin with, conspiracy theories have been around for a long time, even among sophisticated people. Immediately following the 9/11 terrorist attack on the Twin Towers, according to an article in *The Journal of Political Philosophy,* almost half of all New Yorkers believed that the US government was complicit.[1] Roughly about one-third of the US population believes that the Food and Drug Administration is yielding to Big Pharma (by suppressing natural cures for cancer, hiding the facts about radiation from cell phones, suppressing facts about genetically modified foods, for examples).[2] Such theories pervade human society.[3] Many of us may inadvertently believe such theories, not even realizing that they are not true.

The Hard Science of Conspiracy Theory

Now, what are the characteristics that make for conspiracy theories? There are a number; here are five:

1. **Pattern**: There is a pattern that appears to **connect** people and events in a regular and repeated manner,[4] such as the effect of the full moon, giving birth to the term *lunacy.* Pattern-seeking is a universal trait. The brain evolved to find patterns in the natural environment, and we don't always test these patterns. And those who believe one theory are more likely to be susceptible to others as well.

2. **Intention**: The conspirators have clear intentions to create certain events and **deliberate plans** to carry them out.[5]

3. **Coalition**: There are multiple people involved, acting in **coordination** with one another.[6]

4. **Threat**: Beyond being deceptive, their goals are **harmful,** usually to a specified group of people.[7]

5. **Secrecy:** Because there is a lack of open knowledge about the conspirators, the sources of these theories are typically unknown and therefore their theories are **difficult to prove wrong**.

Of course, once a conspiracy theory is open to being tested and proven to be true, or uncovered, it is no longer a theory—case in point, Watergate. And most of them involve powerful groups such as Big Pharma, a deep state within the government, or minorities such as Muslims or Jews, and even celebrities around the globe.

Some Recent Theories

There are always trends in conspiracy theories, often relating to important issues that are in the news. Here are some current ones:

A small group of self-proclaimed medical experts gathered at Capitol Hill to criticize home sheltering and advised against wearing masks, and recommended hydroxychloroquine as a cure for COVID-19. The video of it was broadcast by Breitbart News and became even more popular than the infamous *Plandemic* video.[8]

The *Plandemic* video itself had a life of its own, "starring" discredited medical researcher Judy Mikovits, who proclaimed that wearing a mask activates your own virus and that headliners such as Dr. Fauci and philanthropist Bill Gates were profiting from the whole COVID-19 enterprise. Along with its sequel, *Indoctornation*, these videos had a strong impact, with a quarter of all Americans seeing some truth in it.[9]

Deniers of the pandemic had taken their case to the populace via the strength of Fox News demagogues, such as Tucker Carlson and Sean Hannity, who proclaimed that "coronavirus fearmongering by the deep state will go down in history as one of the biggest frauds to manipulate economies, suppress dissent and push mandated medicines."[10]

Probably the most popular theory in this Age of Mistrust involves Bill Gates's intention to implant microchips in billions of people as they get vaccinated to track them at his will. Unfortunately, according to a new Yahoo News/YouGov poll, 44 percent of Republicans believed this theory to be true.[11]

In this brief chapter on the character of conspiracy theories, I began with one that facilitated the beginning of World War II, when Hitler justified his aggression by using it to his advantage. Then I looked at the five characteristics of all such theories that destroy trust and ended with some relatively recent theories that circulated around the pandemic at its height.

In the next chapter, we'll look at the origins of conspiracy theories in the forms of gossip and what scientists call social vigilance, even occurring among primates prior to the evolution of our own species.

15

The Latest Gossip on Trusting Gossip

"Words have no wings, but they can fly a thousand miles."
—Korean proverb (way before ChatGPT)

"There's a sucker born every minute."
—Banker, DAVID HANNUM, though attributed to P. T. Barnum

Just as some herd animals butt heads or confront one another on an ongoing basis to determine social hierarchy, so do humans sometimes gossip for the same reason, to determine who's up and who's down based on their misdeeds and related intimate secrets. Gossip played a significant role in our primal history of whom to trust as soon as language had developed.

It may have replaced the fur grooming of our primate ancestors to build strong bonds of friendship and trust, enhancing our chances of survival. And we can probably agree that strong friendship without occasional gossip is hard to imagine. Perhaps that was one of the driving forces in the evolution of language, among others—to enhance survival by forming strong bonds for support and a sense of trust. When was the last time you afforded yourself the luxury of gossip with a close friend, or circle of friends? Did you feel closer after that luxury?

Gossip helps us distinguish between close, trustworthy members in a group and the others who are not so close. We need not be vigilant with those in our inner group. But we may need to be vigilant with the others in the group whom we don't trust as much. Gossip and social vigilance, it seems, are inversely related. Without the trust built through gossip or shared intimacy, we don't know enough about the possibility of some social threat by others in the group.

Why We Humans Can Be Paranoid

Research has shown that those who trust one conspiracy theory are more likely to trust other theories, even if they're unrelated, or even incompatible. For example, that Princess Diana staged her own death, or was murdered, or that the pandemic was a hoax while, at the same time, real but the brainchild of Bill Gates.[1]

Such an excessive conspiracy mentality involves low levels of trust as well as an inclination toward paranoid thinking and violence, though very rarely carried out. This mentality seeks out simplistic answers when complex problems lead to fear, and there is a need to put the blame on some well-known figure.

The human brain can be highly susceptible to this paradigm of trust. To the best of our knowledge, humans have the most sophisticated brains in the animal kingdom. Within the realm of predator versus prey, we are both, sometimes hunters, yet sometimes fearful of animals or even other humans who can harm us. Therefore, there is a natural need and ability to be vigilant for our safety, even paranoid, which may play a role in conspiracies.

The Utter Need for Inner Group Trust

When it comes to social groupings, we are concerned about, sometimes obsessed with, where we fit into a social hierarchy. We are particularly sensitive to who gives us a thumbs-up and who a thumbs-down, especially if that "who" is a group that we admire or depend on, and most particularly if we have personal familiarity with such a group but have not yet spent sufficient time to earn its full trust.

We are naturally sensitive to this ongoing evaluation by members of the group, and to nonverbal signals of acceptance or rejection. So, we are highly vigilant about adhering to the norms of our groups on a social basis. We never want to be, or even feel, left out.

What if we felt disenfranchised from governmental considerations because we see ourselves as less educated, less affluent, less powerful than how we visualize the elites in our society, or in terms of our lifestyles or careers? Many would say we're talking about a large group among our citizens. Many of these found solace in successful leaders who finally gave them the recognition and attention they felt they needed and deserved. But the facts weren't always friendly to those leaders. They created narratives to meet their needs for self-glorification even though they didn't always fit with reality. Their own perspectives often didn't match objective reports.

Have You Heard about Herd Mentality?

One of the main higher functions of our brain, as we evolved, was to discern how our social environment could present us with dangerous threats to survival even within our own group, or how opportunities for living and passing on our genes through natural selection could affect future generations. Adaptability to environment—not necessarily physical strength—according to Charles Darwin, was the most significant factor in the survival of a species. Herd animals, usually prey to solitary or pack predators, are particularly vigilant to such dangers.

Even plants, including trees, are known to collaborate to survive and thrive, using chemical secretions through a lattice of fungal networks buried in the soil, sending nutrients and carbon back and forth, primarily to express distress signals, according to ecologists.[2]

Survival requires interdependence, even for trees as well as humans, and so we tend to share beliefs with those we trust, using words instead of fungal networks, even if these words are not always based on facts.

In addition, herd mentality, the urge to remain in the group, gave its members a measure of safety against predators. The success of any hunters depended on singling out an animal from the herd, whether a very young or older member of the herd that could not keep up with its group running from predators. So staying part of the group at all costs has deep, primal roots.

Now, the question remains, are we humans predators or prey? Obviously, we are both. We hunt and we can be hunted down, as previously mentioned. But humans have always lived together, at least in small groups prior to the Industrial Age. How great is our need to socialize? To what extent do we need to be part of a group? Now, with our recent experience of sheltering at home during the pandemic, we have come to realize, painfully at times, how much we crave ongoing social interaction.

In terms of evolution, therefore, it's clear that we need society to immerse ourselves emotionally, particularly in a form that supports us in our values and lifestyles. It's all driven by a fear of rejection and the need to replace that with a sense of trust. To highlight this point, let's take a little side trip to explore the phenomenon of gossip. What is its nature and purpose in the context of trust? Why are we so drawn to it?

The Latest Gossip on Trusting Gossip

According to Merriam-Webster, gossip is simply defined as "rumor or report of an intimate nature," and by Dictionary.com as "idle talk, or rumor, especially about the personal or private affairs of others." In other words, if we may add to the language experts, gossip is a systematic way of judging others' intimate behaviors to place them lower on the social hierarchy because of such personal judgments. We rarely think of gossip as resulting in someone being elevated in the hierarchy. Then it's called praise, admiration, respect, but not gossip.

And when trust in journalism erodes, then there's a greater risk of false accusations. "We've seen what happens when public trust in media erodes," writes Rebecca Jennings, "allegations of 'fake news' can curdle into ambiguousness about what is or is not factual, allowing misinformation to spread unchecked."

Nor did being sheltered at home help any. She goes on to say, "Regardless of what Pope Francis, who described gossip as 'a plague worse than Covid' says, it's clear people are yearning for something to talk about that doesn't involve the latest horrors of the day."[3]

Being Vigilant about Vigilance

So social vigilance, wondering where we stand in terms of trust with our important groups, is a constant awareness for most of us (unless we belong to the group of outliers such as single-minded authors working in solitary fashion on their magnificent books, not to mention their dedicated editors who must slog through the rough copy).

If we can manage to feel supported in our special group by bonding together against a common enemy, that helps us to feel more secure. So that's where conspiracy theories come into play.

Neuroscientists have discovered that as mammals have evolved, those communal animals developed more cerebral neural sophistication for recognizing social signals, versus animals that lived in isolation. It seems that it takes a lot of brain power to recognize where you stand in the group in terms of trusting the hierarchy of dominance/submission.

Such mammals developed highly acute awareness of facial expression of their herd members, involving, for example, the raising of eyebrows, the curve of the lips, the amount of white of the eye showing as eyelids are raised or lowered, the direction of the ears, and the sounds of breathing. Interpretation of all these signals took a significant amount of brain development.

That's why it's not surprising that we humans have the brain power to be very sensitive to issues of trust, where we stand in the groups that are important to us. We watch for social signals such as a subtle pursed lip that could be interpreted as displeasure or an even more subtle nodding of the head with direct eye contact for reassurance.

The more important people are to one another, the more likely is eye contact, sometimes unusually prolonged. (Think of couple actors on the large screen. When eye contact is prolonged, they're described as displaying good chemistry.) So subtle messages of acceptance and rejection are played out continuously. Very rarely are we fully aware of those dynamics as they're occurring. Rejection is a painful experience.

We're vigilant to note if we are being considered for rejection or acceptance, particularly by a powerful member of the group.

This sensitivity to social signals also operates in finding some individuals as undesirable—examples would be if they appear to be visibly suffering from some malady, or seem as untrustworthy by avoiding eye contact, or aggressive if they engage in what seems like too much eye contact with a grimacing demeanor. An instinct for self-preservation would work toward avoiding such individuals and not afford any opportunity for the interpersonal "grooming" of gossip with them.

Beyond common interpersonal transactions, there appear to be certain items about which we are much more vigilant than others—such as spiders and snakes as opposed to ladybugs and squirrels.[4] By the same token, we are sensitive to angry expressions, especially in males, and particularly if they are not in our familiar group, and even more so if they are of a different color.[5]

But often the us versus them vigilance cuts across race when modern political alliances include individuals across racial lines and may break down at such times, replaced by vigilance for political differences rather than race, religion, or social status.[6]

Everybody's Talkin' 'Bout Putin

Let's turn this discussion to focus on current times and discover how vigilance and gossip in political realms can occasionally have positive effects, as citizens of a dictatorship gossip among themselves about their frustration with a dictator who is basically out of touch with their wants and values. This was so eloquently described by Tom Friedman, political columnist for the *New York Times* in his opinion article, "Vladimir Putin is the world's most dangerous fool."

He discusses gossip at the expense of dictator Putin in his column of May 9, 2023. In it, he quotes a key refrain from "Everybody Talks" by his favorite rock group, Neon Trees. The lyrics indicate that it's impossible to hide the truth because gossip is so universal, revealing what is unpublished yet intuitively known.

One of the biggest lessons I've learned [writes Friedman] as a foreign affairs writer reporting from autocratic countries is that no matter how tightly controlled a place is, no matter how brutal and iron-fisted its dictator, EVERYBODY TALKS.

They know who is stealing, who is cheating, who is lying, who is having an affair with whom. It starts with a whisper and often stays there, but everybody talks.

In this modern example, gossip is still playing the same role described earlier in this chapter—a systematic way of judging others' intimate behaviors to place them lower on the social hierarchy because of such personal judgments.

Russian citizens seem to have very little say-so in the dictatorship they inhabit. Their only recourse to regain any sense of personal power, as they see their country flailing in this war against Ukraine, is to gossip. It may have little political impact, but it does have significant psychological impact, mostly reaching out for a sense of power, the bottom line of all gossip.

In this "gossipy" chapter, I focused on the primal need to belong to a primary group for our own sense of emotional security. We evolved brain circuitry to enable us to become acutely aware of whom to trust in our group by sensing subtle facial cues of support or rejection. Perhaps gossip among close friends replaced the grooming of our primal ancestors—a process of social bonding to build trust. I ended with an account of gossiping by Russian citizens to acquire a sense of power over Putin, to "put him in his place," in a secret venture based on the magic power of gossip, among otherwise politically helpless citizens.

In the next chapter, I begin by revealing scientific explorations of war between chimpanzee groups as far back as 6 million years ago. It's based on what scientists refer to as the alliance-detection system, even engaging in politics all these millions of years ago, a result of neurocomputational programs designed by natural selection.

We'll learn how to recognize conspiracy theories more easily and why they play a major role in mistrusting outside groups. As we humans evolved, there was more brain power assigned to the trust process. To bring it to the modern era, I examine a group of wild Japanese snow monkeys as they reveal the politics of status as to who gets out of the cold and into the naturally occurring hot springs. I end on another modern note about trusting conspiracy theories, as they may be generated by chatbots such as ChatGPT and DeepSeek's R1. The battle for trust, embedded in our evolved brains and now emanating from our latest high-tech inventions, is not getting easier.

16

Narcissistic Monkeys and the Evolution of Conspiracy Theory

*"A lie can travel halfway around the world
while the truth is putting on its shoes."*
—MARK TWAIN

Consider that believers in a conspiracy theory trust one another implicitly. They rely on one another for support to promulgate and build on it. Yet there is an absence of trust between the believers and the nonbelievers. When differences become sufficiently intense, each side may see the other as ignorant or evil, or both. Trust between factions becomes very hard to come by. So, we can say that conspiracy theories result in both trust and mistrust, depending on what camp you find yourself in.

Social scientists have come up with the term *alliance-detection system*,[1] in which individuals are vigilant about separating and distinguishing supportive alliances from threatening ones. All these subtle social signals I've been discussing come into play as we make judgments about who is for us and who is against us. In our drive for self-preservation, there is little cost for mistakenly labeling a group judged as nefarious, threatening, or conspiratorial.

The benefit—avoiding physical threat—is greater than the cost—being seen as a bit paranoid. And even when a conspiracy theory is pointed out as such, it doesn't necessarily stop those who assigned the conspiracy label from continuing to believe it, as illustrated by Trump and his followers after losing the 2020 elections.

So how do we get from the us versus them mentality to the initiation of outright violence sometimes ending in war? Two social scientists,

John Tooby and Leda Cosmides, have come up with some concepts that thread the narrative. They believe that wars have a long history, over 6 million years, going back to chimpanzees and their forebears. They postulate "a set of species-typical neurocomputational programs designed by natural selection to regulate within-coalition cooperation and between-coalition conflict,"[2] as well as within-group "politics." If an outside group is seen as threatening in any way, then that is sufficient cause for aggression.

The scientists label the emotions leading to conflict as hate and anger. Hate happens when the outsider group is a threat, and anger occurs due to broken negotiations in the attempt to avoid conflict. Morality as an issue comes into play when the motivation for aggression becomes a strong difference in values. War may start with territorial disputes but, with increasing sophistication in human societies, may also include strong differences of opinion or values.

According to these social scientists, vigilance for those not trustworthy may be the key to understanding the origins of social morality differences and even war. The thinking is that the process of vigilance we've been discussing evolved to work within groups through early evolution. With our sensitivity to social signals pitched so keenly through evolution in modern times, conflict between groups has become much more complex. Now it is characterized by national political factions and stirred up by social media. Therefore, our tendency to categorize groups as us versus them is strong, especially in a political context.[3]

The Evolution of Conspiracy Theory

But the question remains, how strong a factor was this in the social evolution of our very distant ancestors? Was there evolutionary advantage to becoming more vigilant about conspirators looking to harm and possibly kill us? The particular trait we're exploring here is the recognition of potential enemies, through enhanced vigilance, which goes beyond the mere recognition of obvious indications of malevolence.

In other words, it's clear that perceptions of others approaching us with apparent anger and raised fists, so to speak, even with arms such as clubs or AR-15s are easy to discern. But what about the much more subtle awareness of others who are not obvious in terms of their threat but have the potential for lethality? In these modern times, the threat might be to our financial security or access to improved living conditions or education. It might be communicated through racial bias or other prejudices. Did it work, in terms of evolutionary success, for humans to adopt a bit of paranoia to protect imagined versions of ourselves?

Even in ancient hunter-gatherer societies, according to social scientists, privately singling out someone as a malevolent individual prior to any actions to justify that judgment—that is, spreading a conspiracy theory about them—would be acceptable if the larger group were in accord.[4]

To err on the side of caution (in other words, to be a little paranoid and to suspect a conspiracy theory) allows those believing in the conspiracy theory more likely to be successful, live on, and procreate, "justifying" the evolutionary tendency to indulge in such theory. Those who failed to do so and missed the conspiracy theory, which turned out to be real, were more likely to be killed. That trait, of no suspecting, or being too trusting, would eventually decrease. That's why we survivors, or at least some of us, have the tendency to harbor such conspiracy theories.

Where's the proof for such an outlandish theory that conspiracy theories have their basis in the evolution of humanity? After you finish reading the next few sections, you'll know how to recognize conspiracy theories sooner and have a broader range of responses when you confront them. Well, let's take one aspect at a time.

Exaptations

An exaptation is a brand-new use of some trait that evolved in a certain direction but then became useful for another, somewhat unexpected, function. The classical example is the emergence of feathers to help keep birds warmer, but then some birds began to benefit from those feathers when they started to evolve into flying creatures.

By the same token, let's look at the characteristics of conspiracy theories (listed in chapter 14 under the heading, How We Build Trust among Ourselves). Each of those may have evolved in their own right regarding their purpose and function, for example, the abilities to recognize patterns of behavior in social groups revealing our place in the hierarchy, or harmful social threat to our sense of safety. These skills appeared very early in evolution. Once they came into existence and people started using them, others were able to repurpose them.

For example, at some point, all these new skills could be used to form the much more complex sort of vigilance necessary to make up conspiracy theories, for those individuals or groups intending harm with no overt signs.

The skill of vigilance for such subtle behaviors was very different in its complexity than the individual skills that preceded it. It took much more of that evolved brain power to recognize social signals about conspiracies against us. We had to become socially sharper. Such complex recognition skill was an exaptation allowing for using already existing abilities (recall the feathers functioning to maintain warmth, then allowing for the new skill of flying) to form a new skill, the vigilance for conspiracy.[5]

Blame the Narcissistic Monkeys

In order to understand more clearly how subtle vigilance skills evolved from the simpler ability to run from obvious threats, let's take a look at what science reveals when observing some interesting groups of monkeys. We would want to know whether our ancient ancestors, living in small groups, could discern the differences between the more dominant members and the lesser ones. To set the stage, don your fur-lined parkas and mittens. It's going to get cold. But bring along a swimsuit as well.

Research on wild Japanese snow monkeys living in very cold temperatures in the Nagano Prefecture revealed that the opportunity to deal with the freezing temperatures by basking in the naturally occurring hot springs was determined by social ranking. Even in this primitive society, there were haves and have-nots.[6]

And even at this primal level, there was opportunity for conspiracies—making friends with a high-status monkey to spurn a marginally mid-status monkey—in order to gain access to the comforting warmth against the chilly environment, and possibly the vigilance about such conspiracies, which I call theories in this discussion. Do monkeys have the social awareness to figure out how to form coalitions to work the system? Research has indicated that they do.

"Scientists describe Japanese macaque societies as 'despotic' [tyrannical] and 'nepotistic' [favoritism granted to relatives]," says Ben Crair, observing the monkeys firsthand, "and they constantly displaced inferiors to reinforce their rank. The monkeys were vigilant as they picked grain from the snow, constantly looking over their shoulders to keep tabs on their neighbors: A higher-ranking monkey might drag them by the leg or sink its teeth into their neck."[7]

So according to the adaptive-conspiracism hypothesis,[8] there is concern about distress (freezing cold temperatures) and power differences in terms of who gets into the warm water and who doesn't.

Then there is the clear awareness among the monkeys as to who gets the privilege and who does not. Then pattern perception takes over as to who is friend and who isn't, followed by the attempt to make important friends. Finally, there is the decision to either move toward a change in social status or to just accept the grim world of freezing temperatures as inevitable.

Ultimately, the rich reward of warm water may foster some degree of vigilance as to who may be against you and who for you. Here we have the primal beginnings of conspiracy theory and the skill of vigilance to adjust to it, as discovered among early humans, enabling "males of low fighting prowess to cooperatively plan the execution of physically aggressive and domineering alpha males."[9]

Machiavellian Monkeys and Collective Narcissism

Of course, vigilance leading to conspiracy theories is quite different in modern times than it was in ancestral times. In olden times, when we lived in small groups, suspecting someone in the group or a nearby group about possible violence that could lead to murder, then vigilance could save our lives.[10]

But in current times, with large-scale social interaction and social media to reveal almost limitless information (and disinformation), conspiracy theories are less likely to lead to murder and more likely to deal with political outcomes.[11] And these usually involve extremes on the political spectrum,[12] often with the belief that one's own group is superior, what can be considered collective narcissism.[13]

Whether we look at primates or modern-day civilization, conspiracy theories continue to capture our imagination. Almost thirty-five years ago a book by the name of *Machiavellian Intelligence* was published, revealing how important the role of social learning was in primates.[14]

One of the main contributions of this classic book edited by Richard Byre and Andrew Whiten is the presence of theory of mind in primates, that primates can figure out how their group members think from the other's perspective. Hence, the term *Machiavellian* in the title. Primates can figure out what it takes to "work the system" with manipulative social expertise just like the Florentine princes of northern Italy did, such as the powerful Medici family and Niccolo Machiavelli, author of *The Prince,* all about the ruthless tactics in the pursuit of power.

In a follow-up book, *Machiavellian Intelligence II,* the authors state: "In some species, notably chimpanzees, the maneuvering to gain alliances and influence powerful individuals appeared to be so social that the term 'political' and 'Machiavellian' came to be used to describe it."[15]

So, with all this political intelligence, could the chimps figure out where the conspiracies lay and who the culprits were? If so, and that seems to be the case, according to the research, then the chimps fostered conspiracy theories.

Recent research from Canada and Indonesia has revealed that primates have the ability not only to behave politically, but economically as well, which would only enhance their ability to work the system. Long-tailed macaques who live near the Uluwatu Temple in Bali were seen stealing items from tourists and returning the items in exchange for food.

But here's the kicker: The items would typically be returned to the owners for small snacks; but if the items were more costly, such as cellphones or prescription glasses, then the cost was higher. One bartering negotiation lasted twenty-five minutes, including seventeen minutes of negotiation.

Jean-Baptiste Leca and his colleagues saw this as a sign of cultural intelligence, proving "cognitive underpinnings of economic behavior in non-human primates." They conclude that "cognitive skills and temperamental traits exhibited to varying extents by non-human primates engaging in token-aided economic behaviors include preference transitivity, self-control, delay of gratification, action planning and calculated reciprocity."[16] Sounds like conspiracy theories could easily be an outcome of all these sophisticated behavioral awareness skills.

So, what's the point of all this primate research? It's our new understanding that belief in conspiracy theories is at least soft wired in us if not hardwired. This wiring may have formed early in our evolution of learning, if not in our DNA. And it's never going to go away completely. The advantage of getting used to it is that we can learn to deal with it. Going forward, it makes sense to pay attention to what we're learning in this book about how to deal with those deeply immersed in harmful beliefs.

Conspiracy Theories Never Die. They Just Fade Away, but Then . . .

From those early evolutionary days forward, trust, or lack thereof, was a factor in the social lives of primates and, later in history, Italian princes, when the decision whom to trust and whom to distrust had to be made. Niccolo Machiavelli popularized the term *conspiracy* in his book, *The*

Prince,[17] written in the sixteenth century; and later, in the twentieth century, Adolf Hitler used such principles to manipulate his way into power in 1933, using the conspiracy theory mentioned in chapter 15, the dagger stab legend, to start up World War II.

The conspiracy theory started as a way of hiding the German defeat in the previous world war from the citizens of Germany, where there was no fighting as all the war was outside the country. Therefore, with little communication with the outside world, the citizenry could easily be duped by that lie.[18]

This conspiracy theory originated in a discussion between German Army General Erich Ludendorff (who had been feeding lies about the army's remaining strength to the German public) and British General Sir Neill Malcolm when, in response to Ludendorff's explanation of Germany's loss due to political maneuvering, Malcolm responded, "Do you mean, General, that you were stabbed in the back?"[19]

Ludendorff was delighted by this characterization for two reasons—it validated the German sentiment and this by an eminent British general, and it offered a convincing image by which to consolidate the conspiracy theory.

Ludendorff subsequently convinced Germany's President Hindenburg of its effect and thus began the conspiracy theory that gave Hitler the political ammunition to justify the initiation of World War II. In his political treatise, *Mein Kampf,* Hitler wrote about this event and used it as a reason to regain Germany's honor in battle.

The Increasing Power of Conspiracy Theories

Why such a powerful impact by conspiracy theories? Partly to give the populists a sense of power over what they consider the elite power structure. "The Left's successful political recruitment of the universities, the major news media, and some scientific organizations," claims Kevin Williamson, author of *Big White Ghetto*, "has discredited those institutions categorically in the estimate of the populist Right, heightening its preexisting anti-intellectualism," resulting in "the creation of a conspiracy-theory entertainment ecosystem that is both more narratively consistent than in previous eras and also capable of being tailored to particular audiences."[20]

There are also individually directed conspiracy theories in which an individual with grievance toward someone because of being fired from a job or slighted in some way then feels the need for retribution by creating false and maligning stories about a specific individual, or their relatives. Such incidents can be very harmful to one's reputation and even condemn the recipient to loss of job or standing in the community.[21]

"False narratives," as the media refer to them, have powerful consequences.[22] Conspiracy theories just keep on keeping on, struggling against the clear evidence to the contrary.[23] They must be in our DNA, evolved over millennia.

In this chapter, we looked at how conspiracy theories can change history, from providing a reason to start World War II to fomenting a vicious attack on the enemies of Germany in World War I to justify their loss. The evolution of conspiracy theories goes way back in our evolution, and we tracked that through the millennia to more current Machiavellian monkeys ruling such privileges as warm spa-like water holes.

The Age of Mistrust has come into full bloom in recent years, so understanding the beginnings of conspiracy theories has never been more crucial, especially considering their five characteristics: pattern, intention, coalition, threat, and secrecy. This overview is essential to understanding their true nature.

A few years ago, as I've already discussed, there was the advent of ChatGPT, a variant of GPT-3, which came closer to passing the Turing test in which the reader starts to believe that they are communicating with a real person. What is happening to trust here? Can we trust that we are indeed communicating with a sentient, self-aware entity? When asked about whether ChatGPT has self-awareness, here's ChatGPT's answer: "The concept of sentience, consciousness, self-awareness is complex and multi-disciplinary, and they are still not fully understood."[24]

Do you trust that answer?

In the next section, we'll explore how computer technology allows for international shenanigans that simply destroy trust. We'll go into sharp detail as to how this process takes place and how Putin has his hands all over this game of destroying trust. If you're not the detail type, please feel free to just skim this section in cursory fashion, but if you are into the details, then go ahead and enjoy the story of Putin's evil machinations.

I'll also go on to discuss how the Russians experimented with their disinformation process to create conflict in the streets between right- and left-wing factions by pretending to challenge one another to appear at the same place and time for the conflict to take place. This process is called *disaggregation,* and I'll describe it in detail.

PART VII

Cyber Trust: A Very Brief History of Putin's Cybersecurity Threats

Cyber trust: What people feel as they decide to accept what they receive from international hackers, typically Russian or Chinese, on the internet. It also refers to the belief that what is sent to, or received from, others in secret is not being published for all but is kept private and confidential except for the intended receiver of the message. Fake messages can be sent by such hackers to target receivers in the form of propaganda and can create problems if trust in such messages is not scrutinized with care.

> *"The only person who enjoyed that [debate] was Vladimir Putin while he was stroking a cat."*
>
> —JIMMY FALLON, after the presidential debate between Trump and Biden, June 2024

17

Once Upon a Spy

"Why do I have to get tough on Putin? I don't know anything other than that he doesn't respect our country."
—DONALD J. TRUMP

Espionage has always been intriguing, especially in times of international hostility with the possibility of nuclear warfare and is the basis for many a highly engaging spy novel. Well, it turns out that real life is not very far from that.

Putin's Attempt to Create an Alternate Reality to Trust

We hear about the lack of trustworthiness in social media in all countries. With so much misinformation about these crises floating around everywhere, trusting is a daunting challenge. Yet we must finally trust someone at some point. That's why we're often easily seduced into trusting the wrong group.

There had never been a time when mistrust based on misinformation had been a more pressing issue. Russia reported to its citizens that Ukraine was run by a Nazi government, thereby justifying its invasion.

This was not a war, President Vladimir Putin rationalized, while he continued to bomb Ukraine's infrastructure as the bitter winter approached, but rather a "special operation," and legislated a punishment of up to fifteen years in prison if any of its citizens used the term *war* in public to describe it. Journalists in Russia could no longer report the truth. Disinformation became the rule rather than the exception. But this issue was not limited to that international event. Rather, it was endemic to societies around the world, including both democracies and autocracies.

President Putin rattled the sabers of nuclear retaliation should the West continue to reject his alternate reality. The fear of atomic warfare raised its ugly head after decades of calm about that issue. The need to find an alternative to nuclear warfare has become incredibly important. That is one of the key challenges that we'll explore in depth later in the book.

We've learned that Russia's ability to create confusion in the US through this "new espionage" was one of the main benefits of Russia's efforts. Getting information was old stuff, but causing disruption in America's streets and destroying trust in government institutions was the new goal, and the Russians learned quickly how to achieve that in a surprisingly effective manner.

Once Upon a Spy

While opposing Hillary Clinton prior to the 2016 elections, Donald Trump invited the Russians to do his spy work for him. On a TV news conference on July 27, 2016, he publicly requested: "Russia, if you're listening, I hope you're able to find the 30,000 emails that are missing." Whether this was an impulse on his part or well thought out is not known, Trump is likely the most candid, bluntly outspoken president in American history, bar none.

The Russians were accommodating. They responded within five hours of Trump's invitation. They had been very active in the spy game, even more so than the ordinary spy versus spy game of old. The game is now all about the cyber universe and takes some surprising turns. They were not new to the game of cyber espionage—not at all—having used it to spy on the Chechnya Russian Republic separatists as far back as 2009, targeting users of the anonymizing network with malware intrusions in their downloads.

For this assignment, in response to Trump's public request, they used a system called Cozy Bear, which I'll now discuss.

A modular malware implant, it was a bit of a chameleon, running modules from a command-and-control server on demand. The arrows in its quiver included password theft, keylogging, as well as downloading and executing other processes. It contained such hacking tools known as Mimikatz, PSExec, as well as tools labeled by Americans at a Palo Alto research group as SeaDuke, Hammer-Duke, and OnionDuke. Though Cozy Bear hid its identity well for some years, its footprint was finally discovered when part of its system contained user instructions in Russian, saying, in essence, "Title data section must be at least 4 bytes!" Aha, the gig was up. In any case, Cozy Bear was under Russian control, most likely originating with Putin's overview.

In simple terms, here's how the Russians did it:

1. Explored their spy sources to see if they had anyone at the Democratic National Committee on hand to provide the username and password. If not, no problem. Go to the next step.
2. Did reconnaissance: Hacked the committee's computer systems to explore their software characteristics.
3. Customized malware to gain access to their computer emails, so they could see real-time activation on their own screens.
4. Moved through their networks to find what they were looking for.
5. Finally, hid their "footprints" by connecting through cities in the US and a French outfit as a barrier to hide their activity as the source.

The New World of Espionage

In the old world of espionage, there was the KGB, where Putin served and got all his training. Their job was to steal secrets, which spies normally did for a living.

In the new world of espionage, there is the GRU, translated into English as the Main Intelligence Administration, a military-based organization. Alongside that is the SVR, initiated in 1991, a derivative of the former KGB, more like our own CIA, and more traditional than its GRU counterpart, which is much more aggressive and less accountable for its "adventures."

It was the GRU that hacked into the DNC files to get the information that Trump requested and then delivered that information, under the banner of DC Leaks, to Julian Assange at WikiLeaks. According to a US intelligence report, this was done by Putin through a third party.[1]

It was also the GRU that "messed" with Eastern Ukraine in December 2015, turning off their electric grid for a short period, affecting 200,000 people during that cold month.

"While this ended up being a directly disruptive event, the tools deployed and the sequence in which they were used strongly indicate that the attacker was looking to do more than turn the lights off for a few hours," said Joe Slowik, a Dragos analyst who formerly led the Computer Security and Incident Response Team at the Department of Energy's Los Alamos National Laboratory. "They were trying to create conditions that would cause physical damage to the transmission station that was targeted."[2]

This attack was executed by the GRU, according to the British Foreign Office, reporting to *The Register*.[3] Russia even interfered with Ukraine's national elections, electing one of their favorites as leader of the country, until the national government caught on. That hacker group adopted the name Fancy Bear; this same group also hacked into the DNC.

The other group, called Cozy Bear, this one from the SVR, hacked into the files at the Pentagon. Both "Bears" were hacking groups thought to be linked, with 95 percent certainty, to Russian spy agencies that use spear phishing and custom malware software to get to the victims' files. Fancy Bear, affiliated with the GRU, and Cozy Bear, affiliated with the SVR, are known to the Americans as APT28 and APT29, respectively, where APT stands for Advanced Persistent Threat. The aim of both Bears was to steal intellectual property, disrupt organizations, and sow distrust among them. Twelve agents who worked with Fancy Bear were uncovered by the Mueller report and they were indicted. Both Bears were involved in hacking the DNC.[4]

A Hack in the Park

In 2016, as Fancy Bear was hacking into the DNC files, it was ultimately identified by the US as originating from Russia. But Fancy Bear's attempt at deluding the US agents was to refer to itself as a lone rogue by the name of Guccifer 2.0, claiming, "I'm a lone hacker in Rumania."

Why the 2.0? Well, it turns out that there was originally a Guccifer 1.0 whose real name is Marcel Lazar, a Romanian hacker who was arrested in early 2014 and then extradited to the US to stand trial again. The name Guccifer is thought to be a combination of the Gucci brand and the biblical version of the Devil, Lucifer. In May 2016, Lazar told Fox News, true or not, that he had successfully invaded a private email server set up by Hillary Clinton, even while sitting in jail.[5]

This was the origin of the thousands of leaked DNC emails sent to WikiLeaks. These emails revealed that Bernie Sanders had been "thrown under the bus" by Hillary and her associates, creating much conflict in the party. According to political analyst Donna Brazile, an agreement was made between the committee and Hillary's fundraising arm of the campaign in which the fundraisers would assume the DNC's $24 million debt in exchange for control over choice of the Democratic candidate. "Hillary for America (the campaign) and the Hillary Victory Fund (its joint fundraising vehicle with the DNC) had taken care of 80 percent of the remaining debt in 2016, about $10 million, and had placed the party on an allowance," according to Brazile.[6]

Sanders's followers began to claim corruption among Hillary's associates, creating a sense of outrage and disappointment, as they carried placards for Sanders and chanting, "Hillary cheats! Thank you, WikiLeaks!" Whatever the truth of the matter, this certainly embarrassed Hillary's campaign, creating more doubt in her battle against Trump. This is exactly what the Russian military intelligence wanted to accomplish, to undermine her campaign by revealing the inner conflict and lowering the level of trust in her.

To Vladimir Putin, most likely the initiator of all this, what mattered most in the end was the resulting discordant, chaotic public image.[7] He dreams of discrediting the American democratic system, and he never had a more reliable ally than Donald Trump, according to Franklin Foer, writing in *The Atlantic*. The data that Russia gets from America goes through a process of analytic disassembly to figure out what is relevant for the desired outcome, namely, political and social upset. It's called disaggregation.[8]

The Putin "Hands-Off" Leadership Style in Creating His Conspiracy of Trust

Here's how it worked. In 2014, a man by the name of Yevgeny Prigozhin was acting as Putin's chef, but he soon became a close, trusted adviser and gained enough power to initiate different projects, among them the Internet Research Agency, which trolled American targets, focusing on such touchy subjects as immigration and racism.

How Prigozhin was able to achieve such rarefied trust with Putin is an interesting tale of its own and tells us quite a bit about the power dynamics of Putin's "empire." Prigozhin was a ne'er-do-well in his youth. In his teenage years he was convicted of petty crimes and spent most of his twenties in jail. Then he started working in the fast-food industry and, failing at each level, somehow sprung to a higher level in the food industry, getting involved with luxury restaurants, and eventually became a contractor providing food for the Kremlin. It was here that Putin got to know Prigozhin and, since food is such an intimate part of one's life, Putin began to appreciate his trustworthiness.

Pretty soon, Putin trusted Prigozhin enough to allow him to "invest" in certain enterprises, most notably, a company called Concord, providing food for the military services. Once Prigozhin was involved with the military, the next step was the formation of the Wagner Group, a private militia, to do dirty work with which Putin did not want to have direct connection. This was the group sent to eastern Ukraine during the takeover by Russia. With no Russian insignia on their uniforms, Putin could claim innocence for the aggressive actions. This militia was provided with tanks, automatic grenade launchers, and whatever was necessary to overcome any local resistance. Once in place, the militia made sure civil unrest was minimized with the population's fear of unchecked military presence in their midst.

This tale helps us understand Putin's hands-off policy of international manipulation. Those in his power base know they will be handsomely rewarded, with both power and money, if they can achieve what they believe Putin wants. He doesn't have to plan and direct these ventures. He just allows those whom he trusts to "do their thing," and, if they are successful, their power status is rewarded. So when Putin claims innocence regarding hacking other countries or invasions such as that against the Ukraine, he can somewhat honestly do so. In response to questions about the hacking enterprises, Putin has been known to say that such hacking could be done by any nongovernmental hacker, particularly if they are "patriotic," but not his doing.

So that's how Prigozhin got to build his Internet Research Agency. Manned by young Russians looking for low-level IT jobs, its aim was to influence Americans to vote in certain directions by broadcasting interesting messages referencing pop culture, sometimes to the lyrics of Simon and Garfunkel. They were told their job would involve geopolitical marketing, with opportunities for "cartoon artistes." One of the young "artistes" disdainfully referred to his work as "James Bond espionage shit." To ensure their familiarity with their American targets, some coordinators took "educational" trips to various cities in the US to get a better sense of the culture.

No trust lost here.

Both Donald J. Trump and Vladimir V. Putin made enemies of Hillary Clinton. Putin was highly motivated to get his hackers to do what they could to denigrate her in videos aimed at the American voters. The program they used was known as Fancy Bear.

Putin's main intelligence directorate, the GRU, was able to infiltrate the Democratic National Committee's files to get the information that Trump had asked for. This did not help Hillary's campaign at all. Both men proved to be totally untrustworthy with their clandestine attempts at illicitly influencing that election.

Then came Prigozhin, Putin's "chef" who eventually rose to power and became head of the Wagner Group, a military detachment that was heavily involved in the Ukraine war. He became so powerful that he could even challenge Putin as the Ukraine war continued through 2023. At least for most of that time, there was a strong bond of trust between Putin and Prigozhin, though neither of the two could be trusted by any outside party. This is what we refer to as conspiratorial trust, what these two shared and what Putin and Trump shared as well.

In the next chapter, we'll begin by following up with the "techniques" developed by the "cartoon artistes" working under Putin's influence. They experimented with various approaches, a process known as *disaggregation,* to see what worked best in varying locations. Then we'll look at the growing conspiratorial trust between Putin and Trump as they ventured into collaborating on a Trump Tower to be built in Moscow. But then the plot thickened as new characters entered the scene, in addition to Prigozhin, to create a narrative that defied credibility.

18

Fighting in the Streets

"Steal a little and they throw you in jail,
steal a lot and they make you king."
—BOB DYLAN

In 2016, the trolls, led by Prigozhin, were eventually able to create an American persona, a thirty-year-old virtual person named Jenna Abrams who developed a Twitter following of 70,000 people. Besides Twitter and Facebook, there were YouTube, Pinterest, and Reddit as conduits. Interestingly, the trolls aimed at both sides of the political divide, customizing their pop culture messages accordingly.

At the time, if anyone was asked what they thought of the activities of the Internet Research Agency, you'd likely get a blank stare, yet this was changing our political destiny. The IRA was strategic enough to measure its successes state by state. They knew their demographics. For example, with 54 percent of Atlanta being Black, they targeted their "victims" accordingly. The IRA would do so by showering Blacks with enough disinformation to discourage their voting to begin with, thereby skewing the vote in Trump's favor.

They were able to intensify conflict by notifying one group that its antagonist counterpart was meeting at a certain location at a given time. That way, both "warring" groups were positioned to create as much conflict as possible, accomplishing this task all the way from Saint Petersburg (not the city in Florida by the same name). They even sent the same messages to both sides but changed the tone merely by replacing the word *terrorist* for *militia*, depending on the target. The aim was to create hurt and conflict, destroying as much trust as possible. It was becoming clear that they were gaining skills in holding a mirror to our face, **forcing us to see the death of trust** in our two alternate, antagonistic realities.

When confronted about this transmission of disinformation to foster conflict, Putin explained, "At the government level, we never engage in this," claiming that he didn't deny that all this manipulation was going on, but that he clearly would not take responsibility for it, that it was quite possible some "patriotic" Russian citizens might have been doing this on their own.

Disaggregation

When John Brennan, then director of the CIA, became aware of this abuse by disinformation, he had to decide how to respond. He sent a warning to the Russians, but they just denied such activity. He decided that if the CIA were to retaliate in kind, that would only escalate a cyberspace war with Russia and that was in no one's interest, certainly not for the US, and certainly not with the elections coming up. Obama's people were concerned that if they were seen trying to fix all this cyber manipulation, it might look like the government would be using its resources to affect the voting results.

One of Russia's aims was to better understand the current American culture so their cyber activities in broadcasting fake information could be more effective. There was no one method or technique of attack, but rather a set of small ones to see which ended up proving most efficacious. **This is what the disaggregation was all about**, experimenting with various tactics, going with what seemed to work best, and then analyzing what to focus on for the best results for demographic purposes.

One of the outcomes of Russia's cyber activities was learning how easily they could create upset and conflict with American targets. For example, as far back as 2013, the hacker going by the label Guccifer leaked information about Hillary Clinton who used her unclassified private email account to send classified and sensitive information. In July 2016, the Americans discovered that the voter registration systems in Arizona and Illinois had been hacked by the Russians.[1] The following September, they discovered that Fancy Bear had opened other files as well, such as those of the World Anti-Doping Agency and leaked them on the internet. **All this activity resulted in lowering levels of trust in leading political figures.**

No More Mr. Nice Guy

Prior to the 2016 elections, Putin and Hillary Clinton developed an intense dislike for one another. This may have started when Clinton debased Putin as untrustworthy and evil. Putin was extremely offended, especially when he was confronted with her remarks during a press conference in Russia, when the inquiring reporter used Clinton's words verbatim. Putin's demeanor bristled with anger. One could infer his determination to avenge her accusations. She also encouraged pushback against Putin by his local political contenders during his own elections, creating severe problems for him.

At that point, Russian elections were not yet being manipulated as they would later be. Clinton influenced the Russian electorate by sending messages about Putin's tyrannical aspirations. This really put Putin in a bad place, creating large protests pushing against him. Putin later said, "She set the tone for some of the actors inside the country."

I believe it was at this point that Putin became obsessed with destroying her power any chance he could. When it became clear that she would be campaigning against Trump, Putin knew exactly where he would marshal his forces. No more Mr. Nice Guy—Putin would pull no punches. He would use all his influence to attack her, primarily through cyber warfare. Though such cyber activity was not new among nations in conflict, this was a personal matter for him.[2] It may very well be the one factor that undid her chances of becoming president. That's how the dynamic between Putin and Trump began. Putin was clearly determined to do all he could to elevate Trump's chances of succeeding, in part by reducing trust in Hillary Clinton.

Trump Tower Moscow

Enter Felix Sater, a Russian-born businessman raised in the US, highly connected to the Russian mafia in Brighton Beach, New York, where he lived his formative years. He had a rough upbringing, spent some time in jail, and, when work was hard to find, fell into the real estate business. Guess whom he meets and befriends—none other than real estate mogul Donald Trump. Prior to Trump's winning the Republican nomination, it was rumored that the two were planning on building the tallest building in the world—in Moscow.

The plan was to lease the top floor to Putin, not only bringing in loads of money from rent, but also giving the building whatever panache it needed to make it so highly attractive to high-ranking Russian elite tenants. Sater claimed he would have made a $100 million by receiving a portion of the proceeds on the deal and Trump wouldn't do badly either.[3] Sater's office space would have been on the twenty-sixth floor of Trump Tower in Moscow, just seconds away from Trump's offices, giving him precious access to the president, and allowing him to pitch business deals to him. Such access was priceless to Sater.[4]

According to Robert Mueller's team, "If the project was completed, the Company (the Trump Organization) could have received hundreds of millions of dollars from Russian sources in licensing fees and other revenues."[5]

Then the nomination was won by Trump and the project had to be put on hold. But the connection between Trump and the Kremlin was assured.

The Plot Thickens

Now enter Paul Manafort, man about the Communist world, mentor to new leaders who have not yet learned the lifestyle of the rich and infamous. He taught Viktor Yanukovych, then President of Ukraine from 2010 to 2014. Manafort's job was to teach Yanukovych how to dress the part and act according to his newfound power and ensure that he had at least one connection to the US. He had done similar work with other dictators from such countries as Kenya and Nigeria.

When Putin wanted to make a political grab for the eastern part of Ukraine, he wanted to make sure that there would be little backlash from the US government. That's where Manafort came in.

And now enter another character—Oleg Deripaska, a fifty-three-year-old Russian oligarch with a net worth of over $2.5 billion, well known to Manafort, well enough to be in debt to Deripaska for over a million dollars. To make a long financial and political intrigue short, if Manafort could provide a safety net for Putin's continuing attacks against Crimea in Ukraine, then maybe, just maybe, Oleg might forgive that loan owed by Manafort by putting his judgment on hold. Deripaska had already sued Manafort for the debt and had won in court, so it was clearly a debt that had value. Manafort was happy to cooperate. And Putin sent his henchmen into eastern Ukraine to fortify Russian dominance there and basically strengthen Russian control.

In response, the US just yawned despite issuing the Crimea Declaration, giving lip service to Ukraine's rights to the Crimea. Yanukovych hightailed it to Russia before he could get into trouble with the Ukrainians for allowing this to happen. So Manafort was able to absolve his debt, and Putin was able to get Trump's support in his Crimean venture. Another instance of Trump being of service to Putin and Putin being in control, as usual.

Another figure of interest, Konstantin Kilimnik, a fixer, translator, and general "gopher" for Paul Manafort, was a link between Manafort and the Kremlin in the Ukraine takeover. Kilimnik is also believed to have passed American polling information to the Russians and was part of fixing Manafort's debt to Deripaska, sometimes referred to as the secret Kiev payments, earmarked for Manafort to the amount of $12.7 million for "various expenses," recorded in what is known as the Black Ledger. At one point, Kilimnik met with Manafort at the Grand Havana Room, a members-only cigar club, a short walk from Trump Tower, on a twenty-four-hour trip from Russia on July 30, 2016. What transpired there remains in the private realm, but the intrigue remains.

What we do know is that justice finally caught up with Manafort. He was eventually sentenced to seven years in prison for tax fraud, witness tampering, and conspiracy to defraud the US. Trump later pardoned Manafort.

As the years went by, Yevgeny V. Prigozhin, mentioned earlier, who started off as the Kremlin's chef, was gaining more and more power. The 2014 invasion of Ukraine by "little green men" without any identifying insignia on their uniforms was Prigozhin's doing, under the enterprise known as Wagner, now involved in mining activities along with its political influence and use of mercenaries in Africa, even aiding in the takeover of Sudan, so Russia could have easier access to their mined gold supplies[6] and establish a naval base there. With the support of Sudan's ambassador to Russia, Mohamed Siraj, Putin was able to lay claim to the first naval base outside of Russia. Prigozhin had become head of the Kremlin's propaganda machine and its hacking activities.

By 2022, he was more powerful than he ever dared dream, powerful enough to admit in public his direct involvement in interfering with the US elections and other security sites. "We have interfered, are interfering and will continue to interfere," his spokespeople declared, "carefully, precisely, surgically, and in our own way."[7]

Sure enough, in the early summer of 2023, the Americans discovered that the US and other NATO countries had a long-term Russian cyber espionage campaign running against them for quite a while. "The FSB [Russian Federal Security Service] has relied on the Snake malware to conduct cyberespionage against the United States and our allies," reported Assistant Attorney General Matthew Olsen, "and that stops today" [May 9, 2023].[8]

Prigozhin also admitted, for the first time, to founding and financing the Wagner military force, the key group invading Ukraine in 2014.[9] But in January 2023, he suffered his first public embarrassment when one of his commanders, Andrei Medvedev, decided to flee his battalion fighting in Ukraine and seek asylum in Norway, citing mistreatment of frontline Wagner soldiers.[10] This was a great propaganda failure to counteract all the prestige Prigozhin had built over the years.

In the ensuing months, Prigozhin upped the ante. Not only did he follow through to become a more public figure, but he was now seeming to take charge of the war in Ukraine with a demeanor possibly looking to take over the leadership should Putin falter. Using prison convicts as cannon fodder in his Wagner Group in the front lines of the battle in eastern Ukraine and challenging Ukrainian President Zelenskyy to a fighter-jet feud while in the cockpit of a bomber, he was emerging as the face of the Russian Army. He was learning how to play the media.

The Kremlin became concerned. According to Sergei Markov, a former Kremlin adviser and pro-Putin political analyst, "They apparently don't want to bring him [Prigozhin] into the political sphere because he's so unpredictable—they fear him a little bit."[11] Yet President Putin continued to support him despite other Russian leaders' concerns about his increasing bravado.[12]

High Intelligence Official Loses Trust in Putin

Then, on April 4, 2023, a high officer in Putin's elite security service, one Gleb Karakulov, removed himself from an official meeting in Astana, the capital of Kazakhstan, claiming to go look for souvenirs on the last day of the meetings. He clandestinely met with his wife and children and grabbed a taxi to the airport. His heart beating wildly with anxiety, he got through the check-in as demanding texts from his associates started crowding his cell phone, asking where he was.

The five-and-a-half-hour flight was delayed by an hour, adding stress to this dangerous plan. When the family finally landed in Turkey, the fear was that he would be captured by the authorities before he could pass passport control. With his wife near the breaking point of anxiety, they finally got through. And the weight on their collective shoulders finally disappeared. This was a dangerous caper, but Karakulov could no longer justify the hypocrisy of the obvious lies of his Russian superiors. This was a major blow to Putin and his obeisant crew of knowing hypocrites.

"They will be very angry," he told the Western press. "There will be hysterics."[13]

And angry they were. Karakulov, a highly ranked intelligence officer and captain in Putin's Federal Protection Service, was debriefed by Russian opposition figure, Mikhail Khodorkovsky, for over ten hours, disclosing all he knew about Putin, whom he described as "very closed . . . He lives in a kind of information vacuum . . . His perception of reality has been distorted."[14]

In this chapter, we explored how Russian trolls were able to hack American demographics to figure out where the respective antagonistic groups were, state by state, to transmit disinformation to initiate conflict between them, disrupting even further any mistrust between the groups. They used a process known as disaggregation to determine which of their attacks worked most effectively and where, an ad hoc system that allowed them to use what worked best at the time.

We then looked at various characters who helped Putin destroy trust even further, characters like Felix Sater, Paul Manafort, Oleg Deripaska, Konstantin Kilimnik, who aided Putin in mind-bending efforts to undermine American welfare and, finally, the infamous Yevgeny V. Prigozhin, who rose from Putin's chef to leader of the Wagner Group, the cruel warriors who invaded Ukraine in 2014 and who continued to fight fierce battles in 2023 until the mutiny of June 24, which he called the March of Justice.[15]

In the next section, we'll take a close look at how the Russians interfered with American elections, as well as the vulnerability of our cyberspace security.

PART VIII

Conspiratorial Trust:
Behind Closed Doors

Conspiratorial trust: The dynamic between at least two parties who share a belief in a plan to outmaneuver or deceive a large group, or even a nation, to force a designated outcome to the advantage of the conspirators. The foremost example of this is the mutually beneficial working relationship of politics between Presidents Trump and Putin.

19

Collusion? What Collusion? Oh, THAT Collusion!

"Conspiracy works."
—ANNA MERLAN, author of *Republic of Lies*

"Controversy sells."
—KATIE COURIC

The question of collusion between Donald Trump's campaign and the Russian influence has never been proven, for there never was collusion. Trump never had to ask for Putin's help, except for his "request" on the national news conference on TV on July 27, 2016, to find Hillary Clinton's emails.

Putin would help Trump because they both were bitter opponents against Hillary Clinton, Putin's hated enemy, as I explained in the last chapter.

One Example of Conspiratorial Trust

America's low level of trust for government on both sides of the political divide made it a vulnerable target for Putin's cyber tactics. Russia's fake broadcasts reflected America's weaknesses based on this very low level of trust between its political counterparts. America's social media ecosystem made the country vulnerable. The GRU and its virtual persona, Guccifer 2.0, had an easy target. With Assange's cooperation, it was all made easier.

Reality Winner Reveals TOP SECRET

In the summer of 2016, the GRU, Russia's version of America's CIA, had its hackers wreak havoc on American elections at the state and local levels. They had access to the voting machines, with the ability to undermine their integrity by just changing a few numbers, just enough to cast doubt on the integrity of the process. They first got into the databases in such unlikely places as Gila County, Arizona, and in such states as Florida and Illinois. The voting machines were incredibly easy to gain access to, even though they were not ostensibly connected to the internet.

In Georgia, thirty-year-old Reality Leigh Winner (her real name), a former intelligence contractor working as a translator for NSA's Pluribus International Corporation, decided to make some of this information public because, in her own personal opinion, the American public was being lied to. This somewhat pretty, naive-looking blond was arrested for providing information to the Russians. She explained that she did it because she acted out of love for her country. On CBS *60 Minutes*, she stated, "I am somebody who only acted out of love for what this country stands for."

When not at work, Winner was a yoga and fitness instructor and cared for her pets in addition to trying to fulfill her father's wish for her to be a "real Winner." Before leaving work one day at the NSA, she took a document labeled TOP SECRET about Russia's hacking over 100 election systems and tucked them under her dress into her pantyhose before leaving her office at Fort Gordon in Georgia. She was arrested roughly an hour after she released the document and charged under the Espionage Act, enacted during World War I as a punishment for spying at a time of foreign conflict.

Following this, the Russians were able to launch a separate phishing attack targeting 122 local election officials. The hackers got to mess with all the states but did their most damaging work in Illinois. The electoral infrastructure was totally violated by the GRU, according to the National Security Agency.[1]

Despite all the havoc aimed at our electoral process, Senator Mitch McConnell wasn't too eager to pursue investigation into Russian responsibility.[2] When the federal agents tried to warn the states about Russian intrusion, they decided not to mention Russia as the agent for policy reasons. So the states were reluctant to take any action.[3] As a matter of fact, eighteen of the states flatly rejected the offer of help, focusing on states' rights, no doubt. In Georgia, Governor Brian Kemp expressed annoyance, insisting that he could take care of his own terrain[4] for reasons that might have been somewhat suspicious.[5]

A Very Busy Day

President Obama had learned of this capability on Russia's part and, in August 2016, warned Putin about his behavior, threatening deteriorating international relations and pressure on the Russian economy, but Putin was already looking ahead to the next president and making sure it wouldn't be Hillary Clinton.

An investigation into Russia's mischief was in order, but not if Mitch McConnell had anything to do with it. And he did. Did he have foreknowledge of Putin's favoring Trump and the whole Republican enterprise? Probably. As well, Obama was focusing on what appeared to be higher priorities at this point, like Russia's involvement with Syria and the Russian aggression toward Ukraine.

Jeh Johnson, then head of Homeland Security, was sufficiently concerned to make a call to Trump the following October to talk about the issues affecting the election infrastructure. It was the seventh of the month, a very busy day. Hurricane Matthew hit the Florida coast. The Hollywood tapes of Trump's boasting to Billy Bush about his ability to grab women by the p***y and get away with it were just coming out on TV. "When you're a star, they let you do it," he boasted.

At the same time, about twenty-nine minutes after the release of the tapes, WikiLeaks was dumping Podesta's emails with Hillary, revealing such embarrassing details as the source of their contributions from evangelicals, the conflict between Hillary and Bernie Sanders, the

FBI's investigation into Hillary's email accounts, and the politics with "needy Latino" government officials. While torrents of water fell on Florida, torrents of emails fell on Washington.

In testimony before the House Intelligence Committee, Johnson himself recounted, "One of the candidates, as you recall, was predicting that the election was going to be 'rigged' in some way," referring to Trump's unsubstantiated accusation before election day of 2016. "We were concerned that by making the statement we might, in and of itself, be challenging the integrity of the election process itself." Noting that the hacking happened "at the direction of Vladimir Putin himself," Johnson said he was moved to try to shield the nation's election system by the "unprecedented" nature of Russian interference in the 2016 election.[6]

The End or the Beginning?

As if all this weren't enough fodder for the voracious appetite of the media monsters, on October 29, 2016, James Comey reopened the case against Hillary's email leaks via the cell phone of Anthony Weiner's wife, Huma Abedin, a close aide to Hillary, eleven days before the election. One poll indicated that 34 percent of the voters were less likely to vote for her because of this. This was rich fodder for the Russian cyber cannons, leading to accusations of rigged elections and voter fraud.

When Trump won the election in 2016, there were public TV reports of the Russians celebrating with champagne and congratulatory hugs. Even Trump looked somewhat shocked at the first signs of winning. His choice of musical background for his celebratory event was "You Can't Always Get What You Want," probably not expecting to win. Trump was likely thinking that his run would just enhance his brand, even when losing.

On March 22, 2019, the Mueller report was finally complete after two years of intensive investigation. Its conclusion was that, although the Russians may have tried to interfere, there was no collusion to report. Once the redacted version was released by Attorney General

Bill Barr, on April 18, there was not sufficient evidence to warrant treason on Trump's part to impeach him. Trump was quite happy to hold the headline up and wave it to the crowd and TV cameras: Trump Acquitted!

And then, to add insult to injury, James Comey was unceremoniously fired on May 17. Comey first found out about it when it appeared on TV while he was dutifully working on the job.

America's Vulnerable Electric Grids

Was this the last part of Putin interfering in our elections? Well, the problem in 2020 wasn't Putin; it was Trump himself, with the same claims he made in 2016, about rigged elections. But Russia was back just after the 2020 elections, hacking happily into our agencies' sites, as if the 2020 elections weren't worth their energies.[7]

In Trump's last year as president in his first administration, the Russians, believed to be acting through their usual hackers, created the greatest cybersecurity problem the US had to deal with by far. Through a crafty connection with Solar Winds—which offers services to so many companies, it's almost a monopoly—the Russians were able to install malware that went to over 18,000 clients, including the Pentagon, the State Department, and Homeland Security, as well as other government agencies and huge corporations. That enabled the Russians to access great vats of secret information.

What was new about this was not the ongoing problem of hacking from antagonistic nations such as Russia, China, North Korea, and Iran, but rather the size of it and that the spying remained undetected for months. By then, America was vulnerable to foreign attack on its electrical grids, nuclear plants, and dams. In other words, in time of war, our critical systems might be attacked digitally, leaving us extremely vulnerable at a crucial time.

Since the US is such a powerful warrior on the international playing field, why are we so susceptible to these infuriating attacks, which may end up eroding our reputation of strength? There are two main reasons.

One is that we are more susceptible because we are more wired than any other country, thereby providing more access to soft targets. The second is that hackers do not leave calling cards. That factor has to do with the ease of hacking versus the herculean effort of identifying the culprit. Even though we may strongly suspect a country, retaliation, of any kind, would be dangerous if we were mistaken in our attempt to identify the perpetrator.

A very big part of this overwhelming problem is the system of malware development that has grown over the years. The most sophisticated hackers don't work for salaries. They're much better off working as independent contractors, selling their highly prized services to the highest bidder, which is not always the US. For whatever reason, many of these so-called experts work in Russia or neighboring countries friendly with Russia. And even when they are part of the Russian spy system, they are not easily recognized as such.

According to Nicole Perlroth, author of *This is How They Tell Me the World Ends: The Cyberweapons Arms Race*, part of the fault, if not the main cause, was America's decision to use cyber warfare to damage a fifth of Iran's Natanz nuclear enrichment plant in 2009 to dissuade Israel from bombing it. This broke the gentleman's agreement not to cause physical damage to any country through digital means. The moral gate was now opened for similar retaliation.[8]

If Russia were the culprit behind the massive invasion of US cybersecurity, as most experts guess, then one can only imagine that Putin had the temerity to commit this overwhelming assault at the time because he knew that Trump would never allow Putin to be punished for this. His risk of castigation was lower because of that "special relationship" of trust.

If there were any doubt cast on the truth of the Trump/Putin connection of trust, then Bob Woodward's book *War*, published in 2024, put that to rest. Woodward reported that Trump sent Putin some fairly sophisticated Abbott COVID-testing systems for his personal use when the pandemic was at its beginning phase.

In this chapter, I began telling the story of Reality Winner who stole classified documents and sent them to Russia because she disagreed with US government policy. Putin, at the same time, was enjoying his phishing expedition, hacking various states' online systems. This was a period of growing hacking by Russia and other countries before the US government put up strong defenses against it. It was clearly a battle for trust in international relations.

In the next chapter, we'll continue to focus on Putin's strong need to enhance his Russian empire with his aggressive style of cyberattacks against the US and Ukraine. The level of trust was the loser in all this political commotion.

20

Putin's Adventures in Cyberspace

*"There's nothing inevitable about American democracy.
There is a fragile, fallible complicated experience."*
—Jon Meacham

The Beep Goes On

By mid-2021, we were beginning to see a massive increase in ransomware attacks, including government agencies and private industry, with ransoms as high as $70 million. Criminal groups like Ransomware Evil (REvil) sell their wares to smaller entities who share the profits with one another. CNA Financial paid $40 million to get their information back from the cyber criminals. The rise in cryptocurrency has not helped any.

An even worse turn of cyber events is the development of what is referred to as wiping, where cyberwarfare is the purpose rather than financial exploitation. This began with the 2012 wiper attacks by Iran against Saudi Aramco and against Las Vegas Sands Corp in 2014.

Better known is North Korea's wiper attack against Sony Pictures in retaliation for the movie they made that was critical of the leader's regime. Though there's no financial gain for wiper attacks, political fanatics and lone wolves with their own weird motivations can also create massive destruction to the countries they hate. Cyberwar between Israel and Iran in 2020 involved wiper attacks.

If you're still not worried about all this, consider the vulnerability of artificial intelligence (AI) where electronic security devices can be manipulated. Even worse, AI can enhance the power of cyberattacks with smarter and autonomous malware to create more sophisticated phishing attacks and viral tweets that can infect other users.

More recently, firmware, the code that runs between the software and hardware of computers and cell phones, can replace the operating system and take full control.

Once the firmware is under control, hackers can then manipulate such systems as electronic grids, water improvement plants, and other critical networks. This is exactly what the Russians did to Kiev when they blacked out an electric transmission station in the northern part of the city.[1]

And then there are botnets, big networks of enslaved devices that can be used to disrupt connections on the internet by overcrowding them with bogus requests for digital information. Since 5G is ten times faster than 4G, the botnets can be exponentially more destructive in such an electronic environment. And so, the beat goes on, or shall we say, the beep goes on? In late fall of 2021 Russia's intelligence agency, the SVR, was still surveilling American corporate and government networks to sneak into the cloud for all the data they could find.[2]

On a positive note, the United Nations adopted the Convention Against Cybercrime on Christmas Eve, 2024. This document delineates all the aspects of information and communications technology (ICT) and the criminal consequences of abusing such at the international level. It calls for "the prevention, detection, suppression, investigation and prosecution of the offences" of cyberattacks in general.[3] Let's hope all countries sign this very necessary document.

Guess What Putin Desires—Or Else!

Ever since the invasion of Ukraine by Russia, we're learning a lot more about Putin, none of it very good. Putin manages not by direct order but rather by allowing his underlings to imagine what their boss wants and to please him by following up on his demands without Putin having to spell them out, like top captains in the Mafia. This continued during the early parts of the invasion of Ukraine. According to Mikhail Zygar, author of *All the Kremlin's Men*,[4]

[T]he phenomenon of the "collective Putin"—the way his entourage always tried to eagerly anticipate what the president would want. These cronies would tell Mr. Putin exactly what he wanted to hear. The "collective Putin" still exists: The whole world saw it on the eve of the invasion when he summoned top officials, one by one, and asked them their views on the coming war. All of them understood their task and submissively tried to describe the president's thoughts in their own words.[5]

And when his direct reports couldn't articulate Putin's wishes in their own words, he just humiliated them.[6]

The big question involves how to curb Putin's destructive power. Here is one single man who has disrupted the global economy in addition to invading and destroying an innocent nation and committing what many call genocide. So how long will he stay in power? What powers around him might step in to gain a sense of reason in this otherwise sociopathic leadership?

According to a former oligarch, Mikhail Khodorkovsky, who was jailed for ten years for criticizing Putin, Putin's circle of power does not really have much influence over Putin, who is no longer motivated by the accumulation of wealth but rather the dream of leaving a legacy of restoring the power of the former Soviet Union. Putin had built a network of sycophants about him who feared him more than they could share their authentic support.[7] It appears that Putin had built a cocoon about him that prevented accurate news on the Ukraine invasion from reaching him, with his closest advisers even lying to him,[8] and leaving him angry and upset.[9]

Many ask what was going on in Putin's mind. What made him so destructive and uncaring about so many affected by his decisions? Looking at his choices and devastating outcomes, it becomes more and more evident that he has a strong drive to acquire a sense of conquest that could hardly be fulfilled. A need for obvious signs of success in terms of prestige, political power, and riches were obvious. It seemed as if he became noticeably uncomfortable whenever he failed to conquer in Ukraine during the invasion. Yet each victory, as he invaded one territory after another, just fed his need for more conquest.

A book describing the concept called hedonic relativism describes well Putin's need to continually strive for conquest, condemning him "to seek new levels of stimulation" as he vanquished one territory after another, "merely to maintain old levels of subjective pleasure, to never achieve any kind of subjective pleasure, to never achieve any kind of permanent happiness or satisfaction,"[10] as he continued his fantasy of a restored Russian empire. As time went by, this became more and more elusive, as NATO circled him even more closely with Finland able to join the European organization.

Many wondered why Putin wasn't using his country's cybersecurity malware to help fight the war.[11] Perhaps it was his anxiety about the unexpected challenges with which he was confronted that took his attention away from his cybersecurity options.[12] Others thought he might be ill and taking steroids, one of the side effects involving "deeply irrational or paranoid behavior."[13]

But by June 2022, the cybersecurity gloves came off when, according to Microsoft president Brad Smith, "The cyber aspects of the current war extend far beyond Ukraine and reflect the unique nature of cyberspace."[14] Researchers found that 128 organizations in forty-two countries were hacked with stealthy, espionage-focused attacks, though many of the attacks were not successful, at least initially.[15] In 2024, it was discovered that Russian-backed groups were able to hack Microsoft's corporate emails, using what was termed a "password spray attack," including cybersecurity and legal information. This lasted from November 2023 till mid-January 2024.[16]

The cyberwar just continued to escalate, especially against Ukraine and its allies. A particularly sophisticated Russian hacking team known as Sandworm was gearing up to attack Ukrainian supply lines.[17]

Now that we've had a chance, in this section, to explore the complex nature of trust in the world of cyber information, let's move on to the core of the issue. To begin with, how does the current political setting facilitate the decline of trust across the nation, if not the globe in terms of values about free speech? What is it about the sharp, partisan division, often leading to conflict, even insurrection, that has led to our discouragement about the falling level of trust? Does the current political situation have something to do with it? Of course. How close did Trump as president bring us to the brink of nuclear warfare in his first term?[18] And what about the growing division both politically and socially between government control and the freedom of institutions such as education and law?[19]

Let's explore all of this in the next section as we begin to focus on issues of social media free speech and how to deal with the loss of trust.

Why Trust Matters

PART IX

Social Media Trust: The Battle for Free Speech and Artificial Intelligence

Social Media Trust: The extent to which we allow ourselves to trust what we see on our screens from such sites as X (formerly Twitter) and chatbots and to change our beliefs, values, and even our voting choices based on disinformation, especially deepfakes. This is different from cyber trust because of its mostly domestic origins rather than international.

21

Free Speech and the Battle for Trust

When Elon Musk bought Twitter at the above-market price of $44 billion (with a *b*) on October 28, 2022, he likely never imagined what effect he would have on the nature of trust. He was certainly rich enough after his successful exploits with PayPal, OpenAI, SpaceX, Tesla, SolarCity and more with a net worth purported to be over $300 billion.[1] He was determined to bring free speech to the platform by freeing up the guardrails. Within weeks, he began firing employees, including those "who helped fight misinformation" on the site.[2]

Musk was an ardent advocate of free speech. The following November, he ran a poll of the followers of the site, now called X, to see if they would vote for a return of the infamous conspiracy theorist, Alex Jones, who had spent so much time spinning the false story about the Sandy Hook Elementary School shooting tragedy being a hoax. The vote fell in favor of returning Alex Jones to the site and so Musk followed suit. Seventy percent of X's respondents wanted this, and Musk was not about to deny them.

With the guardrails lowered, many of Musk's advertisers chose to leave the site, and Musk tried recruiting smaller businesses to replace this loss of major clients. At the DealBook Summit in New York, when confronted by journalist Andrew Ross Sorkin about the loss of advertisers because of the allowance of anti-Semitic remarks on X, Musk responded that he didn't want those advertisers.

Amazed, Sorkin asked for clarification. "You don't want those advertisers?" he asked in shock.

"Don't advertise," retorted Musk. "If someone is trying to black-mail me with money . . . then go f**k yourself!" Incredulous, Sorkin asked for further clarification, and Musk just repeated his epithet to the amazement of all.

In her description of this event, the columnist Jennifer Zalai later wrote: "By reveling in the chaos, Musk has turned X into an experiment in whether 'the best source of truth' means anything without a foundation of trust to support it . . . about how we know what we know, and why we believe what we do." She went on to comment on the nature of information versus misinformation/disinformation. How much freedom of speech and how much of that should contain false information? If we allow total freedom of speech, then we face the death of trust. She sums up: "This sorting process requires trust—the very thing that Musk spurns."[3]

It's quite clear where Musk stands in the battle between free speech and accountability for trust. "I believe we've got to watch out for the erosion of freedom in America," he stated, making his mark quite clearly.[4] And if the control of "truth" doesn't exist, if all its versions are fodder for the cannon of social media, then do conspiracy theories start to enter our culture of reality? For as long as propaganda has existed, it's well known that repetition makes for belief, no matter how ludicrous the information might be when brought to the light of clear objectivity.

There is more concern and accountability to avoid disinformation in the European Union than there appears to be in the US. In mid-2022, with their Digital Services Act, the EU beefed up its four-year-old code to make high-tech companies increasingly accountable for allowing disinformation. "With the DSA, the time of big online platforms behaving like they are 'too big to care' is coming to an end," reported EU Internal Market Commissioner Thierry Breton.[5]

But back in the US, Musk was railing against the Center for Countering Digital Hate for tracking X and threatening to sue those who opposed his arguably irresponsible approach to free speech.

While attending a conference on global sustainability in Norway, Musk was asked directly, after taking the stage, what he thought of trust. His reply: "I believe in trust and transparency, and the pursuit of truth in general."[6] A politically correct answer, no doubt.

About a year prior to this meeting in Norway, Musk had this to say about trust: "For Twitter to deserve public trust, it must be politically neutral . . . Algorithms must be open source, with any human intervention clearly identified. Then, trust will be deserved."[6]

Trust in the Post-Truth Era

Since 2016, there has been a wide recognition that appeals to emotion can far outweigh rational considerations. Popular reliance on social media and chatbots influenced by artificial intelligence have amplified this effect. The distinction between fact and feelings has become increasingly fluid. This is due to at least three factors: polarization, unregulated social media, and unethical politicians.

If some politicians want to convey their ideas effectively, they are increasingly likely to try and sway their listeners with emotionally laden terms rather than hard facts. Even when confronted by neutral journalists, they use metaphors freely to make their points, without rational backup. Though arguably immoral, this approach tends to win devotion to the cause much more effectively than reasonable arguments. All this leads to a breakdown in social trust.

In his book, *The Believing Brain*, Michael Shermer points out how more susceptible we are to emotional arguments and, once we make such a choice, how unlikely we are to change our minds, regardless of how convincing a rational argument might be.[7]

With the support of certain industries vying for support from government, there is the strong temptation to use public relations as a tool to foment emotionally convincing arguments to rally against true scientific research. In his book, *Post-Truth*, Lee McIntyre writes about this process. He points out how uncomfortable it is for individuals to admit that they've been wrong in their beliefs and political choices. They'd rather use their "ego defenses" to rally behind their original choices than to admit they were wrong to begin with.

The concept of cognitive dissonance refers to the difficulty in having opposing beliefs about your own behavior at the same time. Why did you end up doing something you really don't like? Answer: You just make up a reason to justify your behaviors. Everyone suffers from this from time to time, according to McIntyre. So, we tend to hold onto old beliefs—right or wrong—rather than suffer from cognitive dissonance.

Applied to group affiliation, this phenomenon helps explain why people who belong to groups that are outside the norm in terms of values—such as cults—are reinforced by their fellow members to deny any conflict with normal reality, otherwise known as social conformity.

In 1951 at Swarthmore College, Solomon Asch completed his psychological experiments in which individuals were made to agree with clearly false premises when they were the only ones in the group to see the true reality. When all others in the group—paid actors or "confederates"—professed to see something that wasn't real, the "stooge," or experimental subject, at first expressed surprise and dismay but soon began agreeing with the confederates even though what they were reporting was clearly false (about the length of lines that could easily be seen by the naked eye).

All this, according to McIntyre, largely accounts for what we refer to as confirmation bias, where we tend to believe information that already agrees with our group about what we believe to be true. The influence of others in our midst has an exceptional influence on our choices and ultimately our values.[8] Trust is the ultimate victim here.

One might argue that, with all the options available on social media, we can choose reality-based information more easily, but, as we keep hearing, we instead choose to ignore what we don't already know or agree with, and continue to log onto, the sites that confirm our values and beliefs—manifestations of social conformity and confirmation bias. And if a person of importance, such as a president of the country, has similar beliefs, that just reinforces the whole enterprise significantly.

In his follow-up book, *The Scientific Attitude,* McIntyre defends the scientific approach and the demarcation process necessary to distinguish between science and nonscience falsehoods. We have a tendency to believe what we already "know" to be true, and when emotionally laden issues are put forward in the sheep's clothing of pseudoscience, it's difficult for many to distinguish between the two.[9]

In a *New York Times* column, titled "The American Abyss," Timothy Snyder writes about post-truth that social media "supercharges the mental habits by which we seek emotional stimulation and comfort, which means losing the distinction between what feels true and what is actually true."[10] He discusses Hanna Arendt's depiction of Stalin's lies about the starvation of millions of Ukrainian citizens and Hitler's accounts "proving" anti-Semitism.

The Backfire Effect

The backfire effect is quite simple: When confronted with information that is contrary to people's beliefs, they not only deny it but are actually pushed further in the direction of their original belief system, even though it's contrary to the new information. It is a subvariant of confirmation bias. So those who supported Trump and were faced with his criminal allegations were only pushed further to support him even more strongly. This simple axiom helps explain to the Left why Trump's supporters were so staunch despite, or actually because of, the otherwise negative information. Without this axiom of human behavior, it was quite challenging to understand why his supporters were so devoted.

Social scientist David Redlawsk proved in his lab that "somewhat perversely, motivated reasoners may actually increase their support of a positively evaluated candidate upon learning new negatively evaluated information ... Additional analysis shows that these affective biases may easily lead to lower quality decision making" leading to the question of whether such individuals can vote on a rational basis.[11] In another study, his colleagues found "several instances of a 'backfire effect' in which corrections actually *increase* misperceptions among the group in question."[12]

We're now brought to the point of focusing on the exact dynamics of this phenomenon embracing social conformity and confirmation bias, and how all this relates to our crisis of trust.

One could easily argue that the crisis is not with trust but rather with truth, as in a crisis of truth. Because of the accelerating rate of polarization over the past few years, there clearly appears to be at least two versions of the truth, one on the left and one on the right, to put it in simple terms. This is manifested in two different realities that continue to battle one another via social media.

But each truth has its own history of reality, the result of information that both factions hear and see over time. As mentioned earlier, repetition is a key factor. Joseph Goebbels, the Nazi propagandist, was known to have proclaimed that repetition makes lies believable with sufficient repetitions. Now the technology of social media with its cleverly crafted algorithms make such repetitions even more powerful than radio in Goebbels's time, more powerful in the sense that this technology can reach vastly greater numbers as quickly as electronic communication allows.

But the facts or truths are not in crisis. It is the process by which these truths are made believable. And that process is none other than trust in the origins of conflicting truths. That's precisely why we have our crisis in trust rather than in the words we are made to believe and act on.

In the final analysis, Elon Musk appeared to be politically impartial in former times. He voted for Obama, Clinton, and Biden over the last four elections, but then stated that he might start voting Republican in 2024, supporting, among other Republican values, freedom of speech. He has been accused of wanting to allow conspiracy theories to enjoy freedom of speech and by referring to himself as "a free speech absolutist,"[13] claiming that "free speech is a societal imperative for a function-ing democracy."[14]

As the 2024 elections approached, Musk decided to go all in with Trump, referring to himself as "Dark MAGA," and offering Trump's PAC over $200 million. He also promoted the campaign to his 200 million followers on X. In addition, Musk offered a lottery amount-ing to $1 million a day to one of the individuals who signed a petition pledging support for the First and Second Amendments.

Because of his generous support for Trump's campaign, then president-elect Trump embraced Musk as a confidential partner, allowing him to be present while making the most important phone calls, even handing the phone over to him during a conversation with Ukrainian President Zelenski. Musk's public image exploded with this new political power. His net worth increased by $15 billion in the week following the election. Can we trust Musk's influence on the new administration?

Why the radical shift from progressive to radical right for Musk? Some say that it was in part due to the grave disappointment when his son decided to transition to a woman in 2022, creating a rift between them. Musk decided to join a group of anti-woke ex-Democrats, which included Robert F. Kennedy Jr., to express his displeasure with the far Left. Perhaps he found Trump a welcome break from his frustrations with his personal issues.

So, our crisis of trust is essentially found at exactly this juncture between free speech and the guardrails that keep our media from yelling "Fire!" in a crowded theater. Musk's earnest concerns for free speech brush up against the power of such speech to hurt, even kill, innocent victims of conspiracy theories like those that the Nazis used so efficiently to justify the Holocaust.

I realize we're discussing extremes here, but that is to save the time bickering back and forth about whether hate speech is acceptable at such esteemed institutions of education as Harvard University as long as the purveyors of the hate speech don't act on their diatribes.

With Musk placing himself beside President Trump at the helm of control, and taking charge of the Department of Government Efficiency, it's difficult to predict the future. All we can do is hope and pray for the least harmful outcome.

When Harvard President Claudine Gay testified to Congress and was asked by Representative Elise Stefanik (R-NY) whether calling for the genocide of Jews would violate Harvard's code of ethics, Gay responded that it depends on the context, meaning that this had to be balanced against free-speech protections.[15]

Free speech has been the subject of constitutional and judicial debate at the level of the Supreme Court ever since the First Amendment was introduced. It is a complex and nuanced right, hardly amenable to a congresswoman's request for a yes or no answer as presented to President Gay.

Ultimately, our crisis of trust comes down to the very difficult decision as to what we as a culture allow on social media in terms of what can be referred to as hate speech. Where do the guardrails of our communication systems fall? What are its boundaries? On which side of this slippery slope dare we err? Certainly, we must protect the potential victims of dangerous conspiracy theories and outright lies. But how far can we go in terms of sacrificing at least some aspects of free speech? President Gay didn't have the "right" answer. So, she resigned painfully and perhaps wiser. Our culture is struggling with the very same question. It is our crisis of trust.

In this chapter, we explored the boundaries of free speech, specifically as determined by Elon Musk, the owner of X, previously Twitter. Though originally politically left of center, Musk became entranced with the power of his site and began to insert himself into the political arena by supporting Trump in the 2024 election with his financial influence on potential voters, bordering, some legal experts opined, on legal liability. Trust was the victim when the First Amendment rights took charge over the power of lies and conspiracy theories. Musk decided to allow claims on X that were, to most reasonable people, false and sometimes dangerous. Trust, once again, found itself in the crossfire between polarized parties. But Musk found himself in the center of political power, with Trump welcoming him in the new regime of an oligarchy.

In the next chapter, we'll deal with another aspect of trust on our device screens—the trustworthiness of artificial intelligence. Once again, the power of electronic information would leave trust all beat up and weakened by information that appeared authoritative and official sounding yet could not always be expected to be consistently accurate.

22

Our Growing Crisis with AI

*"Deepfake technology is getting better and better . . .
to create more and more outrageous content."*
—TRISTAN HARRIS, executive director, the Center for Humane Technology

"I cannot see a path that guarantees safety [for AI]."
—GEOFFREY E. HINTON, Nobel Prize winner in physics (2024)

The threat of artificial intelligence (AI) to our experience of trust is becoming more and more apparent. In the summer of 2024, there were over twenty-seven members of the European Union having elections, and all these were seen as being influenced by disinformation amplified by AI. The increasingly aggravating effects of climate change and mass migrations made voters even more susceptible to false information.

Although democracies grew around the globe following the Cold War, there is now a reversal as populist and authoritarian governments appear to be favored by more and more voters across the map. This is influenced by disinformation spread not only by social media but by print, radio, television, and word of mouth as well, according to Katie Harbath, founder of the technology policy firm, Anchor Change. "We're going to hit 2025," she claimed, "and the world is going to look very different."[1]

Hacking into election electronic frameworks is yesterday's game. The claims made about hacking the voting systems were brought to court where over sixty cases claiming voter fraud were dismissed.[2] Nowadays generative AI can spin the truth much more effectively, influencing voting choices as never before at all levels, especially local. A greater concern is disinformation that can sway voters.

"With the evolution of generative AI," writes Adam Marre in *Fortune*, "malicious actors can conjure up fake news articles and social media accounts quicker than ever, easily sowing confusion or swaying public opinion before, during or after an election."[3]

Yet local governments don't have sufficient funds to combat this. And, with generative AI available to the public, anyone can target voters with disinformation. "For the first time," says journalist Rachyl Jones, "AI tools are available to the general public, making it much easier for anyone with a political agenda to spread disinformation."[4]

The Innocence of AI at the Beginning

When AI first arrived on the scene, it was found quite useful for mundane tasks as well as for more sophisticated diagnostic work in a number of fields. (See Chapter Two). Searching through large masses of data, it could identify patterns that transcended human ability, even identifying the success of popular songs through magnetic resonance imaging of listeners.[5] As pointed out earlier, ChatGPT—the letters referring to Generative Pre-trained Transformer—and other chatbots are based on the algorithm functioning as an autocorrection process by which the most likely word to follow a previous word is based on probability of the immense bank of words available (just like on your cell phone, but with incredibly greater power).

In effect, according to Emily Bender, a linguist at the University of Washington, it is acting like a "stochastic parrot."[6] At bottom, the algorithm allows the program to regurgitate what it has in its banks of data by "understanding" words according to a given context, leaving the impression of having understood what it's learned. It's the use of context that is key to the process. That involves taking the probability of word connections to a much greater level of complexity. Yet it does a great job of figuring out solutions to complex problems. Researchers are not quite sure how this gets done. The benefits are many and much appreciated by the various professions that benefit from this.

The Evil Potential of AI

But AI also had applications that transcended human abilities that weren't so benign, especially when it came to influencing voting. Two of these applications were extremely troublesome—deepfakes and human impersonation.

Because generative AI can be used to create credible likenesses of celebrities and well-known politicians, there is the obvious danger of using such images to create disinformation in whatever direction the user chooses. Putting influential individuals in embarrassing scenarios can wreak havoc with these individuals' reputation and perceived morality. Or deepfake images of those in authority can give the false impression that such individuals endorse choices that they never would in reality, thus creating confusion about trust in their integrity.

Human impersonation allows AI to falsely create certain patterns of apparent human activities to generate income for a particular piece of entertainment that gives the impression of a substantial following. Though patently false, this apparent success influences the market for this particular work of entertainment and appears to have growing mass appeal, all of this being artificially created. This clearly upsets normal market patterns to create false impressions that end up stealing the benefits of otherwise normally successful artists. This is one step removed from creating false impressions of political polls, giving unreal impressions that can easily sway otherwise normal patterns of voting.

AI puts power into the hands of unscrupulous and immoral individuals whose interest is to influence human choices by successfully delivering disinformation in an organized, focused manner. To the extent that such endeavors are successful, and there's no reason to imagine they wouldn't be, the ultimate victim is social trust, the essence and basis of the democratic process. If there is no trust in the media that disseminate political messages, then how can a democracy survive?

Criminal individuals and, even more ominous, groups with evil intentions can learn to use AI to their advantage, since AI is amoral.

That is, AI does not take a moral stand on its contribution to progress unless certain guardrails are constructed to curb its potential abuse. If only this were as simple as it sounds at first blush. As AI becomes more user-friendly as it has over time indeed become, as was intended, then a broader spectrum of personalities comes to the AI table to make a greater diversity of its uses, even when the intentions of some of these multitudes of personalities are not so benign. Even as OpenAI tried to create guardrails to prevent election abuse, there were concerns that evildoers could somehow navigate around such guardrails or even use competing chatbots that hadn't yet set up the necessary guardrails.[7]

Though it declared that it had certain usage policies, OpenAI invited their users to report abusers. The clear implication here is that the proposed guardrails were not completely effective. Mekela Pandith-aratne of the Brennan Center for Justice pointed this out quite clearly when she asked, "For example, how exhaustive and comprehensive will the filters be when flagging questions about the election process? Will there be items that slip through the cracks?"[8] Obviously, OpenAI had opened the floodgates for election abuse by making voice-cloning[9] and deepfakes more available and more realistic,[10] and those abuses can be created in seconds.

Deepfakes

Deepfakes come in the form of photos, sound bites, and videos, all managing to give a fairly good impression of disinformation, looking a lot like reality and getting better at it as time goes by. In a process known as generative adversarial networks, or deep learning, computers can bring to visual reality social events that never happened. Any individual's speech habits, facial expressions, lip movements, and overall demeanor can be manipulated into images of events that never happened.

Imagine all the possibilities. Any celebrity can be seen as saying and doing anything you could imagine, being seen as endorsing your favorite candidate, or, worse still, putting that candidate in a very compromising position, such as in porn videos. Deepfakes make photoshop-ping look quaint and harmless. Generative AI allows for deepfakes that are eerily realistic and convincing and can have unexpectedly effective influence in the voting process.

Synthetic media expert Henry Ajder warned us to watch out for "the incriminating, hyper-realistic deepfake of a presidential candidate which swings major voting centers."[11] On January 22, 2024, President Biden can be heard on a fake robocall recommending that people not vote in the New Hampshire caucus election, revealing such abuse for the first time.[12]

In what has been termed the infocalypse, there is the fear that democracy itself is on the brink when we can no longer distinguish truth from deepfakery.[13] When trust in the media, including social media, is so ruptured by abuses of AI that are available to the general public, then trust within our daily world is precariously close to with-ering away. Perhaps the only antidote to this rotting of trust in our society is to transcend the use of social media when it comes to really crucial issues and insist on meetings in person. More on that in the next section, much more.

For the time being, listen to what Rashmee Roshan Lall has to say about this: "Face-to-face interactions, live attendance at political ral-lies, the evidence of one's own eyes and ears will count but not video or audio circulating on news media or social platforms."[14]

Both parties are concerned about the political abuse of deepfakes. Florida Senator Marco Rubio proclaimed that deepfakes could make up "the next wave of attacks against America and western democra-cies."[15] As time goes by, deepfakes get more and more seamless and flawless in their portrayal of manipulated disinformation, making it more and more difficult to trust what we see on our screens. For the time being, one can try spotting them by looking for shimmering or wobbly faces and the absence of blinking. But, as this book, among oth-ers, reaches the public, the creators of deepfakes will work to overcome these tell-tale signs. In general, when a character, whether politician, celebrity or even business executive,[16] seems to act out of character, then this is the time to question what is being revealed before your very eyes.

Many have expressed fears that some deepfake or other image could inadvertently lead to a war, even to the possibility of nuclear conflict. "Deepfakes will be used enormously," according to Bolor-Erdene Battsengel, of the University of Oxford, "adding to existing misinformation and disinformation."[17] In the next section, we'll take a look at the need to use face-to-face interaction to prevent just that.

Other concerns about AI relate to its demand for the use of electrical utilities as over 20 percent of global data-center capacity is utilized by AI; the slow progress of government regulations over AI; the continuing issue of errors; the government's use of AI in benefits and public services; and the growing divide between the two-thirds of the world that have access to AI and the third that doesn't, referred to as the digital divide.[18]

According to Mustafa Suleyman, author of *The Coming Wave*, that title refers to the integration of AI technology and synthetic biology, presenting the ultimate challenge to our society, and the need "to monitor, contain, control, and eventually even close down technologies" with the "growing likelihood that both new technologies . . . might lead to catastrophic and/or dystopian outcomes."[19]

Then there is the long-existing fear of robotic entities taking over the workforce. According to a report by Figure AI, Inc., the most recent versions of robots are capable of much more than what existed to date. These are termed general purpose as opposed to single-purpose robotics. "The potential of general purpose robotics is completely untapped," reported Brett Adcock, CEO of Figure AI. "We look forward to working side-by-side with BMW Manufacturing to integrate AI and robotics into automotive production."[20]

Some scientists are concerned about the evolution of AI models when compared to genetic evolution. Both genetic form and AI evolve in a manner that is unintentional except for the consequence of ultimate survival. There is no preplanning, just the algorithm of repetition, and survival into the next generation. Genetic evolution has taken billions of years, resulting in us humans affecting our planet at an increasingly rapid rate over the past few centuries. Now we have AI evolving at an increasingly rapid tempo over the past decade or so. The successful messenger of evolution is referred to as the replicator. The entire process is mindless yet selfish. Only the successful variations continue to influence the evolutionary process. That's how we evolved and that's how AI evolves. Since we don't know the inner workings of the AI evolutionary process, we can neither predict it nor control it.

So how can we trust the process since it evolves in line with its own benefit rather than ours. Just as our bodies have learned to resist the bad biology of viruses and other pathogens, we can also learn to live with AI by acquiring a technology for our own survival against the dangers of AI. We can hope that the guardrails we implement will help and that our AI technology will give us more predictability and control as we gain more insight into the workings of AI.

Explainable AI (XAI) is an attempt to get into the inner workings of the AI process so we can get a certain sense of understanding, which will hopefully allow us to trust the technical workings in the black box. That might lead to greater trust in the overall process. The machine-learning mechanisms can become better known, though with significant limitations. With greater transparency in the process, we can, at least to some degree, effectively control the evolutionary process and have some degree of trust in the process. By running simulations, we can vie for a greater degree of predictability. By tracing the links between neurons, using a process called Deep Learning Important FeaTures (DeepLIFT), we can better understand what's going on in the otherwise indiscernible black box. The more understanding we can muster, the more we can learn to trust the entire process of AI. This is certainly a challenge but one well worth our efforts if we are to learn to be more trusting of AI, especially as it becomes increasingly more powerful with time.

In this chapter, we looked at the potential dangers of AI, including at the hands of the public as well as foreign enemies, especially around election time. The level of trust becomes lower than ever. With the advent of deepfakes becoming increasingly convincing, the trust level of information relating to elections reaches a nadir in electronic communication. This lack of trust could contribute to the failure of democracy.

In the next section, we transition to a completely different aspect of trust, a much more optimistic one. How can we use our experience and knowledge of trust to improve the likelihood of better communication to save many lives being lost to the ravages of nuclear warfare? Since electronic communication is not always trustworthy, as we've just seen in this last chapter, this would involve meetings on a face-to-face basis, leaving no room for electronic miscommunication.

PART X

Contractual Trust: How to Avoid Nuclear Conflict with Radical Negotiation

Contractual trust: Refers to the ways in which written agreements determine our interactions with, and support of, those with whom we've signed a contract. Contractual trust is evident, for example, in agreements that nations have decided upon to resolve long-standing conflicts of interest. National leaders might negotiate with one another in a chosen, common area to allow for authentic communication about feelings of frustration and defensiveness. The foundation of contractual trust is the hope that when such open communication is allowed in a safe, private place, then differences can be resolved in ways that had previously eluded the participants.

Historically, this may have occurred in transactions such as the Peace of Westphalia, the Potsdam Treaty, the Treaty of Venice, and even the Geneva Conventions. In more modern times, however, diplomats seem to have moved to usurp roles formerly occupied by leaders, and personal meetings between heads of state are fairly rare once conflict has been ongoing. Achieving contractual trust by heads of state is referred to as radical negotiation or, more formally, Track III Diplomacy. The best modern example of this approach is the Camp David Peace Accords, the establishment of which was led by President Jimmy Carter in September 1978. The recommendations in this last section are aimed to promote more successes along these lines with the ultimate goal of preventing nuclear planetary suicide.

> *"Peace cannot be kept by force; it can only be achieved by understanding."*
> —ALBERT EINSTEIN

> *"Our thing was anti-diplomacy, starting with the dress code ... I'd be like, 'I don't need this bullsh-t, break it down in normal terms.'"*
> —Head of Ukrainian delegation DAVYD ARAKHAMIA, negotiating with Russia in 2024

23

One Alternative to Nuclear Planetary Suicide: Restoring Trust

*"Humanity is just one misunderstanding, one
miscalculation away from nuclear annihilation."*
—Antonio Guttierez, Secretary-General of United Nations

"Can we talk to a deaf person?"
—Ukrainian President Zelenski,
discussing the possibility of future negotiations on the war

The personalities of national leaders can influence the outcome of international negotiations. When the war on Ukraine began on February 24, 2022, there was a growing concern among many that President Vladimir Putin might resort to nuclear warfare if resolution to the war were not forthcoming on his timetable. One of the contributing factors was the interaction between Putin and Joe Biden, then new president of the US who had taken office in January of 2021. With Joe Biden in that position, there was some degree of confidence that calm minds would prevail, even though the Kremlin knew that they had a particular adversary in the Democratic administration.

The week before he passed on his power as president to Donald Trump, President Biden shared his thoughts on interpersonal negotiations while being interviewed by Lawrence O'Donnell on MSNBC on January 17, 2025. "It's all about understanding the other man or woman and what their interests are. There are real differences among us, but you can always work something out."

But what if this scenario were played after Donald J. Trump became president for the second time? Or if someone with similar political views were to come into power, such as his vice-president, J.D. Vance? Of course, this would be only one factor.

It's crucial that every effort be made to avoid the slightest possibility of nuclear conflict. The current technology of missile combat makes it impossible to detect incoming armaments in time to make any defensive decisions,[1] sometimes coming in at Mach 5, five times the speed of sound,[2] or even faster as that technology progresses. Despite attempts by NORAD, the Canadian and American front defense lines in the northern part of the American continent, to detect such attacks, these hypersonic missiles are game changers.[3]

Therefore, it is beyond crucial to avoid any scenarios in which misunderstandings could lead to mistrust about first-strike capabilities. "Once they're launched," said Andrea Charron, director of the Centre for Defense and Security Studies at the University of Manitoba, "I don't think anybody has a good solution."[4]

That is why I choose to focus on the personalities of international conflict resolution, and why I will spend significant time looking at the kind of research explored in a popular publication titled *One Alternative to Nuclear Planetary Suicide*.[5]

During the weeks following the invasion of Ukraine by Russia, disinformation played a very large role in people's beliefs about the appropriateness of either side's role in the war. Social media conveyed stories that favored one side or the other. The photos and videos of physical damage were terribly devastating, yet the viewer could get different contexts about culpability, depending on how the narratives were spun, and propaganda played a large role in this. If only all this tragedy could have been prevented.

The big question is whether a negotiated settlement could have avoided the tragedy that followed. I believe such an effort would have been worthwhile. Most effective resolutions of negotiations leave both parties feeling that they gave up more than they expected to or hoped to. Compromise often hurts. To understand Putin's point of view would have taken much effort—getting the other side, presumably either Joe

Biden or one of the leaders of a European organization such as NATO's Secretary-General Mark Rutte, to fully comprehend Putin's basic fear of democracy, in the form of NATO, whose main purpose is to counter Putin's autocratic power.

Without giving conflict negotiation a chance, Putin commenced his plan of destruction soon after entering Ukraine. As the West began its support of the besieged country, Putin announced that Russia's nuclear forces were beginning a phase of "special combat readiness."[6] Of course, that alerted the US to contact its Tiger Team to assess retaliatory responses in worst-case scenarios.[7] Putin's choice not to go to the negotiation table was leading to terrible, unimaginable outcomes, not to mention Russia's bombing of Kiev's power plants in the fall of 2022, creating horrible challenges for staying warm during the Ukrainian winter.[7]

Negotiations by themselves were not very promising, unless a drastically new form of such a process were to be employed. One issue is the intractable nature of President Putin. How can one have a logical debate with someone who appears to be so single-minded and stubborn in his perspective? It's challenging to separate the "villain" from the substance of the debate. Perhaps writer William Saroyan described this challenge best: "Despise evil and ungodliness, but not men of ungodliness or evil. These, understand." And that is the premise of what I refer to as *radical negotiation*.

In this next section, we'll take a close look at the most effective form of international negotiation at the most personal and intimate levels. That's what brings us to the popular publication mentioned before, *One Alternative to Nuclear Planetary Suicide*.[8]

There are many who advocate conflict resolution at the international level, but very few individuals have published their experience of doing so on a personal, intimate basis. One is Carl R. Rogers.

In this part I will share an approach that involves openness and direct expression of the deepest emotions, even though many might argue that this would not work with the Kremlin. It would have to involve mutual assurance backed by verification, of course, and very undesirable consequences for breaking any agreement, or even hindering any verification. Perhaps we can learn to speak from the heart. This is how to *earn* trust. This is the approach to, or pattern of, learning how to trust—learning to be trust*worthy*.

24

Radical Negotiation:
Fear Is the Enemy of Trust

"In nuclear war, all men are cremated equal."
—Dexter Gordon

"We will not learn how to live together in peace
by killing each other's children."
—Jimmy Carter

Our planet is suffering several challenges: climate change, systemic injustice, a pandemic that continues to linger (with variants LP.8.1 followed closely by XEC at the time of this writing), and perhaps the greatest of all, the possibility of nuclear conflict that Putin threatens if the Ukraine conflict, or that Iran threatens if the Israel-Hamas war, remains unresolved (at the time of this writing).

It appears that such nuclear conflict has become more of a threat now than it has for decades. In addition to the friction between Russia and Ukraine and between Israel and Iran, there is Kim Jong Un building his options to threaten the Western nations by offering 3,000 of his troops to Russia and the buildup of nuclear components in Iran.

The Growing Nuclear Threats

This may be the end of what we like to call the Pax EuropAsiAmericana, the relatively peaceful era we have enjoyed since the war in Vietnam. With the wars in Ukraine and the Mideast remaining unresolved as Russia and Israel refuse to negotiate peace, the threat of nuclear warfare continues to simmer just below the boiling point.

When President Vladimir Putin attacked Ukraine on February 24, 2022, President Biden and NATO leaders could only assist Ukraine by sending weapons. Any American boots on the ground would inevitably lead to escalation into full war and then the inevitability of nuclear conflict. This threat is what kept the war to manageable proportions without such unthinkable prospects, as long as US soldiers were not in combat in Ukraine.

When Hamas attacked Israel on October 7, 2023, and the allies of Iran such as Hezbollah in Syria and the Houthis in Yemen began attacking it, the threat of war with Iran escalated significantly.

How dangerous is nuclear threat at this point in our history?

Consider that, aside from bothersome North Korea, the US is facing two potential nuclear enemies—Russia and China. China is aspiring to build over 200 warheads in the coming decade, with new missile designs. But Russia and the US have, between them, over 90 percent of the world's 13,400 nuclear weapons, more than enough to bomb our world population into devastation. France and the United Kingdom are also members of the nuclear club. The saving grace is that these five nations have all signed the Non-Proliferation Treaty, adopted in 1970.

Since then, four more countries have a nuclear arsenal but never signed this treaty: North Korea, India, Pakistan, and Israel (the only country that refuses to acknowledge its nuclear capabilities). And then there is Iran, close to the edge of building their nuclear weapons, not yet considered nuclear warriors.

Now, in this complicated international scenario, consider the potential crises for dangerous conflict between pairs of these nations:

- North Korea's threat to its southern counterpart, South Korea, and then to the US as it sent 3,000 of its troops to Russia, to combat with Ukraine
- Israel's publicly expressed desire to prevent Iran from using any nuclear armaments as attacks between them intensified
- Iran's threats to destroy Israel

- China's well-known desire to "annex" its southern neighbor and historical nemesis, Taiwan
- India's next-door-neighbor disputes with both China and Pakistan

Any one of these scenarios could escalate into a world-war type of scenario.

Of all these possibilities, it could be argued that China's insistence on acquiring Taiwan and Biden's promise to avoid that option from taking place is a clear-cut challenge that might lead to war. Once a war starts between these superpowers, nuclear warfare becomes a dramatic concern. With this in mind, Chinese leader Chairman Xi Jinping has decided, in the public world forum, to fight and win should such a war come about. In order to follow through on that, the Chinese have invested deeply into their defense forces in their attempt to climb to NATO's strength.

In order to anticipate this, the Americans have prepared themselves for a surprise attack by China by designing hypersonic programs spread across the Army, Navy, and Air Force. But China has not been idly sitting by. It has prepared itself by combining resources with its new, yet untested ally Russia. In August 2022, war games were employed by the two countries involving 10,000 troops from both nations to test new weapon systems. The following October they simulated attacks against US submarines, using joint naval exercises involving ten warships. In July 2023, the war games continued.

Since the US withdrew from the Anti-Ballistic Missile Treaty in 2001, Russia and China have had the freedom to build their nuclear weapons without limitation. At this point, the US has the largest stockpile of nuclear weapons. The US defense budget of $733 billion allowed for maintenance of their eleven aircraft carriers while China has only three. But these are only numbers. A nuclear war would devastate all warring nations, regardless of who has more of whatever. So, peace must be maintained before the fog of war has any chance of deepening hostilities to the point of combat. Therefore, the need for a radical approach to building trust among nations.

From Muskets to the Manhattan Project

There is a great need for some sane approach to avoiding any unmanageable outcome such as nuclear war. The results, no matter how one considers them, are not acceptable to any sane leader.

Despite this, as mentioned, it is public knowledge that there now exist over 13,000 nuclear bombs across the planet in such nations as France, India, Israel, Pakistan, China, North Korea, and the United Kingdom, not to mention Russia and the United States, which, between them, own most of the world's supply. And these last two are the ones being threatened with the possibility of using these infernal weapons should the Ukraine invasion grow out of control.

It is devastatingly ironic that this possibility exists when our society has grown so sophisticated with technology of all sorts that makes our world culture more meaningful and internationally cooperative.

Leaders across the globe agree that nuclear warfare is not an option to be considered in any realistic fashion, with the few exceptions such as Putin, Kim Jong Un of North Korea, and possibly former president Ebrahim Raisi of Iran. But all it takes is one nuclear attack and the game, unfortunately, may be over.

If it's hatred between groups geographically divided, hostile feelings between culturally different nations, or religious animosities, the potential for conflict with one of the nuclear countries facing off against one another can trigger a nuclear war.

Hopefully, our world culture has grown beyond the game of throwing sticks and stones at one another, of clashing with swords growing longer and longer, until they're thrown at one another as spears. Then gun powder was invented, and guns became available for warfare about the same time as the printing press allowed for an increase in knowledge.

One of the reasons the American Civil War was so outlandishly deadly was the transition of muskets and breech-loaders, whose accuracy was not great, to deadly weapons of much greater accuracy. The rifling of gun barrels, metallic cartridges, and repeating firearms only made matters worse.

By the time the US was involved in international warfare in the second World War, the Manhattan Project was under way as a response to the news that Germany was working on its own nuclear technology since the 1930s. Tens of thousands of Americans were working on the project in such locations as Oak Ridge, Tennessee; Los Alamos, New Mexico; and Hanford/Richland, Washington.

Fear Is the Enemy of Trust

All this activity was motivated by fear of the enemy's potential for nuclear attack, and fear is the enemy of trust. As a result, the threat of force and intimidation was the rule of negotiation.

There must be another way, one backed by making an attempt at trust rather than fear and intimidation (while maintaining one's defenses, of course, until the negotiations are resolved). In this section, we search for such a solution, with the necessity for the need to develop a more intelligent approach, involving the skills and attitudes of building mutual trust even in the face of historical differences and obvious points of conflict.

There are many schools of thought along these lines already in existence. Many of them outline certain skills or stages of negotiation process, such as preparation, exchanging information, bargaining, and implementation.[1,2] Henry Kissinger was the chief negotiating officer for President Richard Nixon and, being sophisticated in all these skills, did quite well in opening the doors to a former enemy, China.[3] Even at the age of 100, Kissinger was still encouraging improved relations between the US and China, where he was welcomed with open arms in the summer of 2023. There is no shortage of philosophies of international negotiation in which Kissinger played a crucial role.[4]

And yet we see fairly little success in resolving conflict between major countries in conflict. Why is that?

I believe one of the factors relates to the need to adopt a system of negotiation that goes much deeper than existing models allow for, deeper in the sense of personal openness on the parts of the national leaders themselves.

Diplomacy: Tracks I, II, and III

Track I Diplomacy refers to the conventional process of negotiation by professional diplomats along formal lines of process. Track II Diplomacy involves the "back roads" of interaction at a much less formal level to bridge the gap across enemy lines, often run by university scholars and think-tank advocates for humanistic interchange allowing for the opportunity of sharing values on an interpersonal level. What I am proposing here is, for lack of a better term, Track III Diplomacy in which the heads of state meet in an intensely intimate setting to integrate the best of the first two tracks. More on that later.

Those who attain the power of national leadership must have strong egos, the type of self-confidence that is unquestionable in the face of public challenge. So, it goes without saying that such leaders are typically strong personalities who rarely show signs of weakness or vulnerability in public.

There are some exceptions to this rule. Self-effacing humility and openness to opposing ideas as examples among American presidents bring Abraham Lincoln to mind, as well as more modern examples such as JFK and Jimmy Carter.

For the most part, however, when international conflict shows its face, it's typically expressed in terms of us versus them, *us* being the good guys and *them* being the bad guys. As levels of tension rise, insidious propaganda begins to build the case even more strongly. Too often, the fog of war begins to blind people to any possibilities of conflict resolution once the bullets start flying.

In World War II, it was the US against the "Huns" and "Japs." In the Korean and Vietnam wars it was against the "dirty commies." For ten years, we fought the North Vietnamese, bombing their villages and burning their huts only to learn years later how peaceful a culture they lived in. There was an admission of error by many American leaders of the war as to how foolish an endeavor this was,[5] resulting in the loss of over 58,000 American lives, as well as over 2 million Vietnamese lives.[6]

Later it was Ronald Reagan's characterization of the Soviet Union as "the incarnation of evil," while they saw us as aggressors with intent on nuclear war to prove our superiority. There was little opportunity for trust to grow in such a belligerent milieu.

Our point is that most conflicts begin with such divisive emotions based on different cultures, experiences and fears that the other side is evil against our good nature. In order to resolve such deeply ingrained hostilities, there must be an equally intense form of communication allowing for these hostile feelings to be aired under revolutionary safe conditions. Each side must have the opportunity to air its frustrations and hostile feelings fully and openly, giving the other side the opportunity to hear, with some degree of accuracy, what both heads of state are sharing.

But when national leaders lie in public, as Vladimir Putin is reputed to do, then it is extremely difficult to anticipate sincere and authentic negotiations. After the Ukrainian Army bombed the interior of Russia and was then subsequently "punished" by a more thorough shelling of infrastructure, Putin tried to present an image of credible leadership by sending clips of himself reassuring his high officers of their righteous mission.

Putin: "You can't trust anyone . . . You can only trust me."

Where was trust in all this? It was being used in the most egregious manner. "You can't trust anyone," Putin told the Russian media at the end of 2022. "You can only trust me." When the issue of nuclear warfare came up, Putin had previously claimed that he was well aware of the calamitous consequences. He told the world audience, for whom his public meetings were meant, "We're just thinking about it,"[7] *it* being nuclear attack.

At the beginning of 2023, Russia and Ukraine were at each other's throats in the sense that both could claim to have the upper hand. Ukraine was attacking points 300 miles beyond the Russian border, and Russia had virtually wiped out some of Ukraine's infrastructure. If there was any trust in the months prior, it seemed totally eradicated by this point. The bitterness on both sides was too great to allow for any significant degree of trust.

Many may wonder what would bring the leader of a great country such as Russia to invade a much smaller nation without provocation. The simple answer is history. Putin had a strong drive to return to Russia's past glory and power. In his book, *Overreach*, on the war in Ukraine, author Owen Matthews offers his explanation: "The war allowed Putin . . . to fulfill a dream that many old men may aspire to but very few achieve . . . to create a future that reflected an idealized version of their own pasts."[8]

Was Putin's motivation glorious or perhaps more accurate, vainglorious? Many characterize him as psychopathic. According to Cornell University forensic psychiatrist Ziv Cohen, "Putin scores high in the three categories associated with the mental disorder of psychopathy: aggression, narcissism, and lack of empathy." Cohen goes on to say that "you cannot have agreements with them."[9]

So, negotiating with Putin, according to the good doctor, would be fruitless and inexorably frustrating, even though Putin occasionally says he is ready to do so. Toward the end of 2022, Putin declared, "Negotiations will have to be made," at a news conference in Kyrgyzstan. "Now there is a question of trust; it is already almost at zero."[10]

Each side's conditions for beginning peace negotiations were miles apart. Russia insisted on maintaining possession of the four Ukrainian regions to which they had laid claims. Ukraine insisted on Russia facing their war crimes first.

Then, on October 7 of 2023, Hamas attacked Israeli kibbutzim near the border of Gaza. Is there a brief overview account that can explain a bit about the ongoing dynamic of mistrust between Israel and the

Palestinians? Many a university student might benefit greatly by such
an overview, brief as it may be.

When the British Mandate in Palestine awarded land to the Jews
and Palestinians in 1948, the surrounding Arab countries decided to
get rid of the Jews. They surrounded them and decided to drive them
to the sea. The Jews, just a few short years after the Holocaust, felt dif-
ferently and decided to defend themselves, trouncing the Arabs and
gaining a stronger foothold in what is now Israel.

The Palestinians were either driven from their homes or decided to
leave on their own after being warned about the Jews. They intended
to return to their homes within weeks but that was not the outcome.
They were never able to reclaim their land. They were now displaced
migrants, and they've been displaced ever since, living primarily in the
West Bank or to a lesser extent in the Gaza Strip.

This is what gave Hamas the motivation to attack innocent victims
on October 7, 2023. Israel, experiencing the most egregious attack in
its seventy-five-year history, exploded with vengeful anger and began
attacking Hamas wherever they might be found, presumably around
hospitals and other supposedly safe places, such as schools and tem-
ples. If ever there was a vacuum of trust, this was it.

Just as much as the war in Ukraine, this Israel-Hamas/Hezbollah
war could easily spin into a wider conflict, possibly involving Iran, and
then the possibilities of nuclear warfare with Iran's allies could spin
out of control. With the growing alliances among Iran and Russia and
China, this could become even more dangerous, with China building
its nuclear arsenal in anticipation of the conflict regarding the acquisition of Taiwan.[11]

In the summer of 2024, Putin announced that Russia would be
deploying nuclear weapons during its military exercises after the US
was supplying Ukraine with billions of dollars' worth of weapons. Russia's defense ministry claimed that this was in response to provocative
statements and threats by certain Western officials against the Russian
Federation."[12] Between the two of them, Russia and the US had over
10,600 of the world's approximately 13,500 nuclear warheads.

There is little time for hesitation. In the next couple chapters, this brand-new form of negotiation will be put into perspective for its unique character, and how it transcends conventional standards, allowing for personal, intimate interaction between heads of state trying to resolve the conflict between them by using a revolutionary application of trust.

25

A Revolutionary Approach to Resolving "The Troubles" in Ireland

"Democracy is based on trust. Autocracy is based on terror. Dictators systematically destroy trust."
—YUVAL NOAH HARARI, author of *Nexus*

"I think about the rapes and murders of civilians in Israel, about the genocide in Gaza, about the hostages, about the killings in my home city. And I cry."
—West Bank mother, MAI SHAHEEN

Imagine heads of state yelling at one another at the top of their lungs, thumping the tabletop with their white-knuckled fists. This can actually happen, and we'll explore this in detail. But first, here is the outline of the revolutionary form of international negotiations I refer to as Track III Diplomacy.

Fortunately, most national leaders are not crackpots. If we assume that we are to initiate this novel form of negotiation process with "psychologically normal" leaders, then this is how we would proceed. This model is based on the research of Carl Rogers, the results of which were published as a widely read paper titled *One Alternative to Nuclear Planetary Suicide*.[1]

The Four Key Aspects of Carl Rogers's Approach

Let's summarize four key aspects of Rogers's approach to conflict resolution:

1. **Empathy**: the opportunity to create a safe space for opening up about two nations' **leaders' feelings regarding differences in**

beliefs and values, particularly as they concern the politics of the conflict

2. **Unconditional positive regard**: the opportunity to invite both parties in the conflict to share their histories from their own cultural perspectives so that each side can **fully understand where its counterpart is coming from** without allowing its own perspective to allow for unclear judgment or defensiveness

3. **Authenticity**: the opportunity for both sides to become transparent about their initial reactions to hearing the other side's historical experiences and political perspectives, whatever emotions that might lead to, **including anger and hurt** (Here's where a strong personality is required to navigate these treacherous waters to reach the safe harbors of openness and ultimate acceptance.)

4. And finally, a **nondirective approach:** in which each side is given the freedom to determine the direction and pace of their involvement. We will see why it is important not to have an initial point-by-point agenda but rather to leave it open **to allow for an organic development of trust** between the parties.

All this seems deceptively simple at first blush, but this approach allows for the many complicated turns and challenges that make each episode of conflict resolution have its own unique path charted only by the participants themselves.

Carl Rogers wrote about these principles years before they were implemented by President Carter at Camp David. Did these two men influence one another? It's almost impossible to know. It's quite possible that Carter knew of Rogers's work only indirectly because of the latter's worldwide popularity in the 1960s and '70s. By that time, Rogers's work had been so widely adopted that it had become part of the "canon" of the psychology culture of those years, along with the insights of humanists such as Rollo May, Fritz Perls, and behaviorist B. F. Skinner. Regardless of any actual interpersonal connections, Carter's plan for his peace-making mission very closely resembles the work of Rogers.

In my own publication (written with Rogers),[1] we wrote about how nations use threat and intimidation as ways of gaining power. As an alternative option, we offered a model of conflict resolution that focuses on personal authenticity and openness.

We challenged the belief that "We are right, and you are wrong. We are good and you are bad," just as President Reagan characterized the then Soviet Union as "the incarnation of evil." Our hope was that nations in conflict could realize firsthand that each entity attributes the same heinous character to the other. This could be the starting point for more productive dialogue.

Rogers's personal experience included participating as a facilitator between two groups of twenty to twenty-five people who interacted with one another with little personal understanding of the other group. This was a workshop devised by the National Health Council made up of medical and nursing organizations as well as health insurance companies. The purpose was to bring together the health service providers and the consumers to bridge gaps of frustration and misunderstandings of policy. The consumer group was made up of people who came primarily from urban ghettos and rural underprivileged regions. Many were Blacks and Mexican Americans and were mostly lower middle class.

Both groups felt sharp hostility toward one another. According to Rogers, "The bitterness of the poor erupted in full force. Their anger at white professionals . . . was clearly demonstrated." But as time passed and heated vituperations, at times including talk of physical harm, took place, Rogers shared, "Little by little, real interpersonal communication began." In the end, resolutions were devised by the consumers and put into practice. What Rogers learned was that conflict between groups that hate one another can approach resolution when

- the facilitator does not push or prod toward a particular end, but rather
- is sensitive to the organic flow of the interaction, whether rapid or slow,
- does not take sides, and
- does not offer solutions.

This approach allows each group to take responsibility for the end result, and we'll see shortly just how crucially important this is.

A Revolutionary Approach to Resolving "The Troubles"

Rogers had the opportunity to learn even more deeply about the principles of conflict resolution when he was invited to work with a group of Irish citizens, half of whom hated the other half with an intensity that was hard to believe at times.[1] These were the viewpoints during "The Troubles" in Northern Ireland, a term that describes conflicts between the pro-British Protestants and the pro-Irish Catholics. Violence had broken out between these two factions and involved extremist paramilitary groups on both sides. When Rogers became involved, this conflict of violence had been going on for over a decade, and the mutual hatred just grew with the passing years.

In a highly complex and troubled history, it can be understood that the British colonized Ireland in about the eleventh century and conquered Ireland completely in 1652. But political and religious pushback was always problematic, both at the local and central levels. By the mid-1800s, the Great Potato Famine forced a large emigration to England and to the US, and English landlords in Ireland suffered economic losses. By 1865, the Irish began to revolt in significant numbers under the banner of the Fenian movement.

The year 1916 saw the rise of nationalism by the Irish Republican Brotherhood who wanted the British totally out of Ireland. In 1920, Northern Ireland was formed under British rule with its counterpart, the Irish Free State, to the south. The 1960s saw terrible terrorism as both sides suffered mounting casualties until British troops were brought in to try to control the fighting in 1969. This only served to increase the hostilities when British paratroopers killed thirteen Irish citizens on January 30, 1972, in what is known as Bloody Sunday, and the heightening of the modern hostilities known as The Troubles.

This led to urban terrorism in which forty British soldiers were killed. The bombings continued and the killings, on both sides, escalated.

Rogers's group consisted of members of both factions. According to them, residents sometimes had to hide behind mattresses in their homes as bullets flew through the streets. Innocent, nonparticipating residents had to carry bodies torn apart by bombs out of their homes. Gilda, a young Protestant woman participating in the group, shared, "I just get so full of despair, I just give up, you know."

Despite all this hatred, violence, fear, and hopelessness, changes began to be seen after just one weekend of work with Carl Rogers. After only sixteen hours of group interaction, communication across barriers of hatred and despair began to appear. Here are some examples.

Dennis, a Protestant, listened to the story of Becky, a Catholic, as they had "a wee bit of a yarn quietly while you were all away for your dinner." His reaction: "I don't know how I would react if I were one of her lads. I would probably go out and get a gun and finish up doing something radical and end up dead." The degree of violence between the two factions harbored, over time, fantasies of murderous vengeance and revenge. Now a Protestant could more easily understand the primal reactions of a young Catholic boy seeing his parents survive through such onerous threats to their lives.

Becky's reaction: "I think he fully understands me as a person. And for that reason, I am very grateful, and I think I have found a friend." For both, whose feeling represented years of hatred for—and fantasies of—violence to each other's group, a bridge had been crossed, *and it took only sixteen hours.*

What was learned? Based on those critical sixteen hours, Rogers stressed the following key points:

- Feelings based on centuries-old feuds and enmity can be modified and reduced in a relatively short time.
- Both factions need to be entirely removed from their own locales.
- A comfortable residential retreat setting was very helpful.
- Informality is another important factor in the process.

All of this was filmed and subsequently shown to both sides back in Belfast, leading to further discussions about the need to resolve the conflict. There's no record to my knowledge of what effect this had on the two larger groups engaged in the hostilities, whether great or small. But, over a decade later, peace was finally achieved.

On April 10, 1998, the Good Friday Agreement was signed and over 400 political prisoners on both sides were released. Democratic referenda took place a month later. This brought an end to the thirty years of devastating bloodshed.

Finally, on February 10, 2024, almost a quarter of a century later, the Sinn Fein party was elected to run the government of Northern Ireland. The tension between British unionists desiring to remain under British rule and the Irish nationalists whose desire was to unite with Ireland was resolved, at least for the time being.

"This is a historic day," proclaimed Michelle O'Neill, the new first minister, sharing power with Emma Little-Pengelly from the Democratic Unionist Party. "That such a day would ever come would have been unimaginable to my parents and grandparents' generation. Because of the Good Friday Agreement, that old state that they were born into is gone. A more democratic, more equal society has been created making this a better place for everyone."[1]

Rogers had additional experiences that were similar, such as at Escorial in Spain, involving Catholic priests and atheists, communists and conservative businessmen; and in South Africa, involving a group of Blacks and Whites. His experiences made for "a very considerable body of evidence of experience on which to build."[2]

On the final page of that publication, we wrote, "Our modern world will perish in a holocaust unless we learn new and more effective means of reducing and resolving the competitions, hatreds, and enmities that are leading us toward our doom. But the purpose of this . . . is to say—there is hope."[2]

So, let's take this to the next level, applying it to international negotiations to avoid nuclear threat in the present day. Let's see how radical negotiation, an approach otherwise known as Track III Diplomacy, might work to prevent nuclear war.

26

The Revolution of Radical Negotiation to Build Trust between Historic Enemies

"Try to look at the situation through our eyes."
—Mikhail Gorbachev, to President Ronald Reagan
who called Russia the Evil Empire

*"We have a crazy SOB like that guy Putin, and others,
and we always have to worry about nuclear conflict."*
—President Joe Biden

*"There's no good substitute for a face-to-face meeting.
People's minds do change."*
—President of UN Security Council Kishore Mahbubani,
interviewed by Fareed Zakaria on GPS

The Details of Radical Negotiation

It is important to point out that Radical Negotiation is often a last-ditch effort for peaceful negotiation when Track I (through formal attempts involving ambassadors and portfolio officers or cabinet ministers meeting with rigid agendas) and Track II attempts (informal attempts using non-government individuals) have failed.[1,2] Only Track III Diplomacy (also referred to as *Radical Negotiation*) involves the top leaders themselves sitting together in a confidential setting along with a few of their support officials.

The outcomes of these interactions have a sense of finality that transcends the other approaches. There is a sense of do-or-die, an attitude of taking the bull by the horns to resolve a dispute that has avoided resolution for too long a period from both sides' perspectives. Here are the points that both sides must agree on if the process is to have a chance for success.

1. The meetings would need to take place at **a neutral setting** that is comfortable. informal, and free of distractions, like a lodge or retreat. Participants would be able to meet with one another, emphasizing the opportunity to spend some casual time with "the enemy," including shared meals and evening activities such as short hikes, sharing sports such as golf, tennis, pickleball, even checkers and chess. The duration of the entire process is difficult to determine but at least a week should be scheduled, with the option of rescheduling a meeting if necessary.

2. There is an emphasis on **downplaying formality** for the duration of the meeting, including casual wear, sleeping accommodations that are within walking distance of one another, and informal dinner seating arrangements, encouraging both parties to mingle for informal chatting. Formal protocol is not necessary, and political rank even subtly discouraged. Use of first names rather than titles is highly encouraged.

3. Here is a point that is both quite simple and potentially complex. There is an agreement at the outset that everyone **speak openly about political opinions**. The highest-ranking individuals, the leaders, can speak openly about ideas with the understanding that, in most cases, an agreement by their parliamentary bodies would be necessary prior to any closure on informal agreements that do take place. This mode of interpersonal communication is a key component of this novel mode of negotiation, without which this entire enterprise will probably fail. These "negotiations" might take place between two individuals; in small, informal groups at various settings, including dinner time; or in the larger, collective group. This is the place and time not for moralizing or one-upmanship, but rather for realpolitik, the realities of power behind the public niceties. The hope is that the casual, informal approach might lead to

more authentic, open-minded sharing of crucial issues that would otherwise be difficult to resolve.

4. No press allowed. In order for this negotiation process to work, it is essential that all social interactions be kept **confidential** from the public—without exception.

Now, here is the challenge. No computers and no cell phones—at all—can be used during the negotiation process! Otherwise, it just takes one small leak—a phone message to one's spouse or an email to a close friend, and one might as well have a plane writing out something in the big, blue sky that would otherwise remain confidential. This is likely to be the greatest sacrifice of all to the participants, but there can be no exceptions whatsoever. There is a great deal of trust involved in this process and one tiny leak could utterly destroy every semblance of trust so necessary for this to be successful. Then the walls come up and the defensive postures block any further progress.

The only exception is the need for heads of state to be in touch with their government staff to deal with possible timely crises. Here, a commitment to the confidentiality of the mission is critical. A disciplined team should be able to avoid leaks if they are all on the same page. On the other hand, strategic leaks to derail the process might be a challenge.

Only in this fashion, with a commitment to confidentiality, can the participants share thoughts and opinions without judgment of the "outside world," the press and particularly social media, at least until the resolution of the process. It is the confidentiality that allows participants, especially the leaders, to "experiment" with tentative resolutions to otherwise intractable issues of conflict.

If this sounds extreme, it is exactly the intensity of deep trust that is crucial to success here. And there is a cost—the surrender of the comfort and familiarity of electronic communication during the negotiation procedures.

If this feels like creating a bubble of isolation for the duration of the meeting, then that's what it is, as extraordinary as that sounds.

That is one of the more intense components of this very unusual process. Of course, arrangements for emergencies as exceptions are in place.

Before the onset of the negotiation process, the Chief Negotiating Officer (CNO) is responsible for "coaching" both parties how to listen deeply, that is to respond to the other party's statements before following up with their own. This well-known active listening process needs to become second nature to the process for both parties. This is one reason to avoid "leaks" to the public in order to allow participants to articulate what they hear the other side saying without fear of being quoted.

5. Another surprising component of this novel, intense form of negotiation: **No set agenda—except for summaries of the key sources of conflict and issues to be resolved!**

   This is highly unusual. In most normal negotiation processes, the agenda is preset, important and rigid. In conventional settings, everyone knows, before the two parties meet, what is to be discussed, and what the agenda is for each day.

   Not here. In this case, there is, by design and intent, a free flowing process. Although there is no set agenda, the overall goal is to overcome the conflict that brought the parties together, and everyone knows that clearly. It is up to the neutral organizer to initiate the process at the beginning of the first day. Let's refer to that person as the Chief Negotiating Officer or CNO. Though there is no detailed agenda, the CNO is responsible for taking notes during the ongoing negotiations, though a particular individual on the CNO's team might be assigned that task. These notes are designed to help the CNO's team keep track of events but could also be used to share with the separate parties when there is some question about what has been discussed at any particular time, especially when perspectives take separate turns, or to calm down a particularly disruptive session.

6. The **CNO** is an individual with years of experience as a leader of negotiations. That person has a high degree of sensitivity to the nuances in interpersonal communication, what is commonly

referred to as emotional or social intelligence, including the ability to be completely neutral as to the outcome of the negotiations, except that it be successful at the end if at all possible. This may involve some extraordinary skills in understanding the personality characteristics of all the important players.

The CNO is the one who assumes the responsibility not only to bring the parties together on a normal scheduled basis, usually at the same time each morning, and does their best to plan for lunch and dinner at conventional times, but this is not rigid and can be modified by a casual vote as circumstances allow.

The other major responsibility of the CNO is to ensure that both parties feel treated equitably and as warmly as possible, given the circumstances.

In terms of rules of demeanor, the CNO explains that there are two sorts of communication: one that allows for interruptions and the other that does not. Interruptions are allowed most of the time, so that a spontaneous attitude toward communication is encouraged. However, if a speaker has worked on a plan that s/he wants to share with the group, then that individual can request that there be no interruptions until the prepared comments are completed.

Also, interruptions are always aimed at the individual who is speaking at the moment, not as an aside to a neighbor seated to the right or left. It is up to the CNO to maintain this "rule" without exception, lest side conversations become distracting. The CNO might ask something like this, politely, "John, I'd like to know what you're sharing with your associate. It might be of interest to us. Would you mind including the group in your thinking?" This "rule" might be characterized as "focused participation."

The use of humor if it arises naturally is always very welcome. Typically, in a group of ten or so, there will be a few who naturally find humorous comments easy and such individuals are always welcome to share their interesting perspectives.

7. As the process begins to focus on the details of resolution, and handwritten agreements are formulated, emotions may intensify.

Emotional expression is encouraged, and even intense emotions are permitted. The CNO is comfortable with this level of intensity, by training and disposition. If the differences between the parties were not deep and entrenched, there would be no need for this intense form of negotiation. In order to come to a meeting of the minds, emotions must be allowed free rein. Of course, any hint of physical confrontation is quickly defused and becomes material for processing these related deep feelings.

It is not unusual, before the completion of the process, that many a participant will have their tipping point of frustration and show their true colors which were well disguised till that point. Just as the devil is in the details, the points of agreement, when fleshed out on paper, may become sticking points. Attempts at curtailing such emotions may lead to irrational statements, because the intensity of the emotion gives way to speech that isn't always logical at such points. But these are worked out by both parties, as it leads to more authentic discussion.

8. Another important responsibility of the CNO is to use their interpersonal skills to fix things when they break.

When breakdowns occur, and they typically do, s/he should have the necessary skills and motivation to approach the individual involved and "fix" things so that resistance can be transformed into cooperation.

This refers to either party giving up in frustration and deciding to quit the proceedings when the discussions get too overheated, which is expected to occur in most situations. Why? Because of the openness of emotional communication and the unbridled sharing of deeply held emotions that would never surface under normal negotiations (such as Track I or Track II interactions).

At first, when such intense disagreements arise, the CNO can calmly continue taking notes. Sometimes, the CNO can allow a verbal altercation to continue for a while but, before it gets too intense, s/he might ask for an occasion to read the notes and this calm reiteration of the "hot" issues, shared in a cool, calm demeanor, can soften the mood sufficiently for discussion to continue at a smoother pace.

If there is a deep enough rift between members of the parties and one side decides to quit the proceedings, then it is the CNO's job to fix this problem. The CNO can talk with each leader separately to resolve the issue at hand as much as possible until both are assured that continuing the process is in their mutual interest. During these separate communications, the CNO can help each side to understand the perspective of the other, which was not coming through during the normal sessions. Since the entire agenda is fluid, by design, then there is the possibility of the CNO talking with each leader separately from the larger group.

There is also the possibility of having smaller groups meet, possibly while the CNO is meeting with the leaders. The purpose of such smaller groups would be to iron out differences which persist and evade resolutions in the larger meetings. Often there are some participants who aren't as vocal as their associates, and this offers them the opportunity to voice their opinions with insights that may have evaded the larger group process. These smaller groups would typically be facilitated by members of the CNO's team.

This leads directly to the next component.

9. As is becoming clear throughout this description of the novel aspect of Track III negotiations, there is a **"pressure cooker" aspect** to the process. Being together for roughly a week or so without any communication with the outside world is not normal. It is exactly this unique quality that helps arrive at resolutions to conflict that otherwise would evade us.

Given the length of this process and its likely complexities, it is incumbent on the CNO to offer "progress notes" and/or points of agreement at the end of each day to further encourage additional accomplishments.

As the days go by, the relations between the two parties become more intimate, for better or worse. Highs and lows are more intense. That's why breakdowns in communication are to be anticipated.

Two factors prevail to avoid total failure of the process. The first is the sense of togetherness that slowly grows over time and the subsequent feeling of investment of time and energy that begs for resolution. The second is the skill of the CNO to "fix" breaks as described above. There is a negative sense of feeling cooped up, but there is also a complementary sense of "we're in this together till we reach agreement."

The prospect of arriving at a successful end point can be highly motivational for both sides, or they wouldn't have agreed to this unusual and demanding process to begin with.

10. When the process ends with a certain degree of success, it is essential to ensure that both parties, especially their leaders, are credited for their contributions to the entire process. At this point, **the press is invited to report the efforts and victories** of the process, rewarding both sides for their confidence in the proceedings and their efforts to resolve the conflict.

Of course, it goes without saying that both leaders need to be mature, thoughtful and intelligent and stand ready to yield to members of their teams who have these characteristics. Recall how President Trump hit it off with Kim Jong-un. Imagine what could have happened had the governments followed up with details on this camaraderie that had resulted.

In all the daily summaries of the proceedings, the CNO can focus on the more deeply-stated emotional aspects of the messages of both sides, going beyond what is stated verbally to the inner core of the culture which each side's values entail. If those emotional insights can be articulated by the CNO at various points in the discussions, then the opposing sides might develop a greater appreciation of the needs and aspirations of the respective cultures, which can help to focus on the desired outcomes of the proceedings.

Such deep insights into the respective cultures can be brought to bear at times of intense disagreements as the group approaches the details of resolution. The CNO can reach into their own deep understanding of the respective cultures to help the opposing side see that it is not necessarily a zero-sum game in which the gains of one side equal the losses of the other. Rather, a recognition of the need for cultural acceptance, based on the historical development of values, does not detract from the opposing side's success. There are important examples of this, such as the war with American Indians and the war with Vietnam that lasted almost 20 years. We'll deal with the Vietnam war shortly, but let's take a brief look at the lack of social recognition that took place with the American Indian society.

Think, for example, of the Native American Indians whose culture had much to offer the American settlers, yet whose culture was crushed by those early settlers. Over 150,000 children of the Indigenous Americans—roughly a third of all such children—were separated from their families, and forced into government-run schools, often Catholic based, and punished severely for speaking their native language in order to, as US cavalry Captain Richard Henry Pratt put it, "kill the Indian in him, and save the man."[3] This forced assimilation was characterized by the 1902 "haircut order" to force assimilation by destroying the young Indians' self-image and destroying their inner souls.

So, beyond the resolution of political differences between hostile factions, there is the need to recognize the cultures from which they have developed, sometimes over eons of history. That can contribute much to increasing the level of trust between former "enemies."

Some might argue that the national leaders should have the opportunity to discuss the developments of the negotiation process with their direct reports at their home governments, especially as the negotiation process begins to show signs of success. The purpose of this would be to reassess how far they have come from their original positions and to appraise the feedback they might receive upon their return. Such direct reports should be sworn to secrecy about the details but be able to give the negotiation participants a sense of how what they are offering the other side would be accepted in their own countries. This is a sensitive point, as it could potentially derail the hard-earned success of the participants if the feedback is too harsh.

Politics at home need to be taken into consideration, of course, and this is a challenge as well.

In this rather intense chapter, we've laid out the highly unconventional rules of negotiation for a form of communication that sounds incredibly challenging. Great effort and trust are required by both sides. But the payoff, including the opportunity to avoid accelerating conflict leading to warfare, possibly ending up with the ultimate deployment of nuclear arms, makes it all worthwhile. The author of this book is an expert in resolving matters of personal, social and organizational conflict. Now he brings his expertise together in order to "give peace a chance," as the iconic John Lennon put it. No greater success can be aspired to than to save nations from nuclear annihilation. There are increasing risks for that as more nations gear up with nuclear armaments, not only in Europe and the Far East but in the Mideast as well.[4] No other approach seems to get to the basics of international miscommunication as deeply as our proposition. De-escalating potential nuclear conflict (such as the historically classical Cuban missile crisis) is critical now more than ever. Third party mediation is essential, as occurred in the Israel/Hezbollah and Israel/Hamas ceasefires.

Many may see it as a naïve, pie-in-the-sky approach. If it really works, the cynics might point out, why isn't it used more often? How realistic can this approach be? Most national heads of state want more power, the cynics might add. Look at China. Even our own country struggles for more power to influence the rest of the world. Finally, how can you get autocrats to yield their status to compromise with democracies? All these are excellent questions.

There's no doubt that this radical approach can only work with those leaders who are honest in their approach and highly motivated with a basis of deep personal integrity. It is an intensely demanding, complex and arduous process.

There are also those who maintain that war and destruction are intrinsic aspects of human nature and have been present throughout human history. Along with disease and natural disasters, they offer a form of "population control." Whether or not that is the case, we can choose to control our present status regarding our current welfare. Why add to the destructive elements with nuclear disaster in our own time when we have the option of avoiding it by using a form of negotiation that has shown some success in the past?

The United Nations was formed to offer such opportunities for peaceful coexistence, but more is needed. The radical negotiation process offered in this chapter can be the first step in an accord followed by details to be worked out by committees over as much time as needed. This could be the first step in a very complex process.

Consider the alternative. When communications break down and defensive postures are assumed, only one impulsive decision, or even a technical error in the mechanism of aggressive nuclear striking capacity, especially if artificial intelligence is introduced, can lead to immensely regrettable outcomes.

The unconventional option of Track III or Radical Negotiations offered here in this chapter may turn out to be our saving grace.

Let's take a moment to explore the characteristics of this highly unconventional approach to saving our planet from utter nuclear destruction.

Is it different from what exists now?

Absolutely. There are many advocates of negotiations based on interpersonal trust involving the main characters sitting down and exploring their options. And some have been successful. But none of them demands the radical proposition of complete confidentiality, created in part by surrendering all electronic devices for days at a time. This surrender of a technology so dear to our hearts takes a commitment to the deepest levels of trust.

Does it solve an urgent need?

Again, absolutely. What could be more urgent than avoiding the explosion of the first nuclear attack, inevitably leading to retaliation and the possible destruction of civilization as we know it! In the fall of 2024, Putin declared that he was seriously considering using his nuclear arsenal. There is nothing more urgent. "It is proposed that aggression against Russia by any non-nuclear state [Ukraine]," Putin stated, "but with the participation or support of a nuclear state, will be considered as their joint attack on the Russian Federation."[5] Knowing when to initiate radical negotiations rather than back-channel diplomacy is definitely a challenge.

Is this approach easily understood?

For the third time, absolutely. The novel aspect of manifesting a commitment to trust by yielding personal phones and iPads for the duration of the negotiation process is simple enough to comprehend. Its manifestation, however, is revolutionary, bringing the "technology" of trust (or removal of the technology) to a much deeper level of mutual respect and trust than ever imagined in prior negotiation processes.

Most challenging, is it doable?

The first reaction of many might be: "How can you expect national leaders in conflict with one another to give in to this invasive form of negotiation? It's unheard of! It'll never take off." It's like the Wright brothers being told, before their historic first flight in 1903, "How on earth can you expect this seriously heavy wooden contraption to take off and fly through the air? It's sheer madness. You're just wasting everyone's time."

History tells us about that national leaders in conflict with others are not as confident of their position as they appear. Otherwise, why would autocrats like Hitler, Stalin, and Saddam Hussein have murdered so many who were opposed to their ideas? Some leaders, like Khrushchev and Gorbachev were sufficiently open to deal with American presidents to resolve critical issues between them.

The twenty-year-long Vietnam war was, after history revealed the truth, a dreadful mistake. The American paranoia about the spread of communism took over and the United States followed France's failed attempt at trying to dominate Vietnam. In the end, we are now very amicable with the government of that nation. It turns out, according to then Secretary of State, Robert McNamara, that the Vietnam war was a tragic error, as he described in his books, *In Retrospect: The Tragedy and Lessons of Vietnam* (1996) and *Argument without End: In Search of Answers to the Vietnam Tragedy* (1999). All this could have been avoided if there were opportunities for negotiations of deep trust that we are now considering. Presidents Kennedy, and then Johnson, might have negotiated with Ho Chi Minh, a gentle and highly educated man who would have been highly responsive to radical negotiation.

While Vladimir Putin may seem intractable and averse to negotiation, he is nonetheless the leader of one of the most powerful countries. Would he succumb to using nuclear warfare? Is he that mindless as to be unaware of the tragic consequences? Even such a murderous contender must also be aware of such outcomes. In a *New York Times* article, Putin is characterized as someone who poses to be more of a nuclear threat than he really is. "He does not consider himself irrational, but to make his threats credible, he has to rely on his adversaries' thinking that he might be a bit crazy."[6]

So, this radical form of international negotiation is definitely novel, urgently needed, easily understood, and, above all, doable. All it would take is the courageous initiative to propose it to the parties in conflict at the right time.

At the end of the day, there are certain criteria to be met: The national leaders involved must be sufficiently intelligent to understand the complexities of the framework at hand. It must be clear whether the negotiation process is geared towards dealing with an unfolding crisis or with long-term issues. Most important, although there is an aspiration that trust can be built during this intensive negotiation process, it would be naïve to expect that to be the norm. So, the maxims of "Trust but verify" (attributed to Ronald Reagan) and "Good fences make good neighbors" need to be part of the process.

"War may sometimes be a necessary evil," said Jimmy Carter to the Nobel Committee while accepting his Peace Prize. "But no matter how necessary, it is always an evil, never a good. We will not learn how to live together in peace by killing each other's children. The bond of our common humanity is stronger than the divisiveness of our fears and prejudices ... We can choose to work together for peace ... and we must."[7]

27

Trump: Authentic, Confident and Fearless

"Faced with crisis, the man of character falls back
on himself. He imposes his own stamp of action,
takes responsibility for it, makes it his own."
—CHARLES DE GAULLE

Now that you've read this book, I will share with you that I certainly am not a dyed-in-the-wool liberal or conservative; I'm more of a unifier of opposites.

Our political culture has proven itself a 50/50 proposition when you look at so many of our elections that have come close to that split. Neither side is good nor bad, but rather different. Just prior to the 2024 elections, Donald Trump and Kamala Harris were polled at 47 percent each. But Trump prevailed and now we are deeply into a moderately extreme right-wing administration.

The question remains, where will we travel from here? The issues remain what they always were: economics, human welfare, the integrity of institutions. And how do we change existing patterns?

Before saying goodbye, let's take a bit of an overview, a map to give you some idea of where we've traveled together. Perhaps more than ever before, the issue of trust has become quite challenging, both at the political level as well as the societal level. Can we trust one another, our institutions, our politicians? The issue of fake news is a prominent example of mistrust of mainstream media. Now, in the third decade of the twenty-first century, the crisis of trust has become a dominant topic. Distrust is rampant.

A major cause of this is the social climate in which we live. The current political divide has propagated issues of mistrust, promoted bigotry, and claimed that the media are biased and untrustworthy.

The internet, now a major source of information to almost everyone, at times provides unconfirmed information, half-truths, and outright lies that further create a reason for mistrust. It's no wonder so many of us live in a quandary as to what and whom to trust.

E Pluribus, Duo—Dextra et Sinistra

The United States of America has struggled valiantly and successfully to foster its experiment in democracy from the time of its birth. There have been conflicts over the generations, but the institution has persevered, its lowest point coming during the Civil War or, as the South has known it, the War Between the States. At other times, differences of opinion have been tolerated, and even celebrated, as in no other country. The nation's motto, *E pluribus unum*, out of many, one, could be understood to mean this: Out of many opinions, we remain a unified country under a single banner. A more current motto might be, *E pluribus, duo—dextra et sinistra*: Out of many, two—Right and Left.

The Battle for Trust in the Murdoch Empire

Think about it: Why did Fox News not bother airing the January 6 committee hearings with their in-depth findings? In fact, Fox News paid no attention. And those who followed Fox News were unlikely to view the committee's findings.

"Fair and Balanced News" was Fox TV's motto. Then, following the 2020 election, it began using the slogan, "Standing Up for What's Right," with the conservative double entendre staring us right in the face.

Here is the backstory to all this. Rupert Murdoch, former head of Fox News, the *Wall Street Journal,* and the *New York Post,* was certainly in favor of advocating the policies of President Trump and his right-wing followers. But, within Rupert's family, there was an emerging struggle, a battle for trust all its own. One of his sons, Lachlan, was strongly supportive of this company policy. His other son, James, with a greater moral and ethical sensibility, was hoping for change along those lines. For example, when popular commentator Bill O'Reilly was accused of sexual harassment in 2017, Lachlan wanted to delay any decision, lest the company look bad, while James was eager to fire him not only as quickly as possible but loudly as well. When 20th Century Fox studio was up for sale to Disney in 2020, James was all for it, but Lachlan, attracted to the Hollywood glamour of that part of the family business, was against the sale.

In the end, it seemed that Lachlan was the victor. In the summer of 2024, Rupert began legal moves to convert the irrevocable trust in Nevada from being willed to the four children equally, giving no one undue influence over the others, to give Lachlan ultimate control. Rupert's rationale was that the trust would benefit financially with Lachlan's hands on the steering wheel of News Corp. and Fox Corp. and that the other siblings would benefit from this "decanting" of the trust, as it's referred to in legalese, a process only allowable in the State of Nevada.

When the January 6 insurrection took place in 2021, Rupert Murdoch was suffering an existential crisis. He couldn't quite go along with the violence portrayed in the media, yet he couldn't suddenly throw his political "buddy," Trump, under the bus either. This $17.3 billion company had more influence on dividing the country than any other entity, by far. He eventually resolved his crisis by stating, in the *New York Post*, that Trump was "unworthy to be the country's chief executive again," and stopped televising Trump's rallies. And when Trump announced that he was running for the 2024 presidency soon after the midterm elections, the *New York Post* virtually ignored it, only reporting on that political news item on page 26, referring to Trump in a headline as "Florida man."

But there was more trouble for Murdoch. In the early spring of 2023, when it was discovered, during the $1.6 billion legal battle between Dominion Voting Systems and Fox News that key figures at Fox were broadcasting facts that they knew to be falsehoods, and this was verified by texts made public, Murdoch was highly embarrassed. After all, when questioned by the court, he had to admit to being accountable for his employees' actions, according to the plaintiffs: "Even if some of Fox's hosts' statements could qualify as 'opinions,' they are still actionable if—as here—they are based on false and undisclosed facts."[1]

HELP! We're Totally Polarized

But the damage had already been done. And we citizens had been suffering the dramatically divisive effects of the battle for trust for years. What could the American electorate say at this point, having been so greatly influenced into what many feared might result in a new, modern civil war between tribal factions? They might say: "HELP! We're being polarized."

How can we overcome this strong sense of division into two versions of trust that affect our thinking so powerfully that we fear being open about our political opinions when meeting someone new? That is the first thing many of us think about when deciding to be open about our lifestyles and political values. And if we dare venture out with open discussion with that new friend, how do we validate our own way of thinking so that we can communicate it clearly and without fear or rancor in this battle for trust? Relationships are built on trust, but it seems like that's been lost somewhere along the way.

About one-third of all Americans have mixed or moderate views and are not fully represented by either political party, nor do they get as much airtime as the extremes. The other two-thirds end up on one side or the other. The power of tribalization and its evil consequence of setting up conflict in the system of political election cannot be overlooked—all this within the context of growing polarization, at times resulting in the murder of innocent people.

The Consequences of Polarization

One polarizing dynamic leans on the Great Replacement Theory, a conspiracy theory that non-Whites are intent on replacing Whites as the dominant demographic. This idea is responsible for a number of "lone wolf" attacks, such as the murder of eleven worshippers at a Pittsburgh synagogue in 2018; the murder of twenty-three individuals at an El Paso Walmart the following year by another White man, claiming that he was defending his territory against "the Hispanic invasion of Texas"; and then on May 14, 2022, the murder of ten individuals by Payton Gendron at a grocery store in the predominantly Black east side of Buffalo, New York.

After carefully planning his attack for months, eighteen-year-old Gendron, wearing body armor and a helmet fitted with a live-streaming camera, fatally guns down ten citizens of color with his recently purchased Bushmaster XM-15 assault weapon while they innocently shop for their groceries. Was he influenced or radicalized by disinformation on social media by the battle for trust on such outlets as Fox News, Newsmax, and One America News?

Payton had written a 110-page manifesto, proclaiming his racist and anti-Semitic values quite openly, sharing his fear of White replacement. Payton was not a "lone wolf" killer—nor were the perpetrators of the evil acts mentioned here. Rather, they were part of a growing and emerging community of believers in propaganda broadcasts via social media and even supported by mainstream media outlets like Fox News commentators such as Tucker Carlson. The radicalization of Payton Gendron took place in programs openly broadcast to the public at large, not hidden in underground channels such as Reddit and others.

In his manifesto, Gendron mentioned leftist elites and "globalist" Jews who were fostering dark-skinned foreigners to "invade our lands" and "attack and replace our people." (Fortunately, Gendron was tried in a court of law after pleading guilty and sentenced to life without parole by Judge Susan Eagan.)

As an antidote, many viewers tuned in to CNN and MSNBC to hear liberal progressive pundits and their guests talk about how the Great Replacement Theory was influencing the disaffected. Were those viewers being polarized in the battle for trust? Then those same networks aired all the news releases by the January 6 Select Committee while Fox News chose, instead, to air a show with Tucker Carlson (without commercials lest the viewers turn the dial). Were his viewers, in turn, being polarized as well?

The People vs. The Elites

An in-depth survey of 1,500 Americans by the Southern Poverty Law Center revealed that a large majority of Republicans, "67 percent believe the country's demographic changes are being orchestrated by 'liberal leaders actively trying to leverage political power by replacing more conservative white voters.'"[2]

In a study involving 1.6 million tweets sent by every member of Congress between 2016 and 2020, and the links shared to 160,000 articles, the head of the Department of Cognitive Psychology of the University of Bristol in England, Stephan Lewandowsky, found a process he calls participatory propaganda, in which populist demagogues split the political world into two types: "labeling lies and corruption traits of 'The Elites,' and truth and fairness traits of 'The People,' so 'their lies become a signal of authenticity' to the public and accepting the lies becomes a 'signifier of tribal identity.'"[3]

This research on the battle for trust went on to reveal two types of tweets used by both parties: truth-speaking, which involved words like *evidence* and *facts*, and belief-speaking which involved words like *common sense* and *opinion*.

Based on the extensive research on this topic, the social scientists' conclusion was that the "proportion of untrustworthy information posted by Republicans versus Democrats is diverging at an accelerating rate, and this divergence has worsened since President Biden was elected."[4] The battle for trust was becoming wider and deeper over time.

This may have had a lot to do with Trump setting an example of, or model for, consistently pushing his own versions of reality, but aside from Trump's charismatic personality, there may be other factors contributing to the polarization process:

- Our collective inability to navigate social media elegantly with a critical eye—not only us as individuals, but also corporations, special-interest groups, and especially politicians, for example, some political ads prior to elections,
- An irrefutable trend, across the planet, toward nationalistic populism, chauvinism, and bigotry, leading to identity politics, and, finally,
- The lack of privacy laws, allowing so many of us to become targets for exploitation at various levels of social media.

These three factors often lead to personal attacks that make us feel defensive and fearful of, or angry at, the other side. Why? Because of the increasing conflict in politics in general, the sense of loss in democratic principles, and the vulnerability when our privacy is in question.

The Ongoing Battle for Trust

There are two primary ways of being in the world of the battle for trust. One is characterized by reaching out generously to help and support those around us, especially when they seem vulnerable or in need. The other is to dominate with a sense of power even when that involves a defensive, even aggressive approach in the face of challenge to what we hold valuable.

This may be a highly oversimplified view, you may counter, and you'd be right since most of us can relate to either type as life circumstances change. But it does help to understand more clearly the concept of the battle for trust. Along these lines, it also may help to see the reality of our current political dilemma with one faction of Republicans appearing somewhat outspoken and aggressive while Democrats are sometimes criticized for being too gentle in their politics and too generous with public funds, as their respective "primary ways of being."

Some are more prone to being polarized than others. Such individuals may be more easily influenced by social media that tend to foster a growing audience by creating emotional drama, which becomes self-reinforcing. Social media algorithms are constructed to deliver material that mirrors our frustrations and impulses, thereby creating an emotional addiction that keeps us coming back and validating our darker nature. The most glaring examples of that are X and Tik-Tok—"getting affirmation rather than information," as journalist Katie Couric put it so well.

Such polarization processes can result in dire consequences, but there are many that are much more subtle and affect the public at large—you and me—without our full awareness, affecting our political leanings and, eventually, our voting choices.

The battle for trust involves the misplacement of belief in untrustworthy individuals, or entities such as social media, which can use our own information against us, "engagement for profit," as Tristan Harris puts it.[5] "There's so much active misinformation," declared Barack Obama publicly on TV, "and it's packaged so well."

Trump: Authentic, Confident, and Fearless

How can we account for the unique winning power of Donald J. Trump?

Some say that he is more cunning than he appears on the surface, while others marvel at his power to win over so many of the electorate. Those politicians who favored him tended to win at the voting booth; those against him tended to lose, at least until the "anti-Trump revolution" of the 2022 midterm elections. It appeared that many Americans had had their fill of him, some referring to his losing streak as the Trump Factor during the midterms. But then, despite numerous legal challenges coming his way Trump was still running ahead of all others in the run for the Republican nominations as late as the winter of 2024, and then winning the election by what was thought to be a landslide, even the popular vote.

More than that of any other national figure in modern history (except for Joe McCarthy, the senator from Wisconsin who attacked anyone who had any dealings with leftist organizations in the 1950s),

Trump's personality has done more to polarize this nation. What can account for this powerful and persistent influence? Perhaps it's the sense of authenticity in his delivery. He really appears to believe, deep in his soul, that what he says is the unvarnished truth. That sense of conviction is more powerful than the best-thought-out ideas of his opponents, in either party.

Others feel strongly that Trump knows what he is saying is over-simplified, but he also knows what the crowd wants to hear, so he does this on purpose. They also feel that most of the crowd knows the simplified version, but they also accommodate Trump to feel that they're part of the "moral" battle—they enjoy fighting dirty, getting their hands earthy to aid the cause.

His occasional overbearing, and sometimes abrasive manner, according to his opponents, makes him unattractive to many on the Left, but his confident, assertive approach appeals to his followers. To the right wing, he comes across saying, "I'm the only one who can help you. Trust me and you'll be a winner. I'm a winner and I can handle anything better than anyone else." What a contrast to someone like former President Biden who seemed to come across as saying, "I'll try my best to fix the nation's problems. But I'm just human and here's what can go wrong."

Kamala Harris might have been humbler and more thoughtful, but the more buoyantly confident approach often seemed to win the day in terms of popular appeal (for example, with Teddy Roosevelt, or his distant cousin, FDR). A soft-spoken Harris might offer more vulnerability while someone like Trump, though not always accurate, offers a strong sense of conviction and self-assurance—what many of us look for in a leader, at least on the surface.

When the 2022 midterm elections were over, it seemed as if Trump had fallen from grace. One story from Greek mythology illustrates what may have happened to Trump. According to legend, Icarus, attempting to escape the tower in which King Minos had imprisoned him, had wings made for him by his father so he could fly off to freedom. Since these wings were made of feathers, threads, and wax, Icarus's father warned him against too much pride and overconfidence by flying too close to the sun, which might melt the wax, destroying the wings.

And that's exactly what happened. Just like Icarus, Trump showed too much overconfidence, in his case by backing so many election deniers for the midterm elections, and he fell from grace (along with some of his notable favorites, like Adam Laxalt and Kari Lake), rejected by the voters for his hubris. The exit polls revealed, according to CNN reporter Harry Enten, that "more voters said the Republican candidates' views were too extreme."[6]

Despite all this, Trump, at the age of seventy-seven, decided to declare his run for the 2024 presidency. Was he in part motivated to protect himself from the three legal issues he was facing? With all these issues confronting him, he was losing the support of many former supporters, including Rupert Murdoch, who was now showing preference for Florida Governor Ron DeSantis, referring to him as Ron DeFuture on the cover of the November 9, 2022, issue of the *New York Post*.[7]

The Battle for Logic and Facts vs. Emotional Validity

What Nixon referred to as the Silent Majority has now become the Vocal Majority. And this group has been claiming the power it never had before Trump, with a vengeance, perhaps justifying the title, becoming more vocal.

Given these new proportions, the emerging Vocal Majority far outnumber the old political elite. And their version of "the truth," politically speaking, is more emotional than intellectually based, easier to accept at a primal level, without analysis, without data crunching, without ruminating about ethics and morality. It is an easy fix for those who have suffered the political impotence of the "working class" for, lo, these many decades. The national divide between the intellectual elite—the Kennedys, the Bushes, the Clintons, on the one hand, and the populist Trumpers on the other—has given way to this mass polarization. How do we understand this battle of trust between the rational and emotional versions of political truth?

How do we best make sense of the immensely divisive dynamics of polarization? Well, the MAGA crowd has a credible argument to make. The goal of free trade allowed for more labor to be transported overseas, reducing the need for blue-collar workers. More immigration led to fewer jobs, menial as they may be, for American workers. More "woke" values in the entertainment industry made conservatives feel estranged. Decreased segregation and increased feminist progress threatened conservative patriarchal and religious values.

Clear thinking is always necessary in matters of new information, especially in affairs of political trust, no matter what the medium. Awareness is paramount for distinguishing between rational and emotional validity.

Rational validity has to do with critical thinking, involving logic and facts based on evidence. Emotional validity is based on desire, appetite, and fulfillment. Both are important. Both have their place, but they are not interchangeable. Ultimate trust is based on a finely integrated balance between the two.

The battle for trust has resulted in a breakdown of truth that cannot easily be fixed, leaving the Republicans rallying round the banner of success in terms of the damage they've done.[8] And the battle is not over, despite the surprising success of the midterm elections for the Democrats in the Senate in 2022.

And then there is the Chatbot Revolution,[9] where trust finds its ultimate challenge. Here is a new technology that can serve good as well as evil masters. What about its service to politicians vying for our votes, scams vying for our dollars, cyber warriors vying for our belief systems?

"I think we wind up very fast in a world where we just don't know what to trust anymore," says Gary Marcus, AI research scientist. "I think that's already been a problem for society over the last, let's say, decade. And I think it's just going to get worse and worse."[10]

Then there's the ultimate trust issue: How far can we trust the growing power of AI technology such as ChatGPT?

Imagine, for example, that Hamas had the latest version of GPT-4 and asked it how to destroy all Israelis. That would be a simple task for

GPT-4. Now, imagine another greater power, like Putin's Russia, asking a similar question about the US. Again, you or I could even come up with the answer, even without GPT-4, involving destroying their grid and poisoning all water sources. Look what Israel did to the Gaza Strip in terms of withholding resources. ChatGPT would have ways of doing these things much more effectively and efficiently.

Yes, we are challenged. The Chinese military is working frantically on being the first to get the most powerful superintelligence—artificial general intelligence, and so are we and our military, and very likely Russia, Israel, India, and others. Whoever gets there first may master the technology over everyone else.

And GPT-4, along with DeepSeek, mirrors our society's values, which are conquer and master other cultures, as we did to the Native Americans. All we earthlings know is conflict.

How is it that so many Silicon Valley types, who are among the most intelligent, don't realize something that is so obvious? Are we destined to be subjugated by this new technological marvel?

Finally, I shared with you a brand-new recommendation for avoiding nuclear devastation using an approach to international negotiations, employing trust instead of defensive rigidity, for which I offer the term *radical negotiation* or, more technically, Track III Diplomacy, used successfully by President Jimmy Carter in achieving the Camp David Peace Accords.

Unlocking the secrets of those on the other side, in our politically polarized culture, helps us to comprehend their values and how to communicate with them to reach a better understanding of how they see their world. We spent time exploring alternative realities based on emotional gullibility and what Stephen Hawking called "belief-dependent realism."[11]

The us versus them mentality is dangerous enough for the US and China to plan on international talks on limiting the possibility of nuclear warfare "sometime in the near future." For now, there are the meetings sponsored by the Carnegie Endowment for International Peace. In April 2025, Carnegie held its meeting in Washington, DC and was moderated by Senior Fellow George Perkovich. The provocative title of the meeting was Full of Sound and Fury, Signifying … What Exactly?: Russian Nuclear Noise in the Ukraine War. The question remained: Was Russia demonstrating genuine threats or "nuclear manipulation"? Time is of the essence[12] especially with the last major Strategic Arms Reduction Treaty between Russa and the US about to expire in February 2026.[13]

As Presidents Reagan and Gorbachev jointly stated at a summit meeting in Geneva in 1985, "A nuclear war cannot be won and must never be fought."[14]

Our focus was the long story of trust and the dynamics of its polarization, its history through the ages, how easily our trust can be tyrannized by untrustworthy sources, and how it affects us at home as well as in the political and social realms. So how do we find the confidence to trust one another and our society at large?

This confidence rises from within the deepest and often unknowable regions of the body and mind—one might even venture to say the soul—so deep is the abyss of vulnerability that must be crossed. The resolution to trust may be an intuitive release from within rather than an active, logical choice. Like a visceral wellspring, it escapes the limits of reason and wells up with an unanticipated sense of safety, hopeful that the trusted party will not disappoint.

When trust is present and reliable, all things are possible. Without it, dishonesty, dysfunction, and the potential for destruction prevail.

You are now more knowledgeable about these matters and therefore more able to find the dignity of truth in the travesties inherent in the Age of Mistrust. With the knowledge gleaned from this book, our trust can prevail. Onward!

Acknowledgments

I am very grateful to those who have supported me through the process of research, writing, and eventual publication of this book.

First and foremost, to my agent, Kimberley Cameron, who has been the solid rock in the ocean of give-and-take with editors and publishers as we searched for the right home. Equally appreciated is my editor, Sandra Wendel, who improved each chapter magically by making exactly the right recommendations. Then to my colleague, Dr. Gary Botstein, of many high-level talents who was extremely helpful with his fine-tuning and formulation of context.

To all the others who have been so helpful (in alphabetical order):

Wellness coach Martin Becker gave so generously of his time to read some chapters and offer his personal opinions.

Peter Bowerman, author of *The Well-Fed Writer*, and expert on book titles, helped slog through a number of possible titles while we kept one another well fed.

Susan Clymer read much of the material and offered her opinion on what worked and what didn't.

Dr. Janet Colvin, Dean at Utah Valley University, read through each and every chapter to make sure that difficult passages were cleared up.

Dr. Phil Lander, a high school buddy, read through chapters and gave me his undiluted and frank opinions of changes that needed to be made.

Dr. Linda Logdberg, an astute researcher who knows the ways words can make difference.

Goran Matkovic discussed with me his thoughts on almost a daily basis on the subject matter of the book, particularly when it came to the topic of chatbots and AI.

Educational consultant Dr. Steve Preston was incredibly patient in walking me through those passages that needed particularly detailed attention regarding politically historical facts.

Michael Sokolov was kind enough to share his thoughts on the challenges of AI.

Educational administrator Maria Taro helped immensely in formatting the reference section.

Carol and Leslie Toole were kind enough to share their editorial opinions when invited.

Thanks to my fellow speakers at the National Speakers Association for their ongoing support by reading and commenting on the original manuscript, especially Jim Cathcart, former president of NSA.

Notes

Notes for Introduction

1. Denworth, L. Synchronized minds. *Scientific American,* 329(1), July/Aug. 2023, 53.

Notes for Chapter 1

1. Wintour, P. UN says Russian forces have tortured and executed civilians in Ukraine. *Guardian,* online, June 27, 2023.

Notes for Chapter 2

1. Mok, A. What Elon Musk, Bill Gates, and 12 other business leaders think about AI tools like ChatGPT. *Business Insider,* online, Feb. 26, 2023.
2. Tufekci, Z. What would Plato say about ChatGPT? *New York Times,* online, Dec. 15, 2022.
3. Chen, B. X. A.I. bots can't report this column. But they can improve it. *New York Times,* online, Feb. 1, 2023.
4. Klein, E. The imminent danger of A.I. is one we're not talking about. *New York Times, Opinion,* online, Feb. 26, 2023.
5. Thompson, S. A. et al. Conservatives aim to build a chatbot of their own. *New York Times,* online, March 22, 2023.
6. Klein, E. This changes everything. *New York Times, Opinion,* online, March 12, 2023.
7. Bengio, Y. et al. Pause giant AI experiments: An open letter. *Future of Life Institute,* online, March 22, 2023.
8. Metz, C. and Schmidt, G. Elon Musk and others call for pause on A.I., citing 'profound risks to society.' *New York Times,* online, March 29, 2023.
9. Metz, C. Riding out quarantine with a chatbot friend. *New York Times,* online, June 16, 2020.

10. Eloundou, T. et al. GPTs are GPTs. *ArXiv*, online, March 17, 2023.

11. Tang, J. et al. Semantic reconstruction of continuous language from non-invasive brain recordings. *Nature Neuroscience*, online, May 1, 2023.

12. Belluck, P. A stroke stole her ability to speak at 30. A.I is helping to restore it years later. *New York Times*, online, Aug. 23, 2023.

13. Moses, D. A. et al. Neuroprosthesis for decoding speech in a paralyzed person with anarthria. *New England Journal of Medicine*, online, July 14, 2021.

14. Rossi, F. et al. Working together on the future of AI. Announcement by all presidents of the Association for the Advancement of Artificial Intelligence, online, April 5, 2023.

15. Marcus, G. interviewed in Ezra Klein interviews Gary Marcus. *The Ezra Klein Show*, Jan. 6, 2023.

16. Lajka, A. New AI voice-cloning tools 'add fuel' to misinformation fire. *Associated Press*, online, Feb. 10, 2023.

17. Lajka, A. and O'Brien, M. AI tools can create new images, but who is the real artist? *Associated Press*, online, Jan. 19, 2023.

18. Ludes, J. Quoted in Anderson, M. Twitter, Facebook ban fake users; some had AI-created photos. *Associated Press*, online, Dec. 20, 2019.

19. Feldstein, S. *The Rise of Digital Repression*. Oxford University Press, 2021.

20. Mancini, J. IBM plans to replace nearly 1,000 jobs with AI—these jobs are first to go. *Yahoo!Finance*, online, May 5, 2023.

21. Singh-Kurtz, S. The man of your dreams. *The Cut*, online, March 10, 2023.

22. Hinton, G. et al. Statement on AI risk. *Center for AI Safety*, online, May 2023.

23. Roose, K. A.I. poses 'risk of extinction,' industry leaders warn. *New York Times*, online, May 30, 2023.

24. Altman, S. et al. Governance of superintelligence. *OpenAI*, online, May 22, 2023.

25. Gates, B. The risks of AI are real but manageable. *GatesNotes*, online, July 11, 2023.

26. Shevlane, T. et al. Model evaluation for extreme risks. *DeepMind*, online, May 25, 2023.

27. Rajani, N. et al. Red-teaming large language models. *Hugging Face*, online, Feb. 24, 2023.

28. Harris, T. On *Real Time with Bill Maher*. HBO, Oct. 13, 2023.

29. Falk, W. Editor's Letter. *The Week*, 23(1156), Nov. 10, 2023, 3.

30. Butlin, P. et al. Consciousness in Artificial Intelligence: Insights from the science of consciousness. *arXiv*, online, Aug. 22, 2023.

31. Roivainen, E. AI's IQ. *Scientific American, Forum*, 329(1), July/Aug. 2023, 7.

32. Metz, C. A.I. is becoming more conversational. But will it get more honest? *New York Times*, online, Jan. 10, 2023.

33. Friedman, T. Israel is about to make a terrible mistake. *New York Times*, online, Oct. 19, 2023.

34. Howley, D. Generative AI will create a 'tsunami of disinformation' during the 2024 election. *Yahoo!Finance*, online, Nov. 15, 2023.

35. Nicas, J. and Herrera, L. C. Is Argentina the first A.I. election? *New York Times*, online, Nov. 15, 2023.

36. Zhuang, Y. Imran Khan's victory speech from jail shows A.I.'s peril and promise. *New York Times*, online, Feb. 11, 2024.

37. Bunn, C. What AI-generated images of Trump surrounded by Black voters mean for this election. *NBC News*, online, March 8, 2024.

38. Sherman, A. and Sigalos, M. Generative AI dominates Davos discussions as companies focus on accuracy. *NBC News*, online, Jan. 17, 2024.

39. Metz, C. OpenAI unveils new ChatGPT that listens, looks and talks. *New York Times*, online, May 13, 2024.

40. Roose, K. How helpful is Operator, OpenAI's new A.I. agent? *New York Times*, online, Feb. 1, 2025.

Notes for Chapter 3

1. Dolensek, N. et al. Facial expressions of emotion states and their neuronal correlates in mice. *Science*, 368(6486), 2020, 89–94.

2. Burgdorf, J. S., Brudzynski, S. M. and Moskal, J. R. Using rat ultrasonic vocalization to study the neurobiology of emotion. *Current Opinion in Neurobiology*, 60, 2020, 192–200.

3. Serpell, J. et al. Current challenges to research on animal-assisted interventions. *Applied Developmental Science*, 21(3), 2017, 223–233.

4. Darwin, C. *On the Origin of Species by Means of Natural Selection*. NY: Harcourt Brace, 1859.

5. *Merriam-Webster's Dictionary*. Merriam-Webster, 2019.

6. Aguado, L. et al. Effects of affective and emotional congruency on facial expression processing under different task demands. *Acta Psychologica*, 187, 2018, 66–76.

7. Mehrabian, A. *Silent Messages*. Wadsworth, 1980.

8. Plutchik, R. *Emotion*. Harper & Row, 1980.

9. Tomkins, S. S. *Affect, Imagery, Consciousness*. Springer, 1962.

10. Ekman, P. What scientists who study emotion agree about. *Perspectives on Psychological Science*, 11(1), 2016, 31–34.

11. Ekman, P. Expression and the nature of emotion. In K. Scherer and P. Ekman (Eds.), *Approaches to Emotion* (pp. 319–344). Lawrence Erlbaum, 1984.

12. Johnson-Laird, P. N. and Oatley, K. Basic emotions, rationality, and folk theory. *Cognition and Emotion*, 6, 1992, 201–223.

Notes for Chapter 4

1. Rogers, C. R. *Client-centered Therapy*. Houghton Mifflin, 1951, p. 29.

2. Rogers, C. R. *A Way of Being*. Houghton Mifflin, 1980, p. 29 and p. 152.

3. Jourard, S. M. *The Transparent Self*. Van Nostrand, 1964.

4. Maslow, A. H. *Toward a Psychology of Being*. Van Nostrand, 1962.

5. May, R. *Existential Psychology*. Random House, 1961.

6. May, R. *Love and Will*. W. W. Norton, 1969.

7. May, R. *The Meaning of Anxiety*. W. W. Norton, 2015.

8. Reik, T. *Listening with the Third Ear*. Farrar & Straus, 1948.

9. Panksepp, J. *Affective Neuroscience*. Oxford University Press, 1998.

10. Panksepp, J. Affective neuroscience of the emotional BrainMind. *Dialogues in Clinical Neuroscience*, 12(4), 2010, 533–545.

11. Davis, K. L. and Panksepp, J. *The emotional foundations of personality: A neurobiological and evolutionary approach*. W. W. Norton & Co., 2018.

12. Marsalis, W. Episode 6: Swing. In K. Burns, *Jazz* [Film], Florentine Films, 2001.

13. Loehr, J. D. and Palmer, C. Temporal coordination between performing musicians. *Quarterly Journal of Experimental Psychology*, 64(11), 2153–2167, 2011, p. 2154.

14. Carter, J. E. *Keeping Faith*. Bantam, 1983.

15. Motschnig-Pitrik, R. and Barrett-Lennard, G. Co-actualization: A new construct in understanding well-functioning relationships. *Journal of Humanistic Psychology*, 50(3), 374–398, 2010, p. 386.

16. Marsalis, W. Interviewed on *Real Time with Bill Maher*. HBO, Aug. 28, 2020.

17. Bekoff, M. Animal emotions and animal sentience and why they matter. In Turner, J. and D'Silva, J. (Eds.) *Animals Ethics and Trade*. Routledge, 2006, pp. 27–40.

Notes for Chapters 5

1. Logan, R. K. *The Alphabet Effect.* Morrow, 1986.
2. Progovac, L. *A Critical Introduction to Language Evolution.* Springer. 2019.
3. Harari, Y. N. *Sapiens.* HarperCollins, 2015.
4. Puchner, M. *The Written World.* Random House, 2017.
5. HistoryofInformation.com
6. https://houseoftruth.education/en/library/sacred-writings/egyptian-book-of-the-dead-42-negative-confessions
7. https://factsanddetails.com/world/cat55/sub389/entry-5709.html
8. Langbein, J. H., Lerner, R. L., and Smith, B. P. *History of the Common Law: The Development of Anglo-American Legal Institutions.* Aspen Publishers, 2nd ed., 2009.
9. Battles, M. *Palimpsest: A History of the Written Word.* W. W. Norton, 2015.

Notes for Chapter 7

1. Hadas, M. *A History of Latin Literature.* Columbia University Press, 1952, pp. 98-100.
2. *Konrad Zuse Internet Archive.* http://zuse.zib.de/z4
3. Bisharah, J. The era of quantum computing is here. *Quantamagazine,* online, Jan. 24, 2018.
4. Steinberg, S. H. *Five Hundred Years of Printing.* Oak Knoll Press, 2001.
5. Marantz, A. The more things change. *The New Yorker, XCV* (29), Sept. 30, 2019, p. 70.
6. McLuhan, H. M. *The Gutenberg Galaxy.* University of Toronto Press, 2011, pp. 153 and 192.
7. Innis, H. A. *The Bias of Communication.* University of Toronto Press, 2008, p. 30.
8. Sarton, G. *Six Wings.* Indiana University Press, 1957.
9. Carothers, J. C. Culture, psychiatry, and the written word. *Psychiatry,* Nov. 22, 1959, 307–320, pp. 130–131.

Notes for Chapters 8

1. Hodgson, G. M. What are institutions? *Journal of Economic Issues,* 40(1), p. 1–25, 2006.
2. Munster, S. *Della Cosmografia.* University of Basel. Vortecpan, 1558. http://www.columbia.edu/itc/mealac/pritchett/00generallinks/munster/munster.html.

3. Sahut, G. and Tricot, A. Wikipedia: An opportunity to rethink the links between sources' credibility, trust, and authority. *FirstMonday.org*, online, 2017.

4. Sasaki, Y. Publishing nations: Technology acquisition and language standardization for European ethnic groups. Journal of Economic History, 77(4), 1007–1047, 2017.

5. Powell, A. How to build a nation. *Harvard Gazette*, online, Dec. 10, 2012.

6. McLuhan, M. *The Gutenberg Galaxy: The Making of Typographic Man.* University of Toronto Press, 1962.

7. Romano, A. Conspiracy theories, explained. *Vox*, online, November 18, 2020.

8. Miller, Z., Colvin, J. and Seitz, A. Trump praises QAnon conspiracists, appreciates support. *Associated Press*, online, August 19, 2020.

9. Aston, M. *Lollards and Reformers.* Hambledon Press, 1984.

10. Karasapan, O. Social networks and cell phones in the aftermath of the Arab revolutions. *Blogs.worldbank.org*, February 8, 2013.

11. Roos, D. 7 ways the printing press changed the world. *History*, online, Aug. 28, 2019.

12. Ames, T. 6 key changes during the reign of Henry VIII. *HistoryHit*, online, Jan. 11, 2021.

13. Nwanazia, C. Calvinism in the Netherlands: Why are the Dutch so Calvinist in nature? *Dutch Review*, online, March 1, 2021.

14. McLuhan, M. *The Gutenberg Galaxy: The Making of Typographic Man.* University of Toronto Press, 1962.

15. Marino, H. Educational advancement through the printing press. http://web.colby.edu. 2020.

16. Andrews, J. Letter from John Andrews to William Barrell, 6 May, 1775. Massachusetts Historical Society, online, Library Catalog Portal 1791, 1775.

17. Sherman, F. Benefits of the printing press on education, *Bizfluent*, online, Aug. 5, 2019.

18. Alexander, A. P. and Trakhman, L. M. S. The enduring power of print for learning in a digital world. *Conversation*, online, Oct. 3, 2017.

19. Philp, T. Scientific method helps get to the truth. *Expositor*, online, November 29, 2018.

Notes for Chapter 9

1. Shlain, L. *The Alphabet Versus the Goddess*. Viking/Penguin, 1999, p. 1.
2. Levi-Strauss. C. *The Savage Mind*. University of Chicago Press, 1966.
3. Shlain, L. *The Alphabet Versus the Goddess*. Viking/Penguin, 1999, p. 1.
4. Henrich, J. *The Weirdest People in the World*. Farrar, Straus & Giroux, 2020.
5. Friedman, T. L. *Hot, Flat, and Crowded*. Picador, 2006.
6. Shelley, M. W. *Frankenstein*. London: Colburn & Bentley,1831.
7. Verne, J. *Twenty Thousand Leagues Under the Sea*. Seawolf. 1873/2018.
8. Clarke, A. C. *2001*. New American Library, 1968.
9. Gould, C. *Dick Tracy*. *Chicago Tribune*-New York News Syndicate, 1931.
10. Meadows, D. H. et al. *Limits to Growth*. Chelsea Green, i. 2004.
11. Erlich, P. *The Population Bomb*. Sierra/Balantine, 1968.
12. Medieval education and the role of the Church. https://www.encyclopedia.com/humanities/culture-magazines/medieval-education-and-role-church. (n.d.).
13. Public trust in government: 1958-2021. *Pew Research*, online, May 17, 2021.
14. Harvey, C. Climate change—and research—raced forward as Trump turned his back. *Scientific American*, online, November 3, 2020.
15. Kelly, W. C. *Pogo*. Simon & Schuster, 1972.

Notes for Chapter 10

1. Bonner, T. Here's how the American family has changed in the past 50 years. *PennLive, Patriot News*, online, June 15, 2018.
2. Scartascini, C. Testing the impact of social media on trust. *Ideas Matter*, online, October 6, 2021.
3. Yetto, N. QWERTY: Type casting. *Smithsonian*, Sept./Oct. 2023, 34.
4. Appel, G., Grewal, L., Hadi, R. and Stephen, A.T. The future of social media in marketing. *J. of the Acad. Mark. Sci*. 48, pp. 79–95, 2020.
5. Cuthbert, L. and Theodoridis, A. Do Republicans really believe Trump won the 2020 election? *Washington Post*, online, January 7, 2022.
6. Ruth Bader Ginsberg. https://www.oyez.org/justices/ruth_bader_ginsburg. (n.d.)
7. Liptak, A. Barrett's record. *New York Times*, online, October 12, 2020.
8. Baker, P. and Fandos, N. Trump announces Barrett as Supreme Court nominee, describing her as heir to Scalia. *New York Times*, online, September 26, 2020.

9. Luttwak, E. N. The high stakes of quantum computing. *American Affairs,* IV(3), 136–141. 2020.

Notes for Chapter 11

1. Personal communication June 4, 2019.
2. Vincent, L. Everything you need to know about tribal knowledge. *eLearning Industry,* online, April 15, 2022.
3. Logan, D., King, J. and Fischer-Wright, H. Tribal leadership: Leveraging natural groups to build a thriving organization. *Harper Business,* 2008.
4. Chayinska, M., Ulug, O. M., Ayanian, A. H., Gratzel, J. C., Brik, T., Kende, A. and McGarty, C. Coronavirus conspiracy beliefs and distrust of science predict risky public health behaviours through optimistically biased risk perceptions in Ukraine, Turkey, and Germany. *Group Processes & Intergroup Relations,* online, June 15, 2021.
5. Kramer, J. Why people latch on to conspiracy theories, according to science. *Science,* online, January 8, 2021.
6. Uscinski, J. E. and Enders, A. M. The Coronavirus conspiracy boom. *Atlantic,* online, April 30, 2020.
7. Henderson, D. Respect for authority: The case of Canada. *EconLog,* online, February 26, 2013.
8. Pfiffner, J. P. and Hartke, J. The Electoral College and the framers' distrust of democracy. *White House Studies,* 3(3), 261–273, 2003.
9. Karabell, Z. Here's what happens to a conspiracy-driven party. *Politico Magazine,* online, January 30, 2021.
10. Boissoneault, L. How the 19th-century Know Nothing party reshaped American politics. *Smithsonian,* online, January 26, 2017.
11. Mulkern, J. *The Know-Nothing Party in Massachusetts.* Northeastern University Press, 1990.
12. Kranish, M. How Rep. Marjorie Taylor Greene, promotor of QAnon's baseless theories, rose with support from key Republicans. *Washington Post,* online, January 30, 2021.
13. Handler, E. Have you no decency, sir? At long last, have you no sense of decency? *Huffpost,* online, Nov. 10, 2009.

Notes for Chapter 12

1. Evershed, N., McGowan, M. and Ball, A. Anatomy of a conspiracy theory: how misinformation travels on Facebook. *Guardian, Australia News,* online, March 10, 2021.

2. Vinaules, G. and Thomas, V. L. Not so social: When social media increases perceptions of exclusions and negatively affects attitudes toward content. *Psychology & Marketing*, online, February 23, 2020.

3. Public trust in government: 1958-2021. *Pew Research Center*, online, May 17, 2021.

4. Abrams, Z. Controlling the spread of misinformation. *American Psychological Association*, online, 52(2), March 1, 2021.

5. Chan, J. C. In HBO's 'After Truth,' the victims of disinformation campaigns humanize the danger of 'Fake News', *The Wrap*, online, March 18, 2020.

6. Blunt touts top foreign policy accomplishments under Trump administration. http://www.blunt.senate.gov, December 11, 2020.

7. Kemper, M. Stop blaming Trump for spread of the coronavirus/commentary. *Baltimore Sun*, online, April 16, 2020.

8. Trump, M. *Too Much and Never Enough*. Simon & Schuster, 2020.

9. Peale, N.V. *The Power of Positive Thinking*. Touchstone, 1952.

10. O'Harrow, R., Jr. and Boburg, S. The man who showed Donald Trump how to exploit power and instill fear. *Washington Post*, online, June 17, 2016.

11. Krastev, I. and Leonard, M. The crisis of American power: How Europeans see Biden's America. *European Council on Foreign Relations*, online, January 19, 2021.

12. Hannah, M. N. A conspiracy of data: QAnon, social media, and information visualization. *Social Media + Society*, online, August 13, 2021.

13. Rogers, T. B. and Bennett, B. At the Republican National Convention, you might think COVID-19 was over. *Time*, online, August 27, 2020.

14. McDonald, J., Kiely, E. and Robertson, L. Trump's COVID-19 misinformation since testing positive. *FactCheck.org*, online, October 6, 2020.

15. Williams, P. Inside the Lincoln Project's war against Trump. *New Yorker*, online, Oct. 5, 2020.

16. Public trust in government: 1958-2021. *Pew Research Center*, online, May 17, 2021.

17. Brownstein, R. Trump leaves America at its most divided since the Civil War. *CNN Politics*, online, January 19, 2021.

18. Nichols, T. *The Death of Expertise*. Oxford University Press, 2017, p. 214.

19. Kruger, J. and Dunning D. Unskilled and unaware of it. *Journal of Personality and Social Psychology*, 77(6), 1999, 1121–1134.

20. Dunning, D. The psychological quirk that explains why you love Donald Trump. *Politico.com*, May 25, 2016.
21. Haynes, J. Donald Trump, the Christian Right and COVID-19: The politics of religious freedom. *Laws*, 10(1), 6, 2021.
22. Sheldon, O. J., Dunning, D. and Ames. D. R. Emotionally unskilled, unaware, and uninterested in learning more. *Journal of Applied Psychology*, 99(1), 125–137, 2014, p. 125.
23. Hameleers, M., Bos, L. and de Vreese, C. H. "They did it": The effects of emotionalized blame attribution in populist communication. *Communication Research*, 44(6), 2016, 870–900.
24. History.com editors. Treaty of Versailles. *History.com*, online, March 3, 2020.
25. Herma. H. Goebbels' conception of propaganda. *Social Research*, 10(2), 1943, 200–218.

Notes for Chapter 13

1. Lorenz, T., Browning, K. and Frenkel, S. TikTok teens and K-Pop Stans say they sank Trump rally. *New York Times*, online, June 21, 2020.
2. Moster, J. TikTok 'philosophy' is corrupting the youth. *Observer*, online, November 3, 2021.
3. Sanders, S. It's time to put 'woke' to sleep. *NPR*, online, Dec. 30, 2018.
4. Todd, C. et al. Study finds nearly one-in-five Americans believe QAnon conspiracy theories. *NBC News, Meet the Press*, online, May 27, 2021.
5. Donovan, R. Interviewed in Taulli, T. TikTok, *Forbes*, online, Jan. 31, 2020.
6. Bennhold, K. Fertile ground: QAnon thrives with Germans. *New York Times*, Oct. 11, 2020.
7. Kornbluh, K. et al. New study by Digital New Deal finds engagement with deceptive outlets higher on Facebook today than run-up to 2016 election. *The German Marshall Fund of the United States*, online, Oct. 12, 2020.
8. Broda-Bahm, K. Account for proportionality bias: Big events must have big causes. *Holland & Hart Persuasion Strategies, JDSupra*, July 7, 2020.
9. van Prooijen, J-W. and Douglas, K. M. Belief in conspiracy theories: Basic principles of an emerging research domain. *European Journal of Social Psychology*, 48(7), online, 2018, 897–908.
10. Hassan, A. and Barber, S. J. The effects of repetition frequency on the illusory truth effect. *Cognitive Research*, 6, 38, 2021.

11. Isaac, M. Facebook's profit surges 101 percent on strong ad sales. *New York Times*, online, July 28, 2021.

12. Stelter, B. *Hoax.* Atria/One Signal, 2020.

13. Kelly, A. Mothers for QAnon. *New York Times*, Opinion, online Sept. 10, 2020.

Notes for Chapter 14

1. Sunstein, C. R. and Vermeule, A. Conspiracy theories: Causes and cures. *Journal of Political Philosophy,* 17, 2009, 202–227.

2. Oliver, J. E. and Wood, T. Medical conspiracy theories and health behaviors in the United States. *JAMA Internal Medicine,* 174(5): May 2014, 817–818.

3. van Prooijen, J.-W., Douglas K. and De Inocencio, C. Connecting the dots: Illusory pattern perception predicts beliefs in conspiracies and the supernatural. *European Journal of Social Psychology,* 48, 2018, 320–335.

4. Shermer, M. *The believing brain: From ghosts and gods to politics and conspiracies—how we construct beliefs and reinforce them as truths.* Henry Holt, 2011.

5. Douglas, K. M., Sutton, R. M., Callan, M. J., Dawtry, R. J. and Harvey, A. J. Someone is pulling the strings: Hypersensitive agency detection and belief in conspiracy theories. *Thinking and Reasoning,* 22, 2016, 57–77.

6. van Prooijen, J.-W. and van Lange, P. A. M. (Eds.). *Power, politics, and paranoia: Why people are suspicious of their leaders.* Cambridge University Press, 2014.

7. Hofstadter, R. The paranoid style in American politics. In Hofstadter, R. (Ed.), *The paranoid style in American politics and other essays* (pp. 3–40). Knopf, 1965.

8. Robins-Early, N. et al. How quack doctors and powerful GOP operatives spread misinformation to millions, *Huffpost*, online, July 28, 2020.

9. Schaeffer, K. A look at the Americans who believe there is some truth to the conspiracy theory that COVID-19 was planned. *Pew Research Center, Short Reads,* online, July 24, 2020.

10. Cook, J. QAnon's coronavirus-fueled boom is a warning of what's to come. *Huffpost*, online, June 29, 2020.

11. Romano, A. New Yahoo News/YouGov poll shows coronavirus conspiracy theories spreading on the right may hamper vaccine efforts. *Yahoo!News*, online, May 22, 2020.

Notes for Chapter 15

1. Wood, M. J., Douglas, K. M. and Sutton, R. M. Dead and alive: Beliefs in contradictory conspiracy theories. *Social Psychological & Personality Science*, 3, 2012, 767–773.
2. Toomey, D. Exploring how and why trees 'talk' to each other. *YaleEnvironment360*, online, Sept. 1, 2016.
3. Jennings, R. A new era of celebrity tabloids, minus the snark. *Vox*, online, Dec. 11, 2020.
4. Neuberg, S. L. et al. Human threat management systems: Self-protection and disease avoidance. *Neuroscience and Biobehavioral Reviews*, 35, 2011, 1042–1051.
5. Ohman, A. et al. Emotion drives attention: Detecting the snake in the grass. *Journal of Experimental Psychology: General*, 130, 2001, 466–478.
6. Navarrete, C. D. et al. Fear extinction to an out-group face: The role of target gender. *Psychological Science*, 20, 2009, 155–158.

Notes for Chapter 16

1. Pietraszewski, D. et al. The content of our cooperation, not the color of our skin: An alliance detection system regulates categorization by coalition and race, but not sex. *PLOS ONE*, 9, Article e88534. 2014.
2. Tooby, J. and Cosmides, L. Groups in mind: The coalitional roots of war and morality. In Høgh-Olesen, H. (Ed.), *Human morality & sociality: Evolutionary & comparative perspectives* (pp. 191–234). Red Globe Press, 2010.
3. Pietraszewski, D., Curry, O. S., Petersen, M. B., Cosmides, L. and Tooby, J. Constituents of political cognition: Race, party politics, and the alliance detection system. *Cognition*, 140, July 2015, 24–39.
4. Kurzban, R., and Leary, M. R. Evolutionary origins of stigmatization: The functions of social exclusion. *Psychological Bulletin*, 127(2), 2001, 187–208.
5. Andrews, P. W., Gangestad, S.W. and Matthews, D. Adaptationism—how to carry out an exaptationist program. *Behavioral and Brain Sciences*, 25(4), Aug. 2002, 489–504.
6. Matsuzawa, T. Hot-spring bathing of wild monkeys in Shiga-Heights: Origin and propagation of a cultural behavior. *Primates* 59, 2018, 209–213.
7. Crair, B. On the origin of culture. *Smithsonian*, 98–111, January/February 2021, p. 102.

8. Van Prooijen, J-W. and Douglas, K.M. Belief in conspiracy theories: Basic principles of an emerging research domain. *European Journal of Social Psychology*, 48, 2018, 897–908.

9. Wrangham, R.W. Hypotheses for the evolution of reduced reactive aggression in the context of human self-domestication, *Frontiers in Psychology*, 10, 2019, p. 1914.

10. Chagnon, N. A. Life histories, blood revenge, and warfare in a tribal population. *Science*, 239, 1988, 985–992.

11. Li, N. P., van Vugt, M. and Colarelli, S. M. The evolutionary mismatch hypothesis: Implications for psychological science. *Current Directions in Psychological Science*, 27, 2018, 38–44.

12. Van Prooijen, J.-W., Krouwel, A. P. M. and Pollet, T. Political extremism predicts belief in conspiracy theories. *Social Psychological & Personality Science*, 6, 2015, 570–578.

13. Cichocka, A., Marchlewska, M., Golec de Zavala, A. and Olechowski, M. 'They will not control us': Ingroup positivity and belief in intergroup conspiracies. *British Journal of Psychology*, 107, 2016, 556–576.

14. Powell, M. and Gifford, J. *Machiavellian Intelligence*. LID Publishing, 2017.

15. Whiten, A. and Byrne, R.W. (Eds.). *Machiavellian Intelligence II*. Cambridge University Press, 1997.

16. Leca, J-B. et al. Acquisition of object-robbing and object/food-bartering behaviours. *Philosophical Transactions of the Royal Society B*, 376, 2019, online, January 11, 2021.

17. Machiavelli, N. *The Prince*. Luca, Italy: Antonio Blado d'Asola, 1532.

18. Kramer, A. The poisonous myth: Democratic Germany's 'stab in the back' legend. *Irish Times*, online, Jan. 21, 2019.

19. Wheeler-Bennett, J. W. Ludendorff: The soldier and the politician. *Virginia Quarterly Review*, 14(2), Spring 1938, 187–202.

20. Williamson, K. D. Why Americans adore conspiracy theories, *National Review*, online, Feb. 8, 2021.

21. Hill, K. A vast web of vengeance. *New York Times*, online, Feb. 2, 2021.

22. Feuer, A. As right-wing rhetoric escalates, so do threats and violence. *New York Times*, online, Aug. 14, 2022.

23. Confessore, N. and Yourish, K. Creeping into the mainstream, a theory turns hate into terror. *New York Times*, May 16, 2022.

24. Garfinkle, A. An interview with AI. *Yahoo!Finance*, online, Feb. 5, 2023.

Notes for Chapters 17

1. Reuters. U.S. intelligence report identifies Russians who gave DNC emails to WikiLleaks. *TIME,* online, Jan. 5, 2017.

2. Greenberg, A. New clues show how Russia's grid hackers aimed for physical destruction. *Wired,* online, Sept. 12, 2019.

3. Corfield, G. GRU won't believe it. *Register,* online, Feb. 20, 2020.

4. Shead, S. Russia's Fancy Bear and Cozy Bear hacking groups are under the spotlight. *CNBC,* online, July 17, 2020.

5. BBC News. Democratic hack. Online, July 28, 2016.

6. Price, G. Hillary Clinton robbed Bernie Sanders of the Democratic nomination, according to Donna Brazile. *Newsweek, US,* online, Nov. 2, 2017.

7. Amsterdam, R. Vladimir Putin's hacking strategy is to divide and conquer—and it's nothing new. *Newsweek, Opinion,* online, Dec. 23, 2016.

8. Foer R. F. Putin is well on his way to stealing the next election. *Atlantic,* online, June 2020.

Notes for Chapter 18

1. Baezner, M. and Robin, P. Cyber-conflict between the United States of America and Russia. *Risk and Resilience Team/Center for Security Studies.* Zurich, Switzerland: CSS Cyber Defense Project, 2017.

2. Shuster, S. Vladimir Putin's bad blood with Hillary Clinton. *TIME,* online, July 25, 2016.

3. Alexander, D. and Behar, R. The truth behind Trump Tower Moscow. *Forbes,* online, May 23, 2019.

4. Reuters Press. Trump Tower in Moscow. *Independent,* online, March 18, 2019.

5. Walsh, D. 'From Russia with love.' *New York Times,* online, June 5, 2022.

6. *Reuters.* Hemedti says Sudan should be open to naval base accord with Russia, or others. Online, March 3, 2022.

7. *Associated Press.* 'Putin's chef' admits to interfering in U.S. elections. Online, Nov. 7, 2022.

8. Tucker, E. US busts Russian cyber operation in dozens of countries. *Associated Press,* online, May 9, 2023.

9. Engelbrecht, C. Putin ally acknowledges founding Wagner mercenary group. *New York Times,* online, Sept. 26, 2022.

10. Reuters. Former Wagner commander seeks asylum in Norway after fleeing Russia. Online, Jan. 17, 2023.

11. Troianovski, A. Wagner founder has Putin's support, but the Kremlin's side-eye. *New York Times*, online, Feb. 12, 2023.

12. Osborn, A. Kremlin moves to rein in Russian mercenary boss Prigozhin. *Reuters*, online, Feb. 14, 2023.

13. Kinetz, E. 'He's a war criminal': Elite Putin security officer defects. *Associated Press*, online, April 4, 2023.

14. Radio Free Europe. Putin security service officer who defected describes president as 'war criminal.' *Russian Service*, online, April 4, 2023.

15. Atanesian, G. and Korenyuk, M. Wagner mutiny. *BBC News*, online, June 26, 2023.

Notes for Chapters 19

1. Fessler, P. Report: Russia launched cyberattack on voting vendor ahead of election. *NPR*, June 5, 2017.

2. Ackerman, S. et al. Mitch McConnell backs Russia election hack inquiry, but scope remains vague. *Guardian*, online, Dec. 12, 2016.

3. Rohrer, G. Second Florida county hacked in 2016 election, Gov. DeSantis says. *Orlando Sentinel*, online, May 14, 2019.

4. Lee, S. Georgia gov. candidate has been worried about hacking since 2016. *Townhall*, online, Nov. 6, 2018.

5. Blue, V. How Brian Kemp hacked Georgia's election, *Engadget, Bad Password column*, online, Nov. 9, 2018.

6. Huetteman, E. Obama White House knew of Russian election hacking but delayed telling. *New York Times, Politics*, online, June 21, 2017.

7. Sanger, D. E. and Perlroth, N. More hacking attacks found as officials warn of 'grave risk' to U.S. Government. *New York Times, Politics*, online, Dec. 18, 2020.

8. Perlroth, N. *This is How They Tell Me the World Ends*. Bloomsbury, 2021.

Notes for Chapter 20

1. Greenberg, A. 'Crash Override': The malware that took down a power grid. *Wired*, online, June 12, 2017.

2. Sanger, D. E. Ignoring sanctions, Russia renews broad cybersurveillance operation. Online, *New York Times*, Oct. 25, 2021.

3. Guterres, A. *United Nations Convention on Countering the Use of Information and Communications Technologies for Criminal Purposes*. United Nations, June 29, 2021.

4. Zygar, M. *All the Kremlin's Men*. Public Affairs, 2016.

5. Zygar, M. How Vladmir Putin lost interest in the present. *New York Times,* online, March 10, 2022.

6. Walker, S. Putin's absurd, angry spectacle will be a turning point in his long reign. *Guardian,* online, Feb. 21, 2022.

7. Khodorkovsky, M. In an interview with Fareed Zakaria on his GPS broadcast on *CNN.* April 4, 2022.

8. Wickham, A. and Gus, C. Putin advisers mislead Russian leader about Ukraine war status, UK intelligence says. *Politico,* online, March 31, 2022.

9. Berry, L. and Crowther, P. US view of Putin: Angry, frustrated, likely to escalate war. *KTAR News,* March 13, 2022.

10. Brickman, P. and Campbell, D. T. Hedonic Relativism and Planning the Good Society. In *M. H. Appley (Ed.), Adaptation Level Theory: A Symposium* (287–302). Academic Press, 1971.

11. Wolff, J. (2022). Everyone is still waiting for the cyber war. *TIME,* 199(11-12), April 4, 2022, 31-32.

12. Kashin, O. Who will get rid of Putin? The answer is grim. *New York Times,* online, Aug. 18, 2022.

13. Weiss, M. Is Putin sick—or are we meant to think he is? *New/Lines Magazine,* online, May 12, 2022.

14. Siddiqui, Z. Russian cyber spies attack Ukraine's allies, Microsoft says. *Reuters,* online, June 22, 2022.

15. Sanger, D. E. and Barnes, J. E. Many Russian cyberattacks failed in first months of Ukraine war, study says. *New York Times,* online, June 22, 2022.

16. Pereira, I. Microsoft corporate emails hacked by Russian-backed group, company says. *ABC News,* online, Jan. 19, 2024.

17. Bing, C. Russian hackers preparing new cyber assault against Ukraine – Microsoft report. *Reuters,* online, March 15, 2023.

18. Baker, P. and Glasser, S. *The Divider.* Doubleday, 2022.

19. Cottom, T. M. A big TV hit is a conservative fantasy liberals should watch. *New York Times,* online, Aug. 9, 2022.

Notes for Chapter 21

1. Felsenthal, E. The choice, *TIME,* Jan. 3, 2022, p. 34.

2. Wile, R. A timeline of Elon Musk's takeover of Twitter. *NBC News,* Nov. 17, 2022.

3. Szalai, J. The problem of misinformation in an era without trust. *New York Times,* online, Dec. 31, 2023.

4. Felsenthal, E. The choice. *TIME,* Jan. 3, 2022, p. 38.

5. Chan, K. and Casert, R. EU targets Big Tech over hate speech, disinformation. *Associated Press,* online, April 23, 2022.

6. Quoted in Gallagher, B. Elon Musk and what makes an organization trustworthy. *Ethical Systems,* online, March 7, 2023.

7. Shermer, M. *The Believing Brain.* St. Martin's Press, 2011.

8. McIntyre, L. C. *Post-Truth.* MIT Press, 2018.

9. McIntyre, L. C. *The Scientific Attitude.* MIT Press, 2019.

10. Snyder, T. The American abyss. *New York Times,* online, Jan. 9, 2021.

11. Redlawsk, D. P. Hot cognition or cool consideration? *Journal of Politics,* 64(4), Nov. 2002.

12. Nyhan, B. and Reifler, J. When corrections fail. *Political Behavior,* 32, 2010, 303–330.

13. Quoted in Stimson, B. Sorry to be a free speech absolutist. *Fox Business,* online, March 5, 2022.

14. Quoted in Perrigo, B. Twitter employees on why Elon Musk is wrong about free speech. *TIME,* online, April 14, 2022.

15. Borter, G. and Chiacu, D. Harvard President Gay resigns after rocky testimony, plagiarism allegations. *Reuters,* online, Jan. 3. 2024.

Notes for Chapter 22

1. Hsu, T. et al. Elections and disinformation are colliding like never before in 2024. *New York Times,* online, Jan. 9, 2024.

2. Tucker, E. and Bajak, F. Repudiating Trump, officials say election 'most secure.' *Associated Press,* online, Nov. 13, 2020.

3. Marre, A. I'm a former FBI cyber agent. *Fortune,* online, Jan. 12, 2024.

4. Jones, R. Who's ready for the AI election? *Fortune,* online, Jan. 9, 2024.

5. Tu, L. Flop or bop? *Scientific American,* 329(2), Sept. 2023, pp.14–15.

6. Musser, G. An AI mystery. *Scientific American,* 329(2), Sept. 2023, pp. 58–61.

7. Swenson, A. Here's how ChatGPT maker OpenAI plans to deter election misinformation in 2024. *Associated Press,* online, Jan. 16, 2024.

8. OpenAI Blog. How OpenAI is approaching 2024 worldwide elections. Online, Jan. 15, 2024.

9. Lajka, A. New AI voice-cloning tools 'add fuel' to misinformation fire. *Associated Press,* online, Feb. 10, 2023.

10. Riechmann, D. I never said that! High-tech deception of 'deepfake' videos. *Associated Press,* online, July 2, 2018.

11. Quoted in Wong, M. We haven't seen the worst of fake news. *Atlantic*, online, Dec. 20, 2022.

12. Seitz-Wald, A. and Memoli, M. Fake Joe Biden robocall tells New Hampshire Democrats not to vote on Tuesday. *NBC News*, online, Jan. 22, 2024.

13. Schick, N. *Deepfakes: The Coming Infocalypse*. Twelve/Hachette, 2020.

14. Lall, R. Deepfake technology could create huge potential for social unrest and even trigger wars. *The National, Opinion*, online, Jan. 19, 2024.

15. Quoted in Parkin, S. The rise of the deepfake and the threat to democracy. *Guardian*, online, June 22, 2019.

16. Yasoshima, R. et al. ChatGPT, other AI to be studied for military risk by new Japan body. *Nikkei Asia*, online, Dec. 16, 2023.

17. Quoted in Henshall, W. Get ready for the year ahead in AI. *TIME*, Jan. 22, 2024, p. 65.

18. Henshall, W. Get ready for the year ahead in AI. *TIME*, Jan. 22, 2024, pp. 64–65.

19. Suleyman, M. *The Coming Wave*. Crown, 2023, p. vii.

20. Figure AI Inc. Figure announces commercial agreement with BMW Manufacturing to bring general purpose robots into automotive production. *PR Newswire*, online, Jan. 18, 2024.

Notes for Chapters 23

1. Ismay, J. Russia claims to use a hypersonic missile in attack on arms depot in Ukraine. *New York Times*, online, March 19, 2022.

2. Sayler, K. M. Hypersonic weapons. *Congressional Research Service*, online, May 5, 2022.

3. Simon, S. Hypersonic missiles are a game changer. *New York Times*, online, Jan. 2, 2020.

4. Charron, A. quoted in Austen, I. With new threats looming, Canada commits billions to air defense. *New York Times, Canada Letter*, online, June 24, 2022.

5. Rogers, C. R. and Ryback, D. One alternative to nuclear planetary suicide. In R. F. Levant and J. M. Shlien (Eds.), *Client-Centered Therapy and the Person-Centered Approach*. Praeger, 1984.

6. Sanger, D. E. and Broad, W. J. Putin declares a nuclear alert, and Biden seeks de-escalation. *New York Times*, online, Feb.27, 2022.

7. Sanger, D. E. et al. U.S. makes contingency plans in case Russia uses its most powerful weapons. *New York Times*, online, March 23, 2022.

8. Rogers, C. R. and Ryback, D. One alternative to nuclear planetary suicide. In R. F. Levant and J. M. Shlien (Eds.), *Client-Centered Therapy and the Person-Centered Approach*. Praeger, 1984.

Notes for Chapter 24

1. Starkey, B. et al. *International Negotiation in a Complex World, Updated Fourth Edition*. Rowman & Littlefield. 2016.
2. Henard, D. H. *Negotiation: An Artful Science*. Amazon, 2020.
3. Sebenius, J. K. et al. *Kissinger the Negotiator*. Harper, 2018.
4. Colson, A., Druckman, D., and Donohue, W. (Eds.) *International Negotiation*. Republic of Letters, 2013.
5. Blight, J. G. and Lang, J. M. *The Fog of War*. Rowman & Littlefield. 2005.
6. Lawrence, M. A. *The Vietnam War*. Oxford University Press, 2010.
7. Troianovski, A. A chatty Putin's underlying message: I'm still in charge. *New York Times*, online, Dec. 10, 2022.
8. Owens, M. *Overreach*. Mudlark/HarperCollins, 2023.
9. Cohen, Z. Quoted in Rosenberg, R. Russian President Vladmir Putin has features of a psychopath: Expert. *Fox News*, online, March 2, 2022.
10. Simko-Bednarski, E. Putin: Russia ready for Ukraine deal, but partners cheated in the past. *New York Post*, online, Dec. 9, 2022.
11. Buckley, C. Fear and ambition propel Xi's nuclear acceleration. *New York Times*, online, Feb. 4, 2024.
12. Faulconbridge, G. Russia says it's deploying tactical nukes in drills as Ukraine cries blackmail. *USA Today*, online, May 6, 2024.

Notes for Chapter 25

1. Rogers, C. R. and Ryback, D. One alternative to nuclear planetary suicide. In R. F. Levant and J. M. Shlien (Eds.), *Client-Centered Therapy and the Person-Centered Approach*. Praeger, 1984.
2. Melley, B. For the first time, an Irish nationalist will lead Northern Ireland's government. *Associated Press*, online, Feb. 3, 2024.

Notes for Chapter 26

1. Diamond, L. and McDonald, J. *Multi-Track Diplomacy*. Iowa Peace Institute, 1991.
2. Staats, J., Walsh, J. and Tucci, R. *A Primer on Multi-track Diplomacy*. United States Institute of Peace, July 31, 2019.

3. Little, B. Government boarding schools once separated Native American children from families. *History*, online, July 10, 2023.
4. Borenstein, S. Ukraine war moves 'Doomsday Clock' to 90 seconds to midnight. *Associated Press*, online, Jan. 24, 2023.
5. Faulconbridge, G. et al. Putin issues a nuclear warning to the West over strikes on Russia from Ukraine. *Reuters*, Sept. 25, 2024.
6. Freedman L. Putin keeps threatening to use nuclear weapons. Would he? *New York Times,* online, Oct. 3, 2024.
7. Carter, J. *The Nobel Peace Prize Lecture.* Simon & Schuster, 2002, p. 20.

Notes for Chapter 27

1. Dominion's combined Opposition to Fox News Network, LLC's and Fox Corporation's Rule 56 Motions for Summary Judgment, in the Superior Court of the State of Delaware. Feb. 8, 2022, p. 5.
2. Miller, C. SPLC poll finds substantial support for 'Great Replacement' theory and other hard-right ideas. *Southern Poverty Law Center*, online, June 1, 2022.
3. Pazzanese, C. How demagogues wield social media. *Harvard Gazette,* online, Nov. 22, 2022.
4. Lasser, J. et al. Social media sharing of low-quality news sources by political elites. *PNAS Lexus,* 1(4), online, Sept. 2022.
5. Harris, T. Interviewed on *60 Minutes* on Nov. 6, 2022.
6. Enten, H. How Joe Biden and the Democratic Party defied midterm history. *CNN Politics*, online, Nov. 13, 2022.
7. *New York Post* cover for Nov. 9, 2022.
8. Editorial Board. How a G.O.P. faction enables political violence. *New York Times, Section SR*, Nov. 26, 2022, p. 9.
9. Friedman, T. L. Our new promethean moment. *New York Times, Opinion,* online, March 21, 2023.
10. Marcus, G. Quoted in Klein, E. The imminent danger of A.I. is one we're not talking about. *New York Times, Opinion*, online, Feb. 26, 2023.
11. Hawking, S. and Mlodinow, L. *The Grand Design.* Bantam Books, 2010, p. 7.
12. Editorial Board. Nuclear talks with China are essential and long overdue. *New York Times*, online, Nov. 4, 2023.
13. MacFarquhar, N. Russia pulled out of a nuclear test ban treaty. *New York Times*, online, Nov. 2, 2023.
14. Shetty, S. The Reagan-Gorbachev statement. European Leadership Network *Commentary*, Nov. 19, 2021.

About the Author

David Ryback, author of *Putting Emotional Intelligence to Work,* which has been translated into French, German, Danish, Spanish, and Chinese, is an internationally recognized authority on the dynamics of trust in emotional and social intelligence. He remains at the forefront of the latest research on applications of emotional awareness and related aspects of education and executive leadership. Dr. Ryback heads EQ Associates International based in Atlanta, Georgia.

His academic roles include being a professor at Emory University, the University of West Georgia, Georgia State University, and the University of Maryland (Overseas Division).

Dr. Ryback's other published books include *ConnectAbility* (McGraw-Hill), about building strong partnerships with greater trust; *Transforming Communication in Leadership and Teamwork* (Springer), about innovations in person-centered trust; and *Dreams That Come True* (Doubleday), about trusting your dreams, translated into French, German, Danish, and Spanish.

In addition to authoring several books, Dr. Ryback has written more than sixty professional articles, many of which were published in top-tier refereed journals such as the *American Psychologist,* as well as numerous book reviews that appeared in various journals, magazines, and newspapers, including *Psychology Today; Speaker,* the magazine of the National Speakers Association; the *Jerusalem Post;* and the *Atlanta Journal-Constitution.* He served as associate editor for the *Journal of*

Humanistic Psychology and as book editor for *Business to Business* magazine as well as the *American Journal of Family Therapy*.

He is a keynote presenter to such groups as the Federal National Mortgage Association (FNMA) in Washington, DC; RTM in Atlanta; MontCap in Montreal, Canada; educational organizations; and others. In addition, he has presented to such groups as the National Aeronautics and Space Administration (NASA), the National Football League (NFL), the US Air Force, as well as industrial and educational groups in Monterrey, Mexico; Valencia, Spain; Nuremberg, Germany; Vienna, Austria; Milan, Italy; Oslo, Norway; Tel Aviv, Israel; Bangkok, Thailand; and Tokyo, Japan. He delivered a presentation on platform excellence to the annual convention of the National Speakers Association in San Diego.

He earned his BSc with honors in psychology at McGill University, his MS at San Diego State, and his PhD at the University of Hawaii.

Dr. Ryback had his own radio and cable network shows in San Diego and Atlanta and has appeared on select radio and TV programs to publicize his books across the country, in Canada and in Great Britain. In the United States, he has publicized his books on such platforms as ABC TV and CNN as well as many other media outlets.

The successes and rewards of writing about emotional intelligence led Dr. Ryback to found EQ Associates International. He currently offers presentations to corporate and educational organizations across the globe, occasionally at no cost for select entities, depending on need.

www.ingramcontent.com/pod-product-compliance
Lightning Source LLC
Chambersburg PA
CBHW071103050326
40690CB00008B/1103